THE
CANNABIS
BREEDER'S
BIBLE

Also by Greg Green
The Cannabis Grow Bible

THE CANNABIS BREEDER'S BIBLE

The Definitive Guide to Marijuana Genetics, Cannabis Botany and Creating Strains for the Seed Market

BY **GREG GREEN**

GREEN
CANDY
PRESS

PUBLISHED BY GREEN CANDY PRESS
SAN FRANCISCO, CA
www.greencandypress.com

COPYRIGHT ©2005 GREG GREEN
ISBN 1-931160-27-9

Color section photographs © Andre Grossman, Pepper Design Studio, Serious
Seeds, Trichome Technologies and www.Bubblebag.com.
Photographs © Al, Anton, BOG (Bushy Older Grower), Dutch Passion, Eco,
Energy Turtle, Growmaster, HombredelMonte, Honza, Joint Doctor, Kissie,
Kryptonite, Mikal, Mr. Webb, Paradise Seeds, Pepper Design Studio,
Sagarmatha, Sensi Seeds, Strawdog, www.Newlines.nl.

PRINTED IN CANADA BY MARQUIS
MASSIVELY DISTRIBUTED BY P.G.W.

ACKNOWLEDGEMENTS

My thanks to my family and friends for making this book possible.

This book is dedicated to growers and breeders all over the world, of any type of plants. I would like to say thank you to Simi, Moni, Strawdog, Chris, Kissie, Mikal, W. Y. Evans-Wentz, Lama Kazi Dawa-Samdup, Sir John Woodroffe, Mike H, Billy A, Sean C, Nick J, Paul M, John Mc, Mahoona, Cossie, Suz F, Emer D, Mary M, Eug D, Carol L, Arthur C. Clarke, Darra E and Mr. De Butler.

A special thanks to Serious Seeds, Sensi Seeds, Paradise Seeds, Spice of Life Seeds, Nirvana Seeds, Dutch Passions Seeds, Mr Nice, Soma Seeds, Greenhouse Seeds, African Seeds, Flying Dutchmen, Brothers' Grimm, Homegrown Fantaseeds, KC Brains, BOG Seeds and all their breeders for keeping those genetics coming and making them available to all.

My ingratitude goes out to the CIA for refusing to be audited for activities relating to the drug war at the request of the General Accounting Office of America since 1960, making themselves the obvious profiteers of America's spiraling offshore illegal drug trade which creates adulterated cannabis products, the proceeds from which are used to train foreign guerilla forces for a 'cause' which eventually ends up with them rebelling and converting to terrorism that reaches every part of the globe. My ingratitude also goes out to their partners who spread disinformation about the cannabis plant across the world so that the profits can keep rolling in at the expense of human lives. These people should know better than to make money out of mischief.

It's only just cannabis!

I would also like to say a special thanks to my publisher and editor for their always welcome words of wisdom.

This is a book about cannabis breeding and botany, written by people who breed cannabis strains.

TABLE OF CONTENTS

FOREWORD

THIS IS NOT A BEGINNER'S BOOK to cannabis cultivation. This book is about advanced marijuana cultivation and breeding. Although this book will teach you advanced cannabis concepts it will not teach you the basics. If you want to learn growing then get *THE CANNABIS GROW BIBLE: The Definitive Guide to Growing Marijuana for Recreational and Medical Use* by Greg Green (ISBN: 1-931160-17-1), also.

There is still much work that needs to be done to provide a complete reference to everything related to cannabis genetics, marijuana botany and breeding techniques, but that will come in time. You can find entire books dedicated to plant genetics and breeding for most vegetable plants that are ten times more complete than this one. But then most vegetable plants are not illegal in most countries and cultivators and botanists are free to list, classify, grow and distribute their findings. They can also set up companies that freely trade in these genetics across the world without breaking the law. Sadly the same cannot be said for cannabis...until now.

The Cannabis Breeder's Bible is new and truly unique. Those who are willing to take serious risks in getting you this information have discovered most of what you will read and learn here. We listen to and talk with hundreds of such growers and breeders every year. It is with their advice that we can offer you the latest updates on cannabis breeding techniques. The results have been outstanding, and I am very thankful for their fearless contribution to *The Cannabis Breeder's Bible*.

In this book you will read about quite a number of breeding techniques, advanced cultivation methods and botanical aspects of the cannabis plant - probably too much to remember all in one go if this is your first time breeding. That is why I have broken the book into easy-to-follow, step-by-step portions. The book covers cannabis genetics from start to finish. It contains a breakdown of the cannabis plant, its origins, along with a detailed description of its anatomy and how cannabis interbreeds. The chapters are easy to follow and you will find yourself turning to this book time and time again for information about hybrids that you would like to create or advanced cultivation techniques that you need. This is what makes *The Cannabis Breeder's Bible* so accessible and unique. Most cultivation guides lack this very important information or when they touch on this area of expertise they contain information that is exaggerated or even just plainly incorrect. *The Cannabis Breeder's Bible* provides accurate, up-to-date information based on practical experience from breeding strains using multiple techniques. We don't just quote or copy what the breeder or growers has said and we have not taken pages from some web site, book or magazine and simply reproduce them here as if they where gospel truth. We actually test what they say. That is why we can provide you with original and unique cannabis cultivation information that you will not learn anywhere else except inside the book that you are currently holding in your hands.

Don't ever let bad results prevent you from breeding again. That is part of the learning process. However, this book will point out some common mistakes that others have made, so that you don't have to repeat them and learn the hard way. Some seed varieties cost a little more than the price of this book. A handful cost less. Mostly the better strains cost a lot more. Either way, *The Cannabis Breeder's Bible* will be your companion before and after you buy it and nowhere else will you find the unprecedented amount of cannabis genetic information that is contained in this book. We have made the 21st century leap by presenting you the reader and potential breeder with a 'Totally Brand New Understanding of Cannabis Genetics'.

Glance over this book and flick through the chapters. Get a feel for what is going on. Then read it all from start to finish. By the time you turn the last page you will probably have an idea of what breeding techniques suit your needs and maybe even have started creating a new hybrid strain of your own already. If you can do that then please tell people about this book. It is our goal to get everyone participating in breeding the great herb — legally.

This is not the final word on the subject either: this book has been designed to grow! We will be adding new chapters, new pictures, new methods and new theories. That is why *The Cannabis Breeder's Bible* has become the marijuana breeder's handbook of choice.

We hope that you stick with us and we hope that this book will help you to get where you want to go. Happy growing and most of all, remember to ... HAVE FUN!

PREFACE

THIS BOOK HAS BEEN WRITTEN UNDER ADVERSE CONDITIONS. In most countries it is illegal to own cannabis seeds, or to grow or use cannabis. Maybe this will change for you one day if enough people make the effort to have their voices heard. Until that day comes, it is recommended that you verify what your country's legal stance is with regards to cannabis breeding. This book was not created with the intent to encourage anyone to break the law.

The Cannabis Breeders Bible is about cannabis breeding and how it is done. Even though the contents of this book may show you how to acquire seeds, grow them and breed them, ultimately, you are responsible for your own actions. We would like to see you breed bigger, better cannabis plants; however, we don't want to see you break the law.

I would also like to say that many countries have permitted medical users to grow their own personal supplies of cannabis. If this is true of your country then this book will be of massive benefit to you and your health.

A NOTE TO THE READER

Since the release of *The Cannabis Grow Bible* I have received many questions from readers around the globe. I am able to answer most questions by referring to specific pages in the book readers may have missed the first time around or by answering their questions on our website forums at www.cannabisbook.com (thank you everyone for participating by the way and as you know I try to get around to answering every letter). However, I have been totally bombarded with questions related to chapter 15 of that book—How to Breed Marijuana.

The remainder of this book is a companion to chapter 15 of *The Cannabis Grow Bible*. For the benefit of those readers who do not have *The Cannabis Grow Bible*, I have reprinted this classic chapter here as chapter 2, Basic Breeding. This chapter will cover more advanced breeding questions, but it will also provide a glimpse of the breeding market in action and how it works.

PRELIMINARY CONSIDERATIONS

As a breeder, try to avoid using the word *marijuana* too often. There are many marijuana prohibition campaigners who have dedicated whole volumes to listing marijuana slang words so that parents know what the different terms for marijuana are—but what they fail to realize is that the word *marijuana* itself is slang. *Marijuana* is derived from "mari'hwana" which is an American Spanish slang term for cannabis.

The word *marijuana* certainly doesn't sound like the Queen's English, does it? This is exactly why the term was used so widely by cannabis prohibition campaigners from the early 1900s right up until today. Prohibition campaigners quickly devoted themselves to the word *marijuana* wherever they meant to say cannabis in order to affect the American psyche at a basic level. Marijuana sounds new, foreign and strange; the word *cannabis* sounds old, local and scientific.

Early prohibition efforts were always closely knit with racism: marijuana was portrayed as a South American problem that came to America. Nothing could be further from the truth. In the early 1900s American growers had already established many lines of landrace cannabis that were used in the commercial sector. In fact, by the 1930s some cannabis cultivators did not even realize that marijuana prohibition campaigns were directly aimed at their crop!

These wild cannabis plants that have been domesticated by man, but somewhat returned to the wild, tend to be less than uniform in growth when compared to completely domesticated cannabis plants, but are more uniform in growth than wild cannabis populations that have not undergone much interference from mankind.

During the early years of merchant trading systems, landrace strains were mostly used as the basis for domesticating new strains of cannabis. This trend has continued through to this day. Nearly every single domestic cannabis strain has been derived from a landrace strain or, more importantly, a **recombination** of the different landrace strains' genetic material, all of which has more recently been done via breeding selection and not through **genetic modification**.

Most of these landrace strains can still be found in the same places that Occidental man discovered them a hundred years ago or more. To say that Occidental man 'discovered' these strains is a bit like saying that Christopher Columbus discovered America, even though there were Native Americans present when he arrived. We already know that primordial man, through to Bronze Age man and modern man have propagated a lot of landrace cannabis but we do have early wild landrace pockets which still survive to this day.

Europe has not pursued the same kind of radical marijuana prohibition laws as America has. Much of this has to do with Europeans retaining the name cannabis, rather than switching to the term *marijuana*. Thus it would be in the best interests of the growing and breeding community to avoid using the slang term *marijuana* as far as possible—unless you are a Latin American, who should then reintroduce the word as it sounds in your own language! Reintroducing proper language may well help cannabis to once again be seen in the proper light it deserves.

In the 1970s many cannabis growers believed that their only hope in bringing cannabis back from the brink of uncertainty was to establish home breeding projects using landrace strains that had been illegally imported from around the world. The US government had already blindly destroyed its own landrace reserves in a foolish attempt at marijuana extinction. Australia and Europe and many other countries followed suit to some degree. The problem with destroying landrace cannabis is that all that's being damaged is the actual breeding behind specific cannabis strains that were created for various growing environments, and not the cannabis species itself. Imagine for a moment that you develop a new type of apple tree that grows apples that are tasty, nourishing and grow perfectly in your climate. Maybe you have also created a tree that is resistant to pests and can withstand certain common diseases that are found in your area. One day the government comes along and says that apples are bad for people and all apple trees must be destroyed. Does this mean that apple trees will no longer exist? It certainly does not. It just means that your special breed of apple tree is removed. In the early 1930s the US government was hesitant to entirely destroy cannabis, out of fear that it might be needed someday for some technical use. That fear proved correct. The dawn of WW II flung the US agricultural community into panic when it was discovered that fiber reserves were too low to meet demands and external resources were cut off because of the war. Cannabis cultivation was reintroduced to help with the war effort and it met many fiber demands. However, since WW II taxpayers have increasingly found themselves funding the 'war on drugs,' and the US landrace cannabis strains that once saved America have now been lost due to neglect from federal reserve laboratories, which have failed to maintain these strains.

Recent medical discoveries have shown that cannabis is indeed a beneficial herb and, more importantly, that human beings have cannabinoid receptors for processing cannabis chemicals naturally. Since most US landrace strains have been destroyed, the people of the United States are now facing a loss on the medical side of cannabis development. Canada, Alaska, the United Kingdom, Spain, Germany, Holland, Belgium and Switzerland are all making headway in this field of study. Without doubt, to this author's mind, medical cannabis will be widely available to everybody else before the American population takes control of the herb from the federal law enforcers—who are merely playing a game to ensure their share of the tax budget.

Recent failures by federal authorities to preserve landrace strains have set the new cannabis breeding standards for today. The individuals of the new cannabis breeding movement have taken it upon themselves to breed, produce seeds, traffic seeds and share genetics. The results over the past ten years of breeding have been revolutionary. Nowhere in the world can any government-sponsored agriculture body, pharmaceutical firm or plant genetics lab lay claim to such new discoveries, varieties or selections as the domestic cannabis breeding community. They have shown their strength in numbers, production values and efficiency. It is because of their efforts that cannabis remains one of the most sought after plant species in the world today.

The Cannabis Grow Bible went to some lengths to show readers how they can effectively produce and breed cannabis. The following presentation will provide further information to potential breeders as to how they can effectively participate in this process, with all the practical applications and cultivation principles that are necessary to produce high-end cannabis plants. For the professional biologist it will serve to reinforce propagation standards and set about standardizing procedures for the cannabis breeder to adhere to. We are now entering a stage in which genetic manipulation is becoming ever more readily available. We hope to guide the breeder and researcher through the many pitfalls and misconceptions about genetic manipulation that can lead to future problems with the cannabis population. Let this book provide you with standards to adhere to, ones we promise will be both virtuous and profitable.

1 | OVERVIEW OF THE CANNABIS STRAIN MARKET

TO SEED OR CLONE?

There are two basics type of plant reproduction: *sexual reproduction* and *asexual reproduction*. Making seeds is known as sexual reproduction. Cloning is known as asexual reproduction.

First we need to say a few things about the cannabis strain market. Growers who want to produce large quantities of bud choose clones and not seeds as their source of propagation. This is because clones carry the same sex as the parent plant that the cutting was taken from (*CGB*, pp 165-71). Clones flower more quickly too. This means that a grower can keep clones in his grow room and constantly repeat a harvest of the same female plant(s) over and over again.

Because a clone will carry the same genetic material as the parent plant the clone was taken from, the grower does not have to worry about variations in the plants, as they would with seeds from a hybrid strain. In a population of cannabis plants, propagated from seed, a grower will find a good female that appears to have performed better than all the others. The grower will usually keep this plant by cloning it and growing it out into a population of clones that all retain the exact same desired characteristics as that special plant they started with, as long as similar growing conditions are maintained or improved upon. New hybrids and strains do not always faithfully repeat themselves in the offspring through seeds (sexual reproduction) or cannot faithfully repeat themselves in the offspring because the genetic recombination of the parent plants will only result in hidden traits emerging and previously revealed traits disappearing. New hybrids contain variations and sometimes these variations can affect traits that the grower wants to keep. In order to create a hybrid that is uniform, so that its seeds produce very uniform populations, the breeder must learn breeding techniques. Eventually a breeder will be able to stabilize the strain so that all of its offspring are very uniform in growth and the grower does not need to take cuttings or clones because the strain will be consistent in seed form. Why bother creating uniform strains from seed? Why not deal in clones?

SHIPPING CLONES

Shipping a cutting internationally is simply not viable. Forget the legal ramifications of shipping for a moment and think about the state of the clone after it has been shipped from Amsterdam to Alaska. Even if it was shipped first class and packaged with care you still have serious questions to contend with. Anything can happen from point *A* to point *B* and if the clone does not survive transport, then what happens? Does the buyer get his/her money back? How does he prove that the clone did not make it? Who is to blame? Is this really a viable business plan? Will the consumer want to buy clones if he lives far away from the business that sells the clones?

In reality no one sells clones unless the clone is only going to be sent over a short distance or can be handed over to the buyer in person. The risks involved in shipping clones for money simply does not make good business sense. The only time clones are shipped over long distances is if the parties involved are not too concerned with loss or damage to that clone.

Clandestine clones are sent to people in the post all the time. The clone is usually inserted into a small plastic tube no thicker than a pen (A test tube will do just fine). Inside the tube is a tiny amount of water to keep the clone alive. A small piece of wet rockwool is inserted into the plastic tube, blocking the water. A cutting is taken and inserted into the rockwool, with an air-pocket at the top. A thin thread is used to tie the clone's leaves at the top if needed. The tube is then corked or sealed. The tube is then wrapped in a ziplock baggy and a standard A4 bubble envelope is used to send it through the post. This is how cuttings have been transported by growers around the world. You can experiment with this method using non-proscribed plant cuttings. The success rate though is very poor.

A better way to ship clones is to root the clone first in rockwool (*CGB*, p. 167). After a few weeks the clone will take root in the rockwool. The grower then cuts the piece of rockwool down to a smaller size which can easily be inserted into a tube as mentioned above and the same packaging process is repeated. If the sender believes that no moisture will spill from the cloning medium they can choose to leave the tube open and create air pockets in the envelope with a pin to allow the cutting to breathe. This is less secure because of possible smell prob-

These are not just cuttings. These are clones. Note the developed roots on the clone lying down. Hard video boxes can be used to pack more than 1 clone.

Lying the clones down in opposite arrangement prevents overcrowding.

Seal the container with tape to prevent it from opening.

Wrap the container in a plastic zip lock bag and seal it to keep any smells or leakage contained. Procedure and photos by www.Newlines.nl

lems and contamination but should improve the cutting's survival rate. Rooted clones tend to survive transport better than just cuttings.

Obviously clones are not the best option available for breeders to pass on their work. Also finding a good clone mother plant does not revolve so much around breeding techniques as it does just having good growing experience and an eye for spotting worthy plants in large populations, i.e., sizeable selections to choose from. The other option breeders have of making their work available is through seeds. This is a much more feasible process for getting the product to the consumer undamaged and in good condition. Because of these factors seeds have become the standard method of shipping cannabis genetics around the world.

Top breeders and Cannabis Cup winners like Paradise Seeds use large populations for that all-important mother plant selection.

What are the pros and cons of these propagation sources? Let's look at a few important differences between clones and seeds.

Clones
1. Growers must know how to clone if they want to generate more plants from this strain. Most new growers do not know how to clone.

2. Non-hybrid seeds of the clone cannot be made from a female clone without obtaining a male clone of the same strain.* A hybrid can be created by finding any male donor.

3. Clones do not have any diversity. If the clone is from a great mother plant then the clones will also be great female plants. This follows through with our next point.

4. Clones will always carry the same traits through continued cuttings from the original clone.

5. Clones require little to no breeding procedures in order to replicate the mother plant's characteristics. If you find a mother plant that is good then all you need to do is take cuttings from her.

6. Clones can be easily stolen from a breeder and labeled as someone else's produce.

7. If a disease kills a single clone in a grow room, then all the other clones will probably fail too. Clones share the same flaws.

Exceptions to the above statements can occur if a clone suffers some form of mutation. Mutations will be discussed in detail further in this text.

Seeds

1. Growers do not need to know how to clone if they want to generate more plants.

2. Non-hybrid seeds can be made by breeding male and female plants of the same strain during flowering although —

3. Seeds will have variations, losing some traits and gaining some new ones, unless they are **true breeding** (see chapter 2).

4. Seeds require a lot of work if you want the strain to have little or no variations in their offspring.

5. Seeds can be bred in such a way that it is hard to reproduce the mother plant that the seeds came from. This makes the work harder to steal.

6. Most seeds do contain some variations and some might be able to deal with cultivation problems better than others.

These points will give you an idea as a breeder and a consumer of what the market is like and what people prefer. As a breeder, you should not be interested too much in the clone business except for more immediate and viable avenues. You will probably want as many people to get your strain as possible. This means you should go the seed route.

---

* This can be done by forcing the plant to self-pollinate, forcing the clone to become a hermaphrodite, but this is not recommended because the hermaphrodite condition can be passed on to future offspring. For more on selfing, see CGB, p. 230. The hermaphrodite condition is discussed on p. 105 of CGB, and will also be explained further in this book.

WHAT IS A BREEDER?

By definition, a breeder is a person who rears animals and plants. To be more precise, it is a person who breeds a stock of animals or plants of a particular species and who develops that stock by deliberate selection.

What separates the good breeders from the bad breeders? In the world of cannabis breeding the points can easily be listed.

A Good Breeder

1. Does not produce hermaphrodite strains.
2. Only sells viable seed produce.
3. Does not replicate other people's work without their permission.
4. Always selects for traits that he or she likes.
5. Listens to what the market wants if he is breeding for the market.
6. Listens to negative critical comments about his work.
7. Listens to legitimate concerns about his products.

As you can see the overall quality of the final produce does not have much to do with being a good breeder or a bad breeder. Creating a superpotent plant or a high-yield performing plant does not necessarily make you a good breeder.

A good breeder is able to practice breeding in a way that allows him to develop and improve his art. A bad breeder always blows his way around the market, stroking his own ego, telling lies about his produce and generally making other people feel uncomfortable about his presence. The first and most important standards to keep are honesty, sportsmanship and good communication skills.

If you can do this, people will be willing to help you learn more, offer their services, give positive feedback and more than likely BUY YOUR WORK.

I have seen breeders develop fantastic strains only to have their work simply sit on the shelf and not sell because of their social problems, business problems, lack of honesty and overall integrity. If you cannot overcome these personal shortcomings, then hire someone who can. Poor communication skills and lack of social standards will only pull your long-term work down the gutter. Normally reliable seed banks who carry your stock will engage the client on your behalf. The market would rather respond to an honest businessman with average strains than a dishonest businessman with elite strains. This is a reality in the cannabis breeding world. You've got to keep your cool and focus on your work. Find out what you are good at and try to do it the best you can.

Never think you are the best because you have developed something fantastic. Let others do the praising for you. The greatest pleasure you will have as a breeder is seeing other people enjoy your results.

THE MARKET

The market revolves around advertising, and advertising is only really recognized through reputable seed resellers and reputable growing organizations. The people you choose to sell your seeds for you are very important. If they have a bad reputation then they will not be able to sell your work. Seed resellers do not generally breed their own seeds. They simply act as a point of sale for getting your seed produce to the consumer. Seed resellers are also known as seed banks. They are the very same people from whom growers buy their seed stock.

Seeds Of Passion in Maastricht, Holland.

Seedbanks

http://www.geocities.com/stonedas72/AussieSPC.html — Australian Seeds
http://www.africanseeds.com — African Seeds Canada and Europe (Breeders)
http://www.hempdepot.ca — Hemp Depot Canada
http://www.hempqc.com — Heaven's Stairway Canada
http://www.eurohemp.com — Heaven's Stairway UK
http://www.hemcy.com — Hemcy Seeds Holland
http://www.legendsseeds.com — Legends Canada

http://www.emeryseeds.com — Marc Emery Direct Marijuana Seeds Canada
http://www.peakseeds.com — Peak Seeds Canada
http://www.seedsdirect.to — Seeds Direct UK
http://www.worldwideseeds.com — World Wide Seeds Switzerland
http://www.sensiseeds.com — Sensi Seed Bank (Breeders)
http://www.cannabisworld.com/cgi000/auction.cgi — Seed Auction Worldwide
http://www.greenhouse.org — Green House Seeds Amsterdam (Breeders)
http://www.dutch-passion.nl — Dutch Passion Seeds Amsterdam (Breeders)
http://www.seriousseeds.com — Serious Seeds Amsterdam (Breeders)
http://www.flyingdutchmen.com — The Flying Dutchmen Seeds (Breeders)
http://www.homegrownfantasy.com — Homegrown Fantasy (Breeders)
http://www.kcbrains.com — KC Brains Amsterdam (Breeders)

Some breeders decide to sell their own produce without the aid of a seed bank. They do this by setting up a point of sale on the internet or by using a P.O. box address. Most of their advertising is done by word of mouth. Here are the advantages and disadvantages of each method.

Seed Resellers (Seed Banks)
1. Give a percentage based on sales figures.
2. Require testing of your produce before they sell it.
3. Set a fixed price.
4. Sometimes require that you share the product rights with them to prevent you from selling your work elsewhere.
5. Do the advertising for you and promote your work.
6. Act as a point of contact between you and the client, keeping your identity closely guarded.

Self-Marketing
1. You always receive 100% of the money from sales.
2. You do not need to have people test your product before you can sell it.
3. You choose the price.
4. You retain the exclusive rights to your work.
5. You do the advertising.
6. Your identity may be hard to keep undisclosed.

As you can see each method has some good points and some bad points. These pros and cons also depend on the type of seed bank or breeder involved. Most breeders start in the game by giving their seeds away to growers for free before starting to sell their stock. This helps them generate some feedback and also helps them to understand more about consumers and what they like.

Many message board Websites on the internet with large memberships offer these testing services for free. You should try them out if you are interested in getting into the game.

http: //www.cannabisbook.com — Greg Green Cannabis Grow Forums and Website
http://www.hightimes.com — High Times Magazine
http://www.marijuananews.com — Marijuana News and Legal Information
http: //www.cannabistimes.com — Cannabis Times Newspaper
http://www.cannabis.com — General Cannabis Information Website
http://www.yahooka.com — General Cannabis Information Website
http://www.cannabisculture.com — Cannabis Culture Magazine
http://www.overgrow.com — Cannabis Growing Website
http://www.cannabisworld.com — Cannabis Growing Website
http://www.growadvice.com — Cannabis Growing Website
http://www.cannabishealth.com — Cannabis Health Website
http://www.erowid.org — Drug Information Website
http://www.lycaeum.org — Drug Information Website

Your marketing campaign will be aimed at letting people know about you and your strains. You may have to enter cannabis cup competitions and even hand a large quantity of your seeds out for free before you generate any real interest.

If you choose to go the resale route, here are some things that you should know about seed banks before you contact them.

- With a seed bank there is only one knowledgeable person who deals with seed sales—the owner. You should only contact the owner with any queries about selling your seeds. Never deal with anyone else.
- The owner will always use another breeder to test your seeds. You may even be asked to test another breeder's seeds yourself for the owner if you build up a reputation with the seed bank. Remember that the other breeder who will be testing your strain is someone who is respected by the seed bank for his breeding and growing skills.
- Always buy from the seed bank before you ask if you can sell your seeds to them. Buying more than once from them establishes a relationship with the seed bank. It teaches you how they treat their clients and how they ship your seeds. You can also grow out the seeds and check to see if their seeds meet your standards or if yours meet theirs.

- Be aware that when you sell your stock to a seed bank it can take anywhere to a year before the seed bank publishes your strain in its catalogues. This is because seed banks will require a period of testing and evaluation of your produce. You may end up spending a lot of money on developing and sending them seeds.
- The seed bank may ask for exclusive rights and the right to sell your product abroad. The seed bank may ask to simply buy the strain from you outright. They will then breed it under their own name. Or they may just wish to buy the rights for their sales regions, leaving other regions free for you to sell to.
- The big names in the seed bank business never fail. They are only getting bigger. Remember though that your strain may disappear among the vastness of their catalogues.
- You may have to sign a very real contract.

Apart from the commercial aspect, you should be breeding cannabis for yourself and your friends. Most breeders are more than happy to do this just as a hobby and not for profit.

WHY SHOULD WE BREED CANNABIS?

This is the foremost question that a breeder should be asking himself before engaging in a breeding project. It will establish the premise for his breeding ambitions, which may continue for a number of years, with improvements aimed at achieving their objectives along the way. Why should we bother breeding a new strain of Skunk if more than two dozen Skunk strains already exist? Why bother breeding another version of Blueberry when more than thirty Blueberry hybrids already exist? What is the purpose behind creating another Northern Lights hybrid when there are so many NL hybrids on the market?

There are plenty of reasons why breeders should not get involved in a five-year breeding program to begin with, however there are some core reasons why we should breed cannabis plants.

1. To improve a strain's qualities and lock down a trait we like.
2. To create something new.
3. To reproduce something that is lost.
4. To help create strains suitable for specific growing environments.

Let's examine these reasons more closely.

1. *To improve a strain's qualities and lock down a trait we like:* We may have obtained a strain that we like, but in its offspring we may notice that certain

traits are variable, such as potency, flavor or color. We may actually find in the offspring a trait that is better than what the parent plants had to offer. We may find that some of our plants are more potent than the rest.

Since it seems that what we are seeing is a trait that the original breeder did not breed for but is something that we think improves the strain, we can breed this trait true in future populations of this strain. This is why we have so many variations of certain strains like NL#5 and NL#9. When we have identified the trait that we like in the plant we will use breeding techniques to lock down this trait so that any future offspring will only show this specific trait without any variations. This is especially true for strains that are almost stable but contain some variations. When a trait is continued in the offspring without variations the trait is known as true breeding.

2. *To create something new:* The market demands change and growers tire of seeing the same strains over and over again. By breeding strains we can create new hybrids for the market.

If the strain is good the market will respond well. A new addition to the market recently is Blueberry which has done very well. Since then we have even seen numerous hybrid Blueberry plants appear on the market, such as Flo and Shishkeberry.

3. *To reproduce something that is lost:* It does happen that for some reason or another a breeder pulls out of breeding or loses the original parents of a particular strain. If such a situation should arise the breeding community may try to restore the strain again by using genetic material that is related to the lost strain. If both the original parents are completely gone then this can be a very hard task.

4. *To help create strains suitable for specific growing environments:* By breeding a strain under certain conditions we can actually create a strain that grows best under those conditions. Since what we observe in a plant's character is partially genetic and partially due to the growing environment, we tend to breed for traits that are influenced by that environment.

That is why so many strains are labeled as outdoor strains, indoor strains and greenhouse strains. Some strains are even created to suit specific types of grow methods such as **SOG, ScrOG** and **cabinet growing** (*CGB,* pp. 115-19).

If you breed a strain for indoor SOG growing then you are automatically isolating that strain to a specific type of market. Sometimes this can work out very well and sometimes not. Consider the following.

- New growers will probably grow out something like Skunk#1 because seed banks advise them to do so. Skunk#1 is a very stable strain and is very good for the beginner grower because it is easy to grow. The same goes for Northern Lights and Afghani#1.

- Top 44 is a very small plant. It can be flowered completely at only a foot or two in height. Thus it can be grown in very small spaces and is most suitable for that environment. It is also the quickest flowering strain and will finish in 44 days or less—hence the name Top 44.

- Cindy 99, is a plant that does very well in ScrOG setups. Nearly everyone who does ScrOG has tried Cindy 99.

Some nice short Indica plants that are bred for small spaces. Photo by Joe Schmoe.

These are some reasons why we breed cannabis plants and how we can breed cannabis plants to suit a certain area of the market. As a breeder you will probably want to seriously explore these points before you breed anything that you want to sell.

Most good breeders are serious growers or have been growing for quite a number of years. Through their growing experiences they find areas of the market that lack strains to meet their particular tastes and needs. This is when a breeder may develop a winning strain that suits a certain market area.

Breeding is also about knowing when and why you should develop a strain. If you can give good REASONS for creating your strain then you will draw interest to your project.

BREEDING FOR YOURSELF
Some strains that have taken the market by storm have not been planned for the mar-

ket. A breeder may create a strain 'on the fly' and suddenly find that people like it and want to buy it. This type of breeding is hit or miss and you may have to develop twenty or more strains before one of them is discovered as being very suitable for a market area.

THE BASIC CONCEPT OF CANNABIS BREEDING

Cannabis strains are, quite simply, recombinations of each other's genetic material. Actually every cannabis strain is a recombination of cannabis genetic material, but in terms of pure species types, i.e., Pure Indica, Pure Sativa, Pure Ruderalis, they are a recombination of genetic material from that pure species type without influence from another species. That is what makes them pure lines.

All the genes for every cannabis strain
stem from the pure species type gene pools.
The pure species types are the building blocks behind the *mostly*-type strains, i.e., Mostly Indica, Mostly Sativa, Mostly Ruderalis. Without the pure species types we would not have the *mostly* strains. The following chapter will help to explain this further as well.

CANNABIS SPECIES

Originally cannabis was classed by biologists as just *Cannabis Sativa L.* However, today's cannabis researcher has seen this classification further divide into three main species of cannabis that occur naturally in the wild. These are: *Cannabis Sativa, Cannabis Indica* and *Cannabis Ruderalis.*

SPECIES DESCRIPTION TABLE

Species	Height	Nodes	Leaves	Blades
SATIVA	Tall, averaging between 4 and 15 feet	Long internodes between branches, 3 to 6 inches	Pointy leaves with no markings or patterns	Usually between 6 and 12 blades per leaf
INDICA	Small, averaging between 6 inches and 4 feet	Short internodes between branches 3 inches and less	Wide, short and rounded leaves, with marble-like patterns	Usually between 3 and 5 blades per leaf
RUDERALIS	Small, averaging between 6 inches and 4 feet	Very short internodes with much branching	Small and thick	Usually between 4 and 6 blades per leaf

It is generally accepted by most growers that these three species can be obtained in pure form. This means that each species type can be obtained without another species influence. We must remember that historically the different species would have stemmed from the same line; however, evolution and diversity have caused these three species types to develop separately around the globe.

Normally in biology two different species should not be able to crossbreed. However, there are some exceptions to the rule. Cannabis researches and growers see the cannabis species as an exception to the rule. It is for this reason that cannabis breeders also classify their strains according to each of these species types even though mainstream botany science has only one classification for the cannabis species—Cannabis Sativa L.*

Each of these cannabis species is very unique in appearance and growth. They are also very unique in most of their properties including the high type. Each of the species types has a subset of strains that are classed as either a pure species type or a mix of the species. Due to hybridization the subset of each species looks like this:

SPECIES SUBSET TYPES

Pure Indica	A pure Indica species that is either derived directly from a landrace Indica or is mixed with other pure Indica strains.
Pure Sativa	A pure Sativa species that is either derived directly from a landrace Sativa or is mixed with other pure Sativa strains.
Pure Ruderalis	A pure Ruderalis species that is either derived directly from a landrace Ruderalis or is mixed with other pure Ruderalis strains.
Mostly Indica	A mix of Indica and Sativa strains that incline towards Indica characteristics.
Mostly Sativa	A mix of Sativa and Indica strains that incline towards Sativa characteristics.
Mostly Ruderalis	A mix of Ruderalis with either Indica or Sativa strains that incline towards Ruderalis characteristics.
Indica/Sativa	A strain that displays equal amounts of Indica and Sativa characteristics.
Indica/Ruderalis	A strain that displays equal amounts of Indica and Ruderalis characteristics.
Sativa/Ruderalis	A strain that displays equal amounts of Sativa and Ruderalis characteristics.
Indica/Sativa/ Ruderalis	A strain that displays equal amounts of Indica, Sativa and Ruderalis characteristics.

*Many researchers believe that Cannabis Sativa L. is the only recognized species type by Western biologists because of legal ramifications and not because of plant classification systems. When Cannabis Indica was introduced to the occident it was initially presumed to be uncontrolled by cannabis prohibition laws which only stipulated that Cannabis Sativa L. should be controlled. However the courts refused to acknowledge the existence of this separate cannabis species and thus treated all the cannabis species as just Cannabis Sativa L.

Cannabis Ruderalis is not very popular with growers because of its auto-flowering properties (*CGB,* p. 17). This means that the species does not flower according to the **photoperiod** but flowers according to age and maturity. Growers like to control the flowering properties of their plants and so breeders rarely ever use Ruderalis in breeding projects and seed banks rarely ever stock Ruderalis genetics.

It is for this reason that Indica and Sativa strains are not mixed with Ruderalis. In fact, it is now very rare to find Ruderalis strains sold by seed banks because of the strains' unpopularity among cultivators. This means that there are truly only five types of cannabis species subsets being produced by breeders. These are: Pure Indica, Pure Sativa, Mostly Indica, Mostly Sativa and Indica/Sativa varieties.

THE CANNABIS SPECIES PROBLEM*

Because US and other legislations have made specific reference to Cannabis Sativa L. as a proscribed plant, many cannabis cultivators have turned to the use of Cannabis Indica and Cannabis Ruderalis as non-proscribed cannabis species to beat the law. This has resulted in the courts having to dismiss many cases against defendants because of this technicality. R. E. Schultes of Harvard University began testifying in cases in 1972 to show that cannabis could be found in three distinctive species types. A number of respectable botanists including William A. Emboden, also testified in court as to the distinct separate species of cannabis.

In 1975, Ernest Small, while working for the "Canadian Government Commission of Inquiry into the Non-Medical Use of Drugs" was asked to combat this problem by linking Cannabis Indica and Cannabis Ruderalis as just variations of Cannabis Sativa L. and not as separate species. The debate still continues today although it is generally recognized by most cannabis researchers and growers that there are indeed three very distinct species of cannabis.

Carl von Linné (1707–78) or Carolus Linnaeus (Latinized version) was a Swedish botanist and founder of modern systematic botany and zoology. He devised a clas-

---

* The current cannabis species model is classed as follows: Cannabis indica Lam., Cannabis indica Lam. var. kafiristanica Vavilov, Cannabis ruderalis Janisch., Cannabis sativa L. subsp. indica (Lam.) E.Small & Cronquist, Cannabis sativa L. subsp. indica (Lam.) E.Small & Cronquist var. indica, Cannabis sativa L. subsp. indica (Lam.) E.Small & Cronquist var. kafiristanica (Vavilov) E.Small & Cronquist, Cannabis sativa L. subsp. Sativa, Cannabis sativa L. subsp. sativa var. sativa, Cannabis sativa L. subsp. sativa var. spontanea. However, Sativa L only precedes Indica and Ruderalis because it is presumed to be the earlier form of cannabis. This does not appear to be the case. The incorrect current scientific model does not prove whether Sativa or Indica or Ruderalis came first. In Chapter 17 An Introduction to the Sexual Evolution of Cannabis, shows that all these species where derived from separate gene pools and are mutations of another primordial form of cannabis. This has since been proven because of chemical genotype comparisons published in the *American Journal of Botany* A chemotaxonomic analysis of cannabinoid variation in Cannabis (Cannabaceae) by Hillig and Mahlberg Am. J. Bot..2004; 91: 966-975‰ which can be found at http://www.amjbot.org/cgi/content/full/91/6/966

sification system for flowering plants based on stamen type and number of pistils, and became the authority to whom collectors all over the world sent specimens. He described over 7,000 plants, introducing binomial Latin names, although his classification was later superseded by that of Antoine Jussieu. He set out his system in *Systema Naturae* (1735) and other works which are internationally recognized as the starting points for botanical nomenclature respectively. In 1753 he recognized only one species of Cannabis—Cannabis Sativa L.

French naturalist Jean-Baptiste de Lamarck (1744–1829) was an early proponent of organic evolution. Darwin would later draw much from his work. In 1783, Lamarck discovered Cannabis Indica by way of samples that had been sent from India to him by a man named Sonnerat. He published his findings on Cannabis Indica in 1785.

In 1924 the Russian botanist Janischevsky discovered a new species of cannabis growing in Southeastern Russia that he called Cannabis Ruderalis.

The discoveries of Lamarck and Janischevsky contradicted Linnaeus's accepted view that cannabis was a monotypic genus—that genus being Cannabis Sativa L. However Linnaeus had not observed Cannabis Indica nor had he observed Cannabis Ruderalis.

In 1929 Russian botanist Nicolai Vavilov visited northern Afghanistan and discovered the locals cultivating Cannabis Sativa for hashish production. However, east towards the Pakistan border, Vavilov discovered Cannabis Indica in two very unique strain types which appeared to be growing wild. He named the strains Cannabis Indica Afghanica and Cannabis Indica Kafiristanica. Vavilov had discovered Cannabis Indica that was not being used for hashish production and so had found a true wild species of Cannabis Indica. It wasn't until much later that Afghanistan began to process this species into a **cultivar** for hashish extraction. The important point is that Vavilov had found wild Cannabis Indica in 1929 and that the plant did not exhibit any traits of being a cultivar.

The term *Indian hemp* refers to any variation of cannabis that is grown in India. This included both Cannabis Sativa L. and Cannabis Indica, however early botanists sometimes found the term *hemp* confusing and often attributed only Cannabis Sativa L. to it. In fact many went so far as to claim two separate variations of the Indian hemp plant: *Cannabis Sativa L. subsp. culta* and *Cannabis Sativa L. subsp. spontanea*. The subspecies culta referred to cultivated Indian hemp and the subspecies spontanea referred to wild Indian hemp. Today breeders, growers and botanists simply treat both these types of Indian hemp as simply strain types of Sativa or Indica varieties, with cultivars tending to be more uniform in growth than wild or landrace strains.

The main problem with the cannabis species is not cannabis itself but universal discrepancies on what constitutes a species. Taxonomy does not have any clear definitions on what a species actually is. One rule is that a species should not be able to break the confines of what is called a species breeding barrier. This means that species should not be able to breed outside of themselves. Cannabis Indica, Sativa and Ruderalis are all interfertile, meaning that they can breed outside of their species barrier, among themselves, but botanists still remain uncertain as to this definition. One example is that of the horse and the donkey. These are two separate species that can interbreed, however they produce a mule, which is infertile. This led many biologists to explain that "a species consists of those populations that can breed and produce fertile offspring." Since the mule is infertile, the horse and donkey remain two different species. The same also occurs with the 'liger', the offspring of a tiger and lion that produces an infertile 'liger.' However what also must be noted here is that the mule and the liger are artificial creations. In the wild, geographical isolation prevents this from happening. Many biologists believe that geographical isolation eventually creates a complete species breeding barrier that prevents different species from being interfertile and that what we are observing with some species interbreeding is in fact just a moment in their development that allows for interfertility but it will sooner or later become impossible as long as their isolation from one another is maintained. Cannabis Sativa, Indica and Ruderalis do not take advantage of their interfertility in the wild because of geographic isolation but they do when mankind interferes with them. This process is known as a 'ring species.' Salamanders are a very good example of a 'ring species.' Some species of salamander can interbreed while other species cannot. Other examples of a ring species include birds like the gull.

2 | BASIC BREEDING

IF YOU WANT TO CONTINUE GROWING a strain that you enjoy, cloning is your best option. You could also continue the strain by breeding two plants to produce seeds. You won't completely replicate the strain again using the seed method, however, unless the two parent plants are from the same *IBL* (inbred line). Even if the two plants are not IBLs, they should produce seeds that contain most of the parents' features. If you want to create a plant with characteristics from two different strains, breeding the marijuana from seed is your only option. That is the subject of this chapter, which begins with an introduction to simple breeding procedures and then goes on to cover advanced techniques like breeding a true strain and backcrossing.

MAKING SEEDS

How easy is it to make seeds? It's easy if you have healthy plants and a stable growing environment. When your male plants burst their pollen sacks in your grow room they'll pollinate the female flowers. You can also administer pollen directly to your females if you prefer.

COLLECTING AND STORING POLLEN

Pollen can be extracted from male flowers as soon as they open: you'll see the male flower open out from its calyx. It is best to gather pollen after it falls from the pod onto the leaves. You can shake the pollen onto the female flowers to pollinate them or grow your males separately and store their pollen for future use.

Film canisters are great for storing pollen. You can save pollen in a canister for the next harvest. Although it can be stored in the freezer for as long as 18 months, pollen is best used within six months of collection. Pollen has been known to keep for longer than 18 months, but is usually not viable past this time.

COLLECTING AND STORING SEEDS

If you have pollinated your plants, at the end of the flowering stage the bud will contain seeds. The seeds should be gray, tan or dark brown in color. They may also be striped, banded or lined with different colored markings. If they are pale cream or white in color, then they are probably not viable and you have harvested them too early. You should wait until the end of flowering to harvest your seeds.

Your seeds will be mixed in with the bud and it can take quite a bit of time to separate them from their sticky calyx pods. Do not squeeze the calyx directly because you can damage the seed inside. Just tease the seed out from the calyx with your fingers. If you do not want the bud you can brush a seeded flowering branch against some fabric or a sieve to release the seeds from their respective calyx pods. It is easier to remove seeds from dry, cured bud than from freshly harvested plants.

If you plan to use the seeds in more than two years' time, store them in an airtight container and place this in a freezer. If you plan to use the seeds within the next two years, storing them in a standard film canister or similar container will work well. Keep this canister away from heat and direct light and do not let it get damp or you risk spoiling your seeds. Containers placed in the freezer should not be opened until you are ready to use them. Allow the seeds to thaw at room temperature for at least 12 hours before use.

SIMPLE BREEDING

Your approach to breeding will depend on what you ultimately hope to achieve. Do you want to create a new strain, create seeds that are similar to the parents, or cross two plants to create a simple hybrid strain?

CONTINUING A STRAIN THROUGH SEEDS

Say you purchased $120 worth of Silver Haze seeds and you want to make more seeds without any interference from another strain. That's easy. Just make sure that the male and female plants you breed with are from the same strain batch. In this instance the same strain batch would be Silver Haze from the same breeder. If you use Silver Haze from different breeders then the offspring may express a great deal of variation. This is because most breeders create their own versions of a popular strain. Their variety may have dissimilar characteristics from those of other breeders who have bred the same strain.

If you only have Silver Haze from the same breeder in your grow room, then all you need are a group of males and a group of females. Let the males pollinate the females and you will get more Silver Haze seeds, but you will lose some of the features of the original parent plants unless the strain you have is an IBL or from a very stable inbred pure line.

MAKING A SIMPLE HYBRID
Again, making a simple hybrid is easy. Just take a male plant from one strain and a female plant from another, for example Big Bud and Skunk. The result will be Big Bud x Skunk, but there will be differences in the offspring. Some of the plants will exhibit more Big Bud traits and some will exhibit more Skunk traits. Genes not expressed by each of the parents may also appear in the offspring.

If you want to breed for specific traits by eliminating variations, ultimately creating uniform plants or even an IBL, then you should start with a basic knowledge of plant genetics.

INTRODUCTION TO PLANT GENETICS
Genetics can be somewhat difficult to understand at first so we'll start by explaining a few rudimentary concepts and the basic terminology. The explanations for the words below can be treated as a glossary for your benefit.

Genes
Genes are the units of heredity transmitted from parent to offspring, usually as part of a chromosome. Genes usually control or determine a single characteristic in the offspring. There are genes responsible for each feature of your plant to be inherited, including leaf color, stem structure, texture, smell, potency, etc.

Gene Pairs
All of life is made up of a pattern of genes. You can think of this pattern as being similar to the two sides of a zipper. One side is inherited from the mother and the other from the father. Each gene occupies a specific locus, or particular space on the chain, and controls information about the eventual characteristics of the plant. So each gene locus contains two genes, one from the mother and one from the father. These gene pairs are usually denoted by a pair of letters, such as BB, Bb, Pp, pp, etc. Capital letters refer to dominant genes while lowercase letters refer to recessive genes. By way of example, B can represent Big Bud while b can represent small bud. Any letter can be assigned to any trait or gene pair when you are working out your own breeding program.

HYBRIDIZING FOR SELECTION
Hybridizing through multiple selections for better selections.

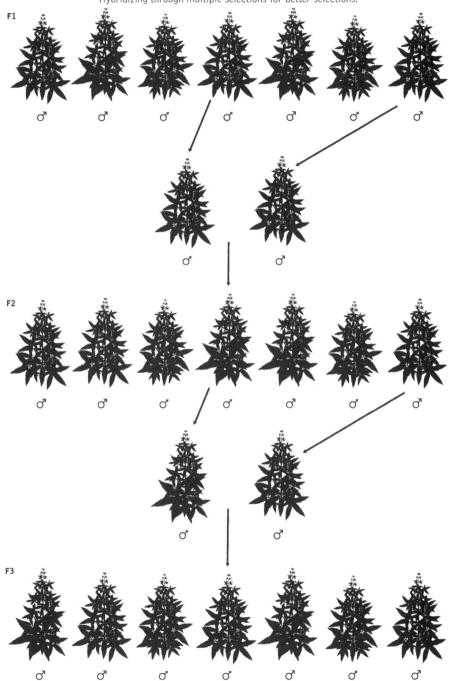

Chromosome
A threadlike structure of nucleic acids and proteins in the cell nuclei of higher organisms that carries a set of linked genes, usually paired.

Locus
A position on a chromosome where a particular gene pair is located.

Allele
Alleles are any of a number of alternative forms of one gene. For example the gene for purple bud color may have two forms, or alleles, one for purple and one for dark red.

Homozygous
Having identical alleles at one or more genetic loci, which is not a heterozygote (see below) and breeds true. Your plant is said to be homozygous for one feature when it carries the same gene twice in the responsible gene pair, which means both genes of the gene pair are identical.

Heterozygous
Having different alleles at one or more genetic loci. Your plant is said to be heterozygous for one feature when the genes of the responsible gene pair are unequal, or dissimilar.

Phenotype
The phenotype is the summary of all of the features you can detect or recognize on the outside of your plant, including color, smell and taste.

Genotype
The *genotype* is the genetic constitution of your plant, as distinguished from the phenotype. The genotype characterizes how your plant looks from the inside. It is the summary of all the genetic information that your plant carries and passes on to its offspring.

Dominant
Dominant is used to describe a gene or allele that is expressed even when inherited from only one parent. It is also used to describe a hereditary trait controlled by a gene and appearing in an individual to the exclusion of its counterpart, when alleles for both are present. Only one dominant allele in the gene pair must be present to become the expressed genotype and eventually the expressed phenotype of your plant.

Recessive

Recessive describes a gene, allele or hereditary trait perceptibly expressed only in homozygotes, being masked in heterozygotes by a dominant allele or trait. A gene is called recessive when its effect cannot be seen in the phenotype of your plant when only one allele is present. The same allele must be present twice in the gene pair in order for you to see it expressed in the phenotype of your plant.

BACKCROSSING
The backcross breeding method.

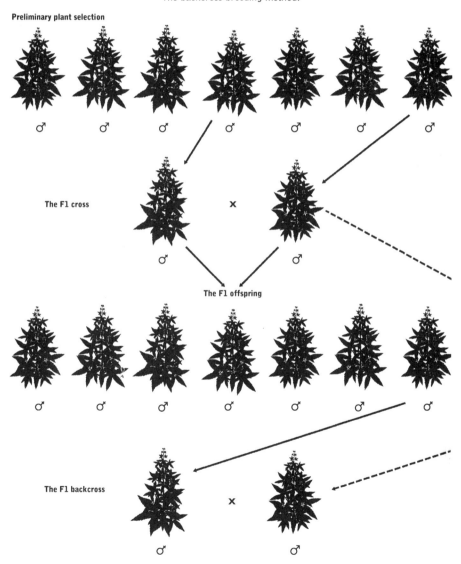

Dominant/Recessive and Genetic Notation

Assume that the dominant 'B' allele carries the hereditary trait for Big Bud, while the recessive 'b' allele carries the hereditary trait for small bud. Since B is dominant, a plant with a Bb genotype will always produce Big Bud. The B is dominant over the b. In order for a recessive gene to be displayed in the phenotype, both genes in the gene pair must be recessive. So a plant with the BB or Bb gene will always produce Big Bud. Only a plant with the bb gene will produce small bud.

Now that we have explained the basic terminology of plant genetics, we can move on to the next step: rudimentary breeding concepts as laid out in the Hardy-Weinberg law of genetic equilibrium.

THE HARDY-WEINBERG MODEL OF GENETIC EQUILIBRIUM

An understanding of plant breeding requires a basic understanding of the Hardy-Weinberg law. To illustrate the value of the Hardy-Weinberg law, ask yourself a question, like: "If purple bud color is a dominant trait, why do some of the offspring of my purple bud strain have green buds?" or "I have been selecting Indica mothers and cross-breeding them with Mostly Indica male plants but I have some Sativa leaves. Why?" These questions can be easily answered by developing an understanding of the Hardy-Weinberg law and the factors that can disrupt genetic equilibrium.

The first of these questions reflects a very common misconception: that the dominant allele of a trait will always have the highest frequency in a population and the recessive allele will always have the lowest frequency. This is not always the case. A dominant trait will not necessarily spread to a whole population, nor will a recessive trait always eventually die out.

Gene frequencies can occur in high or low ratios, regardless of how the allele is expressed. The allele can also change, depending on certain conditions. These changes in gene frequencies over time result in different plant characteristics.

A genetic population is basically a group of individuals of the same species (Cannabis Indica or Cannabis Sativa) or strain (Skunk#1 or Master Kush) in a given area whose members can breed with one another. This means that they must share a common group of genes. This common group of genes is locally known as the gene pool. The gene pool contains the alleles for all of the traits in the entire population. For a step in evolution—a new plant species, strain or trait—to occur, some of the gene frequencies must change. The gene frequency of an allele refers to the number of times an allele for a particular trait occurs compared to the total number of alleles for that trait in the population. Gene frequency is calculated by dividing the number of a specific type of allele by the total number of alleles in the gene pool.

Genetic Equilibrium Theory and Application

The Hardy-Weinberg model of genetic equilibrium describes a theoretical situation in which there is no change in the gene pool. At equilibrium there can be no change or evolution.

RANDOM MATING
Wild non-random mating resulting in unknown male donors.

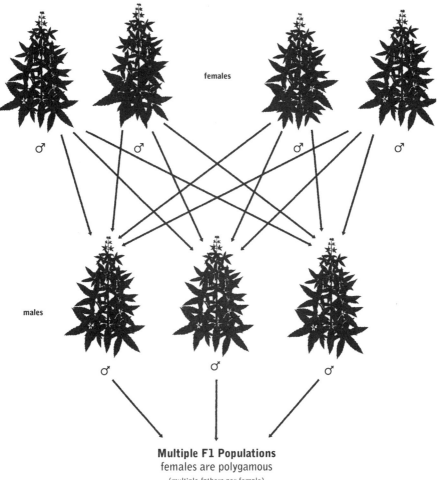

females

males

Multiple F1 Populations
females are polygamous
(multiple fathers per female)

Let's consider a population whose gene pool contains the alleles B and b.

Assign the letter p to the frequency of the dominant allele B and the letter q to the frequency of the recessive allele b. We know that the sum of all the alleles must equal 100 percent, so:

$$p + q = 100\%$$

This can also be expressed as:

$$p + q = 1$$

And all of the random possible combinations of the members of a population would equal:

$$p^2 + 2pq + q^2$$

Where:

p	= frequency of the dominant allele in a population
q	= frequency of the recessive allele in a population
p^2	= percentage of homozygous dominant individuals
q^2	= percentage of heterozygous recessive individuals
$2pq$	= percentage of heterozygous individuals

Imagine that you have grown a population of 1,000 'Black Domina' cannabis plants from seeds obtained from a well-known seed bank. In that population, 360 plants emit a skunky smell, while the remaining 640 plants emit a fruity smell. You contact the seed bank and ask them which smell is dominant in this partic-ular strain. Hypothetically, they tell you that the breeder selected for a fruity smell and the skunk smell is a recessive genotype. You can call this recessive genotype 'vv' and use the formula above to answer the following questions.

Question: According to the Hardy-Weinberg law, what is the frequency of the 'vv' genotype?

Answer: Since 360 out of the 1,000 plants have the 'vv' genotype, then 36% is the frequency of 'vv' in this population of 'Black Domina.'

Question: According to the Hardy-Weinberg law, what is the frequency of the 'v' allele?

WILD POLLINATION
Cannabis pollination and seed production.

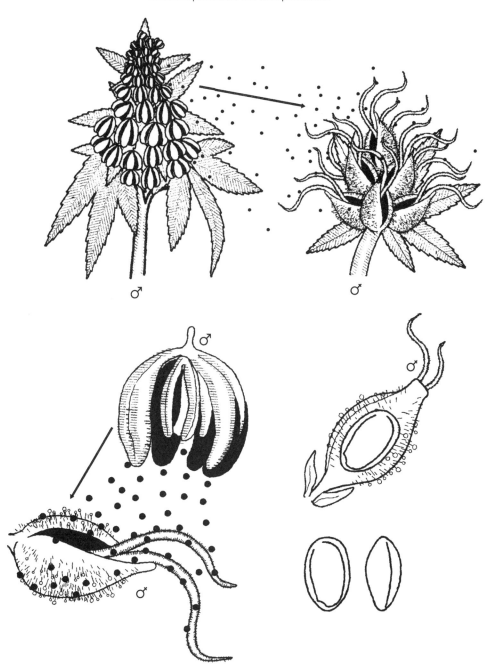

Answer: The frequency of the 'vv' allele is 36%. Since q^2 is the percentage of homozygous recessive individuals, and q is the frequency of the recessive allele in a population, the following must also be true:

$q^2 = 0.36$
$(q \times q) = 0.36$
$q = 0.6$

Thus, the frequency of the 'v' allele is 60%.

Question: According to the Hardy-Weinberg law, what is the frequency of the 'V' allele?

Answer: Since q = 0.6, we can solve for p.

$p + q = 1$
$p + 0.6 = 1$
$p = 1 - 0.6$
$p = 0.4$

The frequency of the 'V' allele is 40%.

Question: According to the Hardy-Weinberg law, what is the frequency of the genotypes 'VV' and 'Vv'?

Answer: Given what we know, the following must be true:

$VV = p^2$
$V = 0.4 = p$
$(p \times p) = p^2$
$(0.4 \times 0.4) = p^2$
$0.16 = p^2$
$VV = 0.16$

The frequency of the genotype 'VV' is 16%

$VV = 0.16$
$vv = 0.36$
$VV + Vv + vv = 1$

0.16 + Vv + 0.36 = 1
0.52 + Vv = 1
Vv = 1 − 0.52
Vv = 0.48 or 48%

Or alternatively, 'Vv' is 2pq, therefore:

Vv = 2pq
2pq = 2 x p x q
2pq = 2 x 0.4 x 0.6
2pq = 0.48 or 48%

The frequencies of V and v (p and q) will remain unchanged, generation after generation, as long as the following five statements are true:
1. The population is large enough
2. There are no mutations
3. There are no preferences, for example a VV male does not prefer a vv female by its nature
4. No other outside population exchanges genes with this population
5. Natural selection does not favor any specific gene

The equation $p^2 + 2pq + q^2$ can be used to calculate the different frequencies. Although this equation is important to know about, we make use of other more basic calculations when breeding. The important thing to note here is the five conditions for equilibrium.

Earlier we asked the question: "I have been selecting Indica mothers and cross-breeding them with mostly Indica male plants but I have some Sativa leaves. Why?" The Hardy-Weinberg equilibrium tells us that outside genetics may have been introduced into the breeding program. Since the Mostly Indica male plants are only Mostly Indica and not Pure Indica, you can expect to discover some Sativa characteristics in the offspring, including the Sativa leaf trait.

THE TEST CROSS
Some of you may be asking the question: "How do I know if a trait such as bud color is homozygous dominant (BB), heterozygous (Bb) or homozygous recessive (bb)?"

If you've been given seeds or a clone you may have been told that a trait, such as potency, is homozygous dominant, heterozygous or homozygous recessive. However, you will want to establish this yourself, especially if you intend to use those specific traits in a future breeding plan. To do this, you will have to perform what is called a test cross.

Determining the phenotype of a plant is fairly straightforward. You look at the plant and you see, smell, feel or taste its phenotype. Determining the genotype cannot be achieved through simple observation alone.

Generally speaking, there are three possible genotypes for each plant trait. For example, if Golden Bud is dominant and Silver Bud is recessive, the possible genotypes are:

Homozygous Dominant: BB = Golden Bud
Heterozygous: Bb = Golden Bud
Homozygous Recessive: bb = Silver Bud

The Golden and Silver Bud colors are the phenotypes. BB, Bb and bb denote the genotypes. Because B is the dominant allele, Bb would appear Golden and not Silver. Most phenotypes are visual characteristics but some, like bud taste, are phenotypes that can't be observed by the naked eye and are experienced instead through the other senses.

For example, looking at a Mostly Sativa species like a Skunk plant you will notice that the leaves are pale green. In a population of these Skunk plants you may notice that a few have dark-green leaves. This suggests that this Skunk strain's leaf color is not true breeding, meaning that the leaf trait must be heterozygous because homozygous dominant and homozygous recessive traits are true breeding. Some of the Skunk's pale-green leaf traits will probably be homozygous dominant in this population.

You may also be asking the question: "Could the pale-green trait be the homozygous recessive trait and the dark-green leaf the heterozygous trait?" Since a completely homozygous recessive population (bb) would not contain the allele (B) for heterozygous expression (Bb) or for homozygous dominant expression (BB), it is impossible for the traits for heterozygous (Bb) or homozygous dominant (BB) to exist in a population that is completely homozygous recessive (bb) for that trait. If a population is completely homozygous for that trait (bb or BB), then that specific trait can be considered stable, true breeding or 'will breed true.' If a population is heterozygous for that trait (Bb) then that specific trait can be considered unstable, not true breeding or 'will not breed true.'

If the trait for Bb or BB cannot exist in a bb population for that trait, then bb is the only trait that you will discover in that population. Hence, bb is true breeding. If there is a variation in the trait, and the Hardy-Weinberg law of equilibrium has not been broken, the trait must be heterozygous. In our Skunk example there were only a few dark-green leaves. This means that the dark-green leaves are homozygous recessive and the pale-green leaves are heterozygous and may possibly be homozygous dominant too.

You may also notice that the bud is golden on most of the plants. This also suggests that the Golden Bud color is a dominant trait. If buds on only a few of the plants are Silver, this suggests that the Silver trait is recessive. You know the only genotype that produces the recessive trait is homozygous recessive (bb). So if a plant displays a recessive trait in its phenotype, its genotype must be homozygous recessive. *A plant that displays a recessive trait in its phenotype always has a homozygous recessive genotype.* But this leaves you with an additional question to answer as well: Are the Golden Bud or pale-green leaf color traits homozygous dominant (BB) or heterozygous (Bb)? You cannot be completely certain of any of your inferences until you have completed a test cross.

A test cross is a performed by breeding a plant with an unknown dominant genotype (BB or Bb) with a plant that is homozygous recessive (bb) for the same trait. For this test you will need another cannabis plant of the opposite sex that is homozygous recessive (bb) *for the same trait.*

This brings us to an important rule: *If any offspring from a test cross display the recessive trait, the genotype of the parent with the dominant trait must be heterozygous and not homozygous.*

In our example, our unknown genotype is either BB or Bb. The Silver Bud genotype is bb. We'll put this information into a mathematical series known as Punnett squares.

	b	b
B		
?		

We start by entering the known genotypes. We do these calculations for two parents that will breed. We know that our recessive trait is bb and the other is either BB or Bb, so we'll use *B?* for the time being. Our next step is to fill the box in with what we can calculate.

	b	b
B	Bb	bb
?	?b	?b

The first row of offspring Bb and Bb will have the dominant trait of Golden Bud. The second row can either contain Bb or bb offspring. This will either lead to off-spring that will produce more Golden Bud (Bb) or Silver Bud (bb). The first possible outcome (where ? = B) would give us Golden Bud (Bb) offspring. The second possible outcome (where ? = b) would give us Silver Bud (bb) offspring. We can also predict what the frequency will be.

Outcome 1, where ? = B:
   Bb + Bb + Bb + Bb = 4Bb
   100% Golden Bud

Outcome 2, where ? = b:
   Bb + Bb + bb + bb = 2 Bb + 2bb
   50% Golden Bud and 50% Silver Bud

Recall:
   Homozygous Dominant: BB = Golden Bud
   Heterozygous: Bb = Golden Bud
   Homozygous Recessive: bb = Silver Bud

To determine the identity of B?, we used another cannabis plant of the opposite sex that was homozygous recessive (bb) *for the same trait.*

Outcome 2 tells us that:
• Both parents must have at least one b trait each to exhibit Silver Bud in the phenotype of the offspring.
• If any Silver Bud is produced in the offspring then the mystery parent (B?) must be heterozygous (Bb). It cannot be homozygous dominant (BB).

So, if a Golden Bud parent is crossed with a Silver Bud parent and produces only Golden Bud, then the Golden Bud parent must be homozygous dominant for that trait. If any Silver Bud offspring is produced, then the Golden Bud parent must be heterozygous for that trait.

To summarize, the guidelines for performing a test cross to determine the geno-type of a plant exhibiting a dominant trait are:

1. The plant with the dominant trait should always be crossed with a plant with the recessive trait.
2. If any offspring display the recessive trait, the unknown genotype is heterozygous.
3. If all the offspring display the dominant trait, the unknown genotype is homozygous dominant.

The main reasons behind performing a test cross are:

1. When you breed plants you want to continue a trait, like height, taste, smell, etc.
2. When you want to continue that trait you must know if it is homozygous dom-inant, heterozygous or homozygous recessive.
3. You can only determine this with certainty by performing a test cross.

We should mention that, as a breeder, you should be dealing with a large popula-tion in order to be certain of the results. The more plants you work with, the more reliable the results.

HARDY-WEINBERG LAW, PART 2

The question may arise: "How do I breed for several traits, like taste, smell, vigor and color?" To answer this question, you will need to learn more about the Hardy-Weinberg law of genetic equilibrium.

If you breed two plants that are heterozygous (Bb) for a trait, what will the off-spring look like? The Punnett squares can help us determine the phenotypes, genotypes and gene frequencies of the offspring.

	B	b
B	BB	Bb
b	Bb	bb*

*Take special note of this offspring and compare it with the parents.

In this group, the resulting offspring will be:

1 BB - 25% of the offspring will be homozygous for the dominant allele (BB)
2 Bb - 50% will be heterozygous, like their parents (Bb)
1 bb - 25% will be homozygous for the recessive allele (bb)

Unlike their parents (Bb and Bb), 25% of offspring will express the recessive phe-notype bb. So two parents that display Golden Bud but are both heterozygous (Bb) for that trait will produce offspring that exhibit the recessive Silver Bud trait, despite the fact that neither of the parents displays the phenotype for Silver Bud.

Understanding how recessive and dominant traits are passed down through the phenotype and genotype so that you can predict the outcome of a cross and lock down traits in future generations is really what breeding is all about.

When you breed a strain, how do you know that the traits you want to keep will actually be retained in the breeding process? This is where the test cross comes in. If you create seeds from a strain that you bought from a seed bank, how can you be sure that the offspring will exhibit the characteristics that you like? If the trait you wish to continue is homozygous dominant (BB) in both parent plants then there's no way that you can produce a recessive genotype for that trait in the offspring, as illustrated in the Punnett square below.

	B	B
B	BB	BB
B	BB	BB

It is impossible for the recessive trait to appear. And if both parents contain the recessive trait then they cannot produce the dominant trait.

	b	b
b	bb	bb
b	bb	bb

In order to breed a trait properly you must know if it is homozygous, heterozygous or homozygous recessive so that you can *predict* the results before they happen.

MENDEL AND THE PEA EXPERIMENTS

Gregor Mendel (1822-1884) was an Austrian monk who discovered the basic rules of inheritance by analyzing the results from his plant breeding research programs. He noticed that two types of pea plants gave very uniform results when bred within their own gene pools and not with one another. The traits he noticed were:

PEA PLANT #1	PEA PLANT #2
Solid seed shells	Wrinkled seed shells
Green seeds	Yellow seeds
White flowers	Purple flowers
Tall plants	Short plants

He noticed that the offspring all carried the same traits when they bred with the same population or gene pool. Since there were no variations within each strain he guessed that both strains were homozygous for these traits. Because the pea plants were from the same species, Mendel guessed that either the solid seed shells were recessive or the wrinkled seed shells were recessive. Using the genotype notations SS for solid seed shells and ss for wrinkled seed shells, he knew that they couldn't be Ss because one lot didn't exhibit any of the other strain's phenotypes when bred within its own gene pool.

Let's illustrate this using two basic Punnett squares where SS is pea plant #1 with the trait for solid seed shells and ss is pea plant #2 with the trait for wrinkled seed shells.

Pea plant #1 results:

	S	S
S	SS	SS
S	SS	SS

All the offspring will be SS.

Pea plant #2 results:

	s	s
s	ss	ss
s	ss	ss

All the offspring will be ss.

The First Hybrid Cross (the F1 Generation)
Mendel made his first hybrid cross between the two strains and the results were all solid seeds as seen in the chart below.

	s	s
S	Ss	Ss
S	Ss	Ss

Up until this point, he didn't know which trait was recessive and which was dominant. Since all the seeds shells were solid, he now knows with certainty that pea plant #1 contained the dominant genotype for solid seed shells and pea plant #2 contained the recessive genotype for wrinkled seed shells. This meant that in future test crosses with other pea strains, he could determine if a particular seed shell trait was homozygous or heterozygous because he had identified the recessive trait (ss).

The Second Hybrid Cross (the F2 Generation)

The offspring in the F1 cross were all Ss. When Mendel crossed these offspring he got the following results:

F2 Cross	S	s
S	SS	Ss
s	Ss	ss*

*Take special note of this offspring and compare with parents.

Mendel had mated two pea plants that were heterozygous (e.g., Ss) for a seed shell trait. In this group, the resulting offspring were:

25% of the offspring were homozygous for the dominant allele (SS)
50% were heterozygous, like their parents (Ss)
25% were homozygous for the recessive allele (ss)

In his first cross to create the hybrid plant, Mendel ended up with no recessive traits for seed shape. But when he crossed the offspring, because they were heterozygous for that trait, he ended up with some having the homozygous recessive trait, some having the homozygous dominant trait and some continuing the heterozygous trait. In correct breeding terms his first cross between the plants is called the F1 cross or F1 generation. The breeding out of those offspring is called the F2 cross or F2 generation.

Now since he has Ss, ss and SS to work with you could use Punnett squares to determine what the next generations of offspring will look like. Compare your results with what you have learned about ratios and you'll be able to see how it all fits together.

More on Genetic Frequencies

Take a look at the cross below between two heterozygous parents. If two heterozygous parents are crossed, the frequency ratio of the alleles will be 50% each. Remember the genotype can be Ss, SS or ss, but the allele is either 'S' or 's.'

	S	s
S	SS	Ss
s	Ss	ss

We can see S S S S (4 x S) and s s s s (4 x s). This means that the frequency of the allele 'S' is 50% and the frequency of the allele 's' is 50%. See if you can calculate the frequencies of the alleles 'S' and 's' in the following crosses for yourself.

	S	s
S		
S		

	s	s
S		
s		

Recall that the Hardy-Weinberg law states that the sum of all the alleles in a population should equal 100%, but the individual alleles may appear in different ratios. There are five situations that can cause the law of equilibrium to fail. These are discussed below.

1. **Mutation.** A mutation is a change in genetic material, which can give rise to heritable variations in the offspring. Exposure to radiation can cause genetic mutation, for example. In this case the result would be a mutation of the plant's genetic code that would be transferred to its offspring. The effect is equivalent to a migration of foreign genetic material being introduced into the population. There are other factors that can cause mutations. Essentially a mutation is the result of DNA repair failure at the cellular level. Anything that causes DNA repair to fail can result in a mutation.

2. **Gene Migration.** Over time, a population will reach equilibrium that will be maintained as long as no other genetic material migrates into the population. When new genetic material is introduced from another population, this is called introgression. During the process of introgression many new traits can arise in the original population, resulting in a shift in equilibrium.

3. **Genetic Drift.** If a population is small, equilibrium is more easily violated, because a slight change in the number of alleles results in a significant change in genetic frequency. Even by chance alone certain traits can be eliminated from the population and the frequency of alleles can drift toward higher or lower values. Genetic drift is actually an evolutionary force that alters a population and demonstrates that the Hardy-Weinberg law of equilibrium cannot hold true over an indefinite period of time.

4. **Nonrandom Mating.** External or internal factors may influence a population to a point at which mating is no longer random. For example, if some female flowers develop earlier than others they will be able to gather pollen earlier than the

rest. If some of the males release pollen earlier than others, the mating between these early males and females is not random, and could result in late-flowering females ending up as a sinsemilla crop. This means that these late-flowering females won't be able to make their contribution to the gene pool in future generations. Equilibrium will not be maintained.

5. **Natural Selection.** With regard to natural selection, the environment and other factors can cause certain plants to produce a greater or smaller number of offspring. Some plants may have traits that make them less immune to disease, for example, meaning that when the population is exposed to disease, less of their offspring will survive to pass on genetic material, while others may produce more seeds or exhibit a greater degree of immunity, resulting in a greater number of offspring surviving to contribute genetic material to the population.

HOW TO TRUE BREED A STRAIN

Breeding cannabis strains is all about manipulating gene frequencies. Most strains sold by reputable breeders through seed banks are very uniform in growth. This means that the breeder has attempted to lock certain genes down so that the genotypes of those traits are homozygous.

Imagine that a breeder has two strains: Master Kush and Silver Haze. The breeder lists a few traits that he particularly likes (denoted by *).

MASTER KUSH	SILVER HAZE
Dark-green leaf	Pale-green leaf *
Hashy smell *	Fruity smell
White flowers	Silver flowers *
Short plants *	Tall plants

This means he wants to create a plant that is homozygous for the following traits and call it something like Silver Kush.

SILVER KUSH
Pale-green leaf
Hashy smell
Silver flowers
Short plants

All the genetics needed are contained in the gene pools for Master Kush and

Silver Haze. The breeder could simply mix both populations and hope for the best or try to save time, space and money by calculating the genotype for each trait and using the results to create an IBL.

The first thing the breeder must do is to understand the genotype of each trait that will be featured in the ideal "Silver Kush" strain. In order to do this the genotype of each parent strain for that same trait must be understood. Since there are four traits that the breeder is trying to isolate, and 4 x 2 = 8, eight alleles make up the genotypes for these phenotype expressions and must be made known to the breeder.

Let's take the pale-green leaf of the Silver Haze for starters. The breeder will grow out as many Silver Haze plants as possible, noting if any plants in the population display other leaf colors. If they do not, the breeder can assume that the trait is either homozygous dominant (SS) or recessive (ss). If other leaf colors appear within the population, the breeder must assume that the trait is heterozygous (Ss) and must be locked down through selective breeding. Let's look closely at the parents for a moment.

	S	SS
S	SS	SS
S	SS	SS

If both parents were SS there wouldn't be any variation in the population for this trait. It would already be locked-down and would always breed true without any variations.

	S	s
S	SS	Ss
S	SS	Ss

With one SS parent and one Ss parent, the breeder would produce a 50:50 population—one group being homozygous (SS) and the other heterozygous (Ss).

	S	s
S	SS	Ss
s	Ss	ss

If both parents were Ss, the breeder would have 25% SS, 50% Ss and 25% ss. Even though gene frequencies can be predicted, the breeder will not know with certainty whether the pale-green leaf trait is dominant or recessive until he performs a test cross. By running several test crosses the breeder can isolate the plant that is either SS or ss and eliminate any Ss from the group. Once the genotype has been isolated and the population reduced to contain only plants with the same geno-type, the breeding program can begin in earnest. Remember that the success of any cannabis breeding program hinges on the breeder maintaining accurate records about parent plants and their descendents so that he can control gene frequencies.

Let's say that you run a seed bank company called PALE-GREEN LEAF ONLY BUT EVERYTHING ELSE IS NOT UNIFORM LTD. The seeds that you create will all breed pale-green leaves and the customer will be happy. In reality, cus-tomers want the exact same plant that won the Cannabis Cup last year or at least something very close. So in reality, you will have to isolate all the 'winning' traits before customers will be satisfied with what they're buying.

The number of tests it takes to know any given genotype isn't certain. You may have to use a wide selection of plants to achieve the goal, but nevertheless it is still achievable. The next step in a breeding program is to lock down other traits in that same population. Here is the hard part.

When you are working on locking down a trait you must not eliminate other desir-able traits from the population. It is also possible to accidentally lock down an unwanted trait or eliminate desired traits if you are not careful. If this happens then you'll have to work harder to explore genotypes through multiple cross tests and lock down the desired traits. Eventually, through careful selection and *record keeping* you'll end up with a plant that breeds true for all of the features that you want. In essence, you will have your own genetic map of your cannabis plants.

Successful breeders don't try to map everything at once. Instead, they concentrate on the main phenotypes that will make their plant unique and of a high quality. Once they have locked down four or five traits they can move on. True breeding strains are created slowly, in stages. Well-known true breeding strains like Skunk#1 and Afghani#1 took as long as 20 years to develop. If anyone states that they developed a true breeding strain in 1 or 2 years you can be sure that the genetics they started with were true breeding, homozygous, in the first place.

Eventually you will have your Silver Kush strain but only with the four genotypes that you wanted to keep. You may still have a variety of non-uniform plants in the group. Some may have purple stems, while others may have green stems. Some may be very potent and others not so potent. By constantly selecting for desired traits you could theoretically manipulate the strain into a true breeding strain for every phenotype. However, it is extremely unlikely that anyone will ever create a 100% true breeding strain for every single phenotype. Such a strain would be called a perfect IBL. If you're able to lock down 90% of the plant's phenotypes in a population then you can claim that your plant is an IBL.

The core idea behind the true breeding technique is to find what is known as a donor plant. A donor plant is one that contains a true breeding trait (homozygous, preferably dominant for that trait). The more locked down traits are homozygous dominant the better your chances of developing an IBL, which does not mean that the line of genetics will be true breeding for every trait, but rather that the strain is very uniform in growth for a high percentage of phenotypes.

Some additional advanced breeding techniques that will help you to reduce or promote a trait in a population are discussed below. Using these techniques may not create a plant that is true breeding for the selected traits, but it will certainly help to make the population more uniform for that trait.

ADVANCED BREEDING TECHNIQUES
Simple Backcrossing
Our first cross between the Master Kush plant and the Silver Haze is known as the F1 hybrid cross. Let's pretend that both traits are homozygous for leaf color: the Silver Haze is pale green and the Master Kush is dark green. Which is SS or ss? We won't know until we see the offspring.

F1 Hybrid Cross	s	s
S	Ss	Ss
S	Ss	Ss

This F1 cross will result in hybrid seeds. Since S is dominant over s, we'll know which color is more dominant and from which parent it came from. In this example, the overall results are pale green. Thus, the pale-green allele is dominant over the dark-green.

S = Silver Haze pale-green leaf trait is dominant
s = Master Kush dark-green leaf trait is recessive

We also know that because no variations occurred in the population, both parents were homozygous for that trait. However, all the offspring are heterozygous. Here is where we can take a shortcut in manipulating the gene pool for that population. By cloning the parent plant SS, we can use this clone in our cross with the Ss offspring. This is known as a backcross. Obviously, if our parent is female then we'll have to use males from the Ss selection in our backcross, and vice versa.

F2 Backcross	S		s
S	SS	Ss	
S	SS	Ss	

Now our first backcross will result in 50% homozygous (SS) offspring and 50% heterozygous offspring (Ss) for that trait. Here all the offspring will exhibit the pale-green leaf trait. If we didn't backcross but just used the heterozygous offspring for the breeding program we would have ended up with 25% homozygous dominant (SS), 50% heterozygous (Ss) and 25% homozygous recessive (ss), as shown below.

F2 Hybrid Cross (without backcrossing)		S		s
S	SS	Ss		
s	Ss	ss		

Backcrossing seriously helps to control the frequencies of a specific trait in the offspring. The F2 hybrid cross produced some plants with the dark-green leaf trait. The F2 backcross did not.

The F2 backcross above is an example of simple backcrossing. Let's see what happens when we do our second backcross (F3) using the same original parent kept alive through cloning. Our second backcross is referred to as *squaring*. Since we're dealing with only two types of offspring Ss and SS, we'll either repeat the results of the F2 backcross...

F3 Backcross with heterozygote		S		s
S	SS	Ss		
S	SS	Ss		

...or we will successfully lock down the desired trait as follows:

F3 Backcross with homozygote		S		S
S	SS	SS		
S	SS	SS		

In the F3 backcross with the homozygote, all of the offspring are homozygous dominant (SS) and thus true breeding for that trait. These offspring are the result of squaring and can never produce the ss traits because the SS trait is now true breeding and stable. The F3 backcross with the heterozygote has some Ss offspring. If we breed the Ss and Ss offspring we can produce the ss trait. This line would not be stable.

HOW TO GENERATE A CLONE MOTHER

The best way to generate a clone mother is to grow a large population of plants from the same strain. If the strain is an IBL then you should find that the plants do not exhibit much variation. It can be difficult to find a clone mother from an IBL strain, though, because IBLs are created to provide a population of plants from seed from the F3 Backcross with the homozygote, which all resemble the clone mother that the breeder enjoyed and wanted to share with you.

The best way to generate a clone mother is to select her from a large population of F1 hybrids. If you do not find a clone mother in the F1 population then allow random mating to occur and see if you can generate a good clone mother in the F2 population. If you do not find the clone mother in the F2 population then either grow a larger population or select different parents to create a new F1 population.

A clone mother is only as good as the environment she is grown in. The environment influences how the genotype is displayed in the phenotype. Although indoor plants can grow outdoors and outdoor plants can grow indoors, the expressed phenotype of the genotype may change because of the diversity in growing conditions. This is why breeders urge that you grow their strains in the recommended environment.

Selfing

Selfing is the ability of a plant to produce seeds without the aid of another plant and refers to hermaphrodite plants that are able to self-pollinate. Hermaphrodite plants have both male and female flowers. This usually means that the hermaphrodite plant is monoecious. Most plants are dioecious and have male and female flowers on separate plants.

Monoecious cannabis strains will always display both sexes regardless of the growing conditions. Under optimal growing conditions a monoecious cannabis strain will still produce both male and female flowers on the same plant. Under optimal growing conditions a dioecious cannabis strain will produce male and female flowers on separate plants.

Stressful growing conditions can cause some dioecious cannabis strains to produce both male and female flowers on the same plant. Manipulating an irregular photoperiod during the flowering stage is an easy way to encourage the dioecious hermaphrodite condition. Not all dioecious cannabis strains can become hermaphrodites. The dioecious cannabis strain must have a preexisting genetic disposition to become hermaphrodite under stressful conditions in order for male and female flowers to appear on the same plant.

If you find a dioecious cannabis strain that has the hermaphrodite condition you can separate this plant from the rest and allow selfing to occur. If the male pollen is viable on this plant then the hermaphrodite will produce seeds. Selfed plants that produce seeds will eventually generate offspring that:

1. Are all female
2. Are all hermaphrodite
3. Produce male, female and hermaphrodite plants because the environment also influences the final sexual expression of the selfed plant
4. Express limited variation from the original selfed plant

Breeders should note that it is nearly impossible for a hermaphrodite to create male plants although environment can influence males to appear. Hermaphrodites usually create female-only and hermaphrodite seeds. The female-only seeds often carry the hermaphrodite trait. Selfing has become popular among those who wish to breed all-female or feminized seeds. Unfortunately feminized seeds do very little for the cannabis gene pool as the hermaphrodite condition prevents growers from generating a sinsemilla crop.

Well-informed breeders tend to shy away from producing feminized seeds. Feminized seeds should only be used for bud production and not for breeding. Generating seeds from feminized plants is only advised for personal use and not for distribution.

NOTES ON SELFING BY VIC HIGH
[These notes were taken from an online interview and provided by Vic High, BCGA breeder.]

100% Female Seeds
Posted by The Silicon Magician on February 13, 1999 at 05:17:41 PST
As some of you may know I've been a regular in the chat room for a while and I spend a large amount of time in there. I have had the extreme pleasure of

speaking to Mr. XX over the last few nights for many hours and have gotten to know him quite well via email and the chat. He has confided in me and in a few others about his process for coming up with 100% female seeds.

Mr. XX is a very nice guy, funny too and it's always a pleasure to speak with him. He doesn't speak English too well, but his wit comes through the rough language and he's a riot. He's a pure lover of cannabis and feels that everyone should share and share alike. He simply wants to share his knowledge with the cannabis community, and because he's spent 15 years researching this, I spoke about it with him in depth.

He has stressed literally hundreds of plants with irregular photoperiods. What he does is put the lights on 12/12 for 10 days. Then he turns the lights on 24 hours, then 12/12 again for a few days, then back to 24 hours for a day, then 12/12 again for a few weeks. If he does this and no hermaphrodites come up, he has found a 100% XX female that can't turn hermaphrodite naturally. He claims that your chance of finding a 100% XX female is vastly increased when using Indica genetics. He also informed me that the more Afghani or Nepalese genetics the plant has, the better the chances of finding a natural XX female. In his own words: "Where did nature give weed a home originally?" I tried to get him to narrow it down to a ratio, but he never specified just how many plants per are XX females. He claims there are plenty of XX females for everybody, and that's all he will say on the subject. It takes a lot of time and a lot of plants to find that one female.

He then uses gibberellic acid, mixing 30 centiliters of water with 0.02 grams of gibberellic acid and 2 drops of natruim hydroxide to liquefy the gibberellic. Then applies as normal and creates the male flowers. He has gotten down to the 4th generation without loss of vigor, and with no genetic deficiencies and hermaphrodites. He claims that the plants are exact genetic clones of one another, complete sisters. Basically it's cloned from seed instead of from normal cloning methods.

Posted by The Silicon Magician on February 13, 1999 at 05:17:41 PST

Mr. XX also says that it's easy for the home grower to find an XX female. It's a very time-consuming process but a straightforward one. He advises home growers to confine themselves to a single strain. Mr. XX used a Skunk#1 x Haze x Hawaiian Indica. He says to separate those plants from your main grow and *stress them severely. Do this repeatedly with every new crop of seeds you get of that strain until you find the XX female. While this is time consuming it is by no means impossible.*

CONCLUDING THOUGHTS ON BREEDING

Experimentation results in new hybrids. Stabilized hybrids result in new strains. It is far better to generate one excellent stable strain than to generate several unstable average ones. Breeding is a long-term commitment. Many breeders stop breeding after only a few years because of lack of time, space and money. Although they may have learned something about breeding in that short a time, they will not have had the opportunity to put it into practice. If you want to breed cannabis then be prepared to spend a few grows getting the basics right first.

Breeding is all about recognizing which traits are worth continuing. Do not be afraid to admit that you do not have anything worth breeding. Some of the best breeders have gone through dozens of different populations before finding a plant that stands out from the rest.

There are many reasons to breed your own strain of cannabis. Try to find an original idea for breeding your own cannabis strain. Original ideas always seem to work out best.

3 | DONOR PARENTS, POLLINATION AND SEEDS

USING PARENT PLANTS TO CREATE MORE THAN ONE STRAIN

The previous chapters have helped us develop a notion of what breeding is all about and what principles are involved in breeding strains for traits that we want to see produced in a population of cannabis plants. A breeder only needs two parent plants to create the final produce.

However you may find that a breeder uses a mother plant to produce several different products (strains/hybrids). Let's imagine that a breeder sells the following items: Masterkush, Blueberry and Kushberry.

You can probably guess that the breeder is using a similar template for each strain, although some breeders are clever and may give their strains different names to make it seem like these strains are all developed from different parents.

Let's say for a moment that each strain is known to be related to similar parent plants and it is our goal to figure out what those parents are.

Masterkush is probably a true breeding strain for a large percentage of its traits. The same applies to Blueberry. By doing a little research and asking around we may find that the breeder released these strains first. These two strains are very different in their phenotypes so we can guess that the breeder has two parents for each strain. These are:

Masterkush = Masterkush female parent #1 x Masterkush male parent #1. Through breeding both parents the breeder produces Masterkush seeds.

Blueberry = Blueberry female parent #1 x Blueberry male parent #1. Through breeding both the parents the breeder produces Blueberry seeds.

So for these two strains the breeder has four parent plants on the table as his main breeding stock.

When we grow out a large population of Kushberry we may notice that the strain has some variations. If so, then we know that the Kushberry's parents do NOT breed true for certain traits. This means that the Kushberry's parents are probably:

   Masterkush female parent #1 x Blueberry male parent #1

or

   Masterkush female parent #1 x Blueberry male #1.

In this case we can guess that the breeder has only the four parent plants for their Masterkush, Blueberry and Kushberry strains. Only two of these strains are considered stable by definition—the Masterkush and the Blueberry.

The Kushberry is an F1 hybrid!

If we grow out a large population of Kushberry and notice that there are no variations in any of the traits then we know that the breeder has actually developed parents for the Kushberry that will breed true for the Kushberry traits. This means that the breeder has not four parent plants, but six.

If you are asking the question if there is a difference between using the male or female version of each parent for the resulting hybrid the answer is in what you have already learned in the previous chapter. Let us look at the Punnet tables for each.

Masterkush has BB for brown bud color. Blueberry has bb for blue bud color. Since both strains are stable there is no Bb in their individual populations.

   Masterkush male #1 x Blueberry female #1

	b	b
B	Bb	Bb
B	Bb	Bb

Blueberry male #1 x Masterkush female #1

	B	B
B	Bb	Bb
b	Bb	Bb

It seems like both ways will produce Bb, brown bud color, so there it makes no difference which male or female we use. However let us continue on with another trait. Masterkush has cc for a small calyx. Blueberry has CC for big calyx. Since both strains are stable there is no Cc in their individual populations.

Masterkush male #1 x Blueberry female #1

	c	c
C	Cc	Cc
C	Cc	Cc

Blueberry male #1 x Masterkush female #1

	C	C
c	Cc	Cc
c	Cc	Cc

It seems like both ways will produce Cc, big calyx, so it makes no difference which male or female we use. This means that in stable strains, without variations in the populations, the male or female selection does not change the resulting offspring. The resulting offspring will only change with the different male and female selection if we breed the resulting offspring or if we are use heterozygous traits to begin with.

	C	c
C	CC	Cc
C	CC	Cc

	C	c
c	Cc	cc
c	Cc	cc

This will help you understand more about the actual propagation of genetics. You may be wondering at this point: *Is it possible for the breeder to create a true breeding hybrid if by some fluke of nature the two parent plants combine in such a way that no heterozygous genotypes are produced?* We already know from chapter 2 that the very term *true breeding hybrid* is untrue. It simply does not exist, so this statement is not possible.

THE STRAIN'S PARENTS

Ideally a strain should have two parents that are unique only to that strain. Nowadays it is very common to see well-liked strains produce new hybrids that have some association with the well-liked strain's parents. A good example of this would be to take two very popular strains like Northern Lights and Haze. Recently NL x Haze has come onto the market and has gained some popularity. It is highly unlikely however that NL x Haze is as stable as NL or Haze. There will probably be variations in the population until such time as the breeder develops NL x Haze parents that are unique to that line and breed true.

This is very important to know about, especially in situations where a breeder has developed two very popular strains only to produce a third cross between the two. This third cross is usually less stable than the line from which it came, although over time the breeder will undoubtedly develop separate parents to make this line more uniform in growth. One very popular strain that is being developed for more stability at the moment is Jack Flash from Sensi Seeds. Jack Flash is a very popular variation of the famous Jack Herer strain that revolutionized the industry. Every year Jack Flash becomes more stable. This suggests that the breeder is making headway in developing two unique parents that will eventually combine to create a Jack Flash that is very uniform in its traits.

The Male Parent

Because the female parent is generally the parent that we are trying to improve on, or recreate, we have a problem with selecting the right male for the job. Male plants do not exhibit female floral traits and so the initial selection of the contributing male is blind.

In order to assess the male plant's breeding qualities you must perform test crosses and consider the results in the offspring*. This is very dependant on the female and how the male's genes combine with those of the female to produce various traits. Testing males is just as important as testing females. By making the right male selection you can enhance your strain in almost every single trait.

The more males that you work with, the better your chances are of finding a male

---

* Avoid trying to Herm the male as Hermaphrodites will not give you true female floral results.

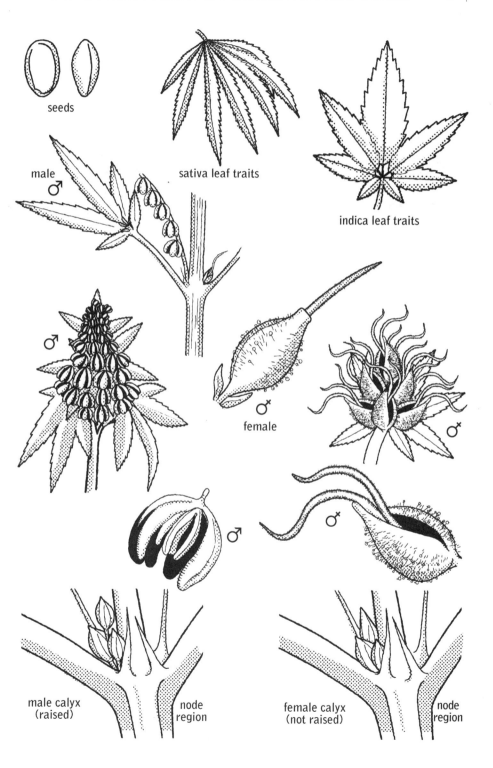

seeds

male ♂

sativa leaf traits

indica leaf traits

♂

♂

female ♀

♀

♂

♀

male calyx
(raised)

node
region

female calyx
(not raised)

node
region

donor parent that gives very unique properties to the offspring. Some males are so helpful in increasing yields and potency that they become as important as a good clone mother.

This male is only a day or two away from producing pollen. Photographs by Kissie.

Pollinating

Males can drop pollen anywhere between 12 hours and 3 weeks from initial calyx development. For this reason breeders and growers want to get to the males as soon as possible. The problem with male identification is that initial calyx development is subtle and although there are signs that a given plant could be a male in the initial stages of calyx development, the definitive factor is in the actual flowering phase.

Males tend to grow taller than females but this is tentative. Males also tend to show their sex before females but again this is not definitive. Males also have a raised calyx on a short stem but sometimes the odd female can show this too. Growers and breeders should endeavor to tag males in the early days of calyx development or even remove them from the grow area until such time as the flowers actually show. Never put all your eggs in one basket until you know for sure (*CGB*, pp. 100-103).

Male calyx development also usually occurs in clusters very quickly—so if you see more than one calyx developing at the node you can be almost sure that the plant is male.

As noted above, most males can be very quick to shed pollen. In the initial stages of calyx development a male will often start to produce pollen right away. I personally have witnessed males shedding pollen within a day after initial calyx development, although it typically takes a few more days than just one. The moral here is to keep an eye out for calyx development as you near the end of vegetative growth.

Is this a male or female cannabis plant? It is too early to tell because this plant is still in the vegetative stage of growth and has not produced any calyxes.

Males can produce pollen without need for a 12/12 flowering photoperiod—they can also drop pollen under the 24/0 or 18/6 vegetative photoperiods—but under the 12/12 photoperiod males tend to produce *more* flowers and thus *more* pollen. Males will continue to drop pollen throughout the flowering phase (for more flowering information see *CGB,* pp. 103-111).

Indoor males can easily be moved away from the female plants. Indoor window light is enough to keep the males producing pollen. Even when kept in a dark closet, males can continue to produce pollen and flowers for at least a few days.

Males that are left in the breeding room will only pollinate everything around them. If you want your males to do this, fine, but this is not selective breeding. If you want to engage in selective breeding, you need to move and segregate your males from the females.

Outdoor male segregation can be a hard task. The best way to control pollen outdoors is to take cuttings from the males in the early stages of calyx development and then cull the male doners shortly after you do this. Root and flower the cuttings in a separate grow area. Flower the males by putting the male clones under 12/12 light exposure one week after rooting and you will have controllable males from which you can extract pollen. Basic fluorescent lighting of the cool white type between 30W and 60W should suffice. Window light can also be adequate.

This very short Ruderalis Hybrid - Lowryder, from The Joint Doctor, www.highbred.net, is fully flowered at less than 12 inches. This male was selected for pollen production. As you can see even a short little plant like this one can produce quite a lot of pollen to work with.

Some growers like to 'bag' the male flowers. This involves tying a small paper or plastic bag envelope around the male flowers and allowing the pollen to drop into the bag. This works, but has two problems. The first problem is that the male flowers do not receive any light and so produce far less pollen, if any at all. The second problem is that the bag needs to let some air in to allow the flowers to grow properly. This means a small hole has to be cut in the side of the bag. Although pollen may not flow from the hole, this certainly is not a secure way to ensure that selective breeding takes place, rather than wild, random pollination.

The best way to collect male pollen is to use small black film canisters and a small pair or tweezers. Be sure to label the canister to correspond with the male that you are taking the pollen from. Hold the canister under the male flower and gently tap the flower with the tweezers. The male flower should drop pollen into the canister. If it does not, wait a day and try again. Keep doing this until the male releases its pollen. All it should take is a little tap of the tweezers. If you tap too hard the male flower may fall off.

If you are afraid that you will miss out on the pollen dropping overnight then simply get a white piece of paper and place this around the plant's base on top of the pot. You can rip the sheet of paper halfway down the middle so that it slides easily around the stem. Remove the fan leaves and any other large leaves from the male or else they will catch the falling pollen instead of the paper. Come back the next day and some of the pollen will be caught on the paper. Gently remove the sheet of paper and curve it slightly. Empty the pollen into a black film canister. Make sure not to use fans in the grow room or else pollen with be blown around. Even extractor fans cause the pollen to spread. It is also important to prevent moisture and light from coming into direct contact with the pollen after collection. Store the pollen using the methods described in chapter 2.

Male flowers open at different times so it may take a few days of pollen collection for you to end up with a workable amount from one male plant.

The application of pollen to the females is easy, but must be done with care and with timing in mind. You should try to pollinate your females at least four weeks before the end of harvest. Pollinating females any later than this can result in nonviable seeds around harvest time. Sometimes it can even take six weeks for the female to create viable seeds.

Only the flowering areas of the females that receive pollen will produce seeds. It is very easy to keep a number of colas sinsemilla by not applying pollen directly to them. The best way to apply pollen is to use a cotton swab or a small paintbrush. Dip the swab or paintbrush and lightly brush the pollen onto the selected areas of the female. Make sure to label the female with the corresponding male pollen that she has received. Using a small piece of tape can help remind you which branches have been pollinated.

For heavier pollination you may wish to remove your female from the grow room to avoid inadvertent pollen contamination of other females. When you have finished brushing pollen from the film canister onto the female simply blow the excess pollen away from the leaves before returning the female to the grow room*. You might also choose to let your plant rest for a day before returning her to the grow room.

Female pistils that have received pollen tend to change color although this is not always the case. The best way to mark pollinated areas is, again, by using tape and labels.

Pollen can easily be removed from the females by washing them down with water. This renders the pollen nonviable. Simply dip the pollinated female flowering areas in water or spray them down with water. This may damage some of the trichomes but it will prevent the bud from producing seeds.

Pollinated female flowers should be given adequate amounts of light to produce seeds. If a pollinated bud area does not receive adequate amounts of light then the seeds may be rendered nonviable, so you need to make sure that pollinated areas receive light. You may have to tie back certain branches in order to ensure that they do.

It is very important to maintain the 12/12 photoperiod with females that have received pollen. If you revert to vegetative growth or disrupt the 12/12 photoperiod it can have an adverse effect on the production of seeds. Also the plant may produce hermaphrodites because of photoperiod related stress and you will only end up with selfed seeds and standard seeds that are indistinguishable from one another. A suspect hermie can render an entire breeding period void and the breeder will have to start that term over again.

It is also worth keeping in mind that even in optimal environmental conditions some sinsemilla branches from certain strains can produce hermaphrodites. Although there may be only one male flower per cola of bud, if the pollen is viable then that branch may produce some seeds. Avoid using these seeds in any breeding program. The pollen may also spread to other branches. This means that there

---

* You can also use a fan to remove excess pollen.

may be a chance that some hermaphrodite pollen has contaminated another branch on the same plant or has traveled to a neighboring plant. Sinsemilla branches are best avoided in breeding environments. If you are going to pollinate your plant try and pollinate the whole plant. The other way to prevent this minor percentage of hermaphrodite seeds is to simply keep a close eye on your females for any signs of male flowers and clip them away as quickly as possible.

2 weeks, 4 weeks and 6 weeks flowering out of a total 8 week flowering time. Pollination is best done before the last picture as it may be too late to produce viable seeds before harvest.

CANNABIS POLYGAMY

As a breeder you may be asking yourself the question: Is cannabis polygamous?

Polygamous:
1. *Practicing polygamy; of, pertaining to, or involving polygamy. Having more than one mate of the opposite sex.*
2. *Bearing male, female, and hermaphrodite flowers on the same or on different plants. Flowers that contain seeds made from different male parents.*

Cannabis *is* polygamous and it is more than capable of producing several types of hybrids on one plant. Take for example Northern Lights. If you applied Haze pollen to one branch, Skunk pollen to another, and Blueberry to another, then you would end up with NL x Haze, NL x Skunk and NL x Blueberry offspring. You must, however, ensure that each branch is labeled correctly or else you will end up mixing the seeds and growing out an unknown progeny. Any wind movement in the grow room may also send pollen from one branch to another. Always allow your pollinated females to rest for a few days in a quiet and calm room if possible.

Dutch Passion use a seed counting machine to sort and pack all of their seeds.

REMOVING SEEDS FROM THE BUD

The single best way to remove seeds from the bud is to harvest, manicure and cure your bud as normal (see CGB, pp. 195-206). It is far easier to remove seeds from cured bud than it is to remove them from wet flowers. When the bud is dry you can easily tap the seeds from it. You may also find that seeds have already come loose and are in the bottom of the canning jar. Seeds also tend to mature during this process. Even though the plant has been harvested, the seeds many continue to develop during curing.

Make sure to label your canning jars so that you know what the seeds are. If you are having trouble removing seeds from the bud then you may wish to screen the bud. Screening (see *CGB,* pp. 242-45) for seeds has two advantages.

1. You do not destroy the bud as you would if you used your fingers to get at the seeds.
2. It is gentler on the seeds.

Professional breeding outfits use automatic screening machines to produce seeds. These machines actually sieve the seeds from the bud. Seeds should be stored as directed in chapter 2.

VIABLE AND NONVIABLE SEEDS

Most viable seeds are dark in color, feel firm and have a rough feeling. Most non-viable seeds appear pale white or a light green although some strains do create viable seeds that look this way. The only surefire way to know if your produce is viable is to test your seeds. You should always test a few seeds from EACH female to ensure that your produce is viable.

Nonviable seeds should be discarded, never be sold or distributed. Maintain high standards and only distribute tested viable seeds.

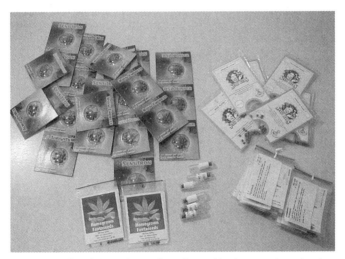

Some various breeder's packaging from the seed bank – www.hempdepot.ca.

BREEDER'S PACKAGING

Packaging your seeds in a breeder's pack is always a good idea. It helps to avoid unscrupulous breeders ripping off your strains. Most seed packs are roughly 3.5" by 2" in size and should contain a placeholder card with the strain's name, description and your logo. Shop around from official breeders to see what they use. Do not use bags that have a zip lock because these are easy to open. Instead you will have to heat seal your bags. Heat sealers are relatively inexpensive and a must for any semiprofessional or profes-sional breeder looking to distribute his seeds. If you can follow these packaging standards then it is harder for a fraudulent breeder to mimic your packaging. It is still not impossi-ble for them to do it but it makes the job a lot harder for them than if your packaging was just a small zip lock bag with the name of the strain in black ballpoint on the front.

Seed pack counts are a matter of discretion, but the most common amounts contained in seed packs are 10, 15 and 16 seeds. Preferably you should sell your seeds in batches of 16 to ensure a good female plant selection, although most breeders are now using 10 seeds as the norm.

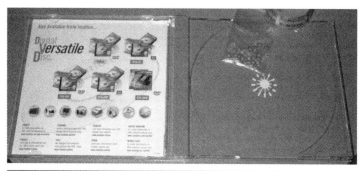
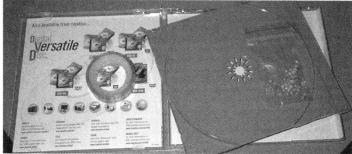

CD/DVD boxes make great secure seed packages. All you need is tape.
Unclip the disc holder from the box and turn it over. Tape the seed pack to the back of the holder.
You can get up to 4 seed packs on the back of these. Clip the disc holder back into the box,
write something on the disc and you are done.

STEALTH

Batches of seeds as large as 1000 or more should not be sent through the post if you think that there is a possibility that the seeds will not make it to their destination. Most seed banks have collectors who are more than willing to travel to pick up large amounts of seeds. The best way to send bulk seeds in the post is by boxing the seed packs together inside a videocassette box. You may have to send several boxes in order to send large amounts. The cassettes will be hard enough to ensure that the seeds get through undamaged. There are many other items you can use to send seed bulk seed orders and I am sure that by using a little inge-nuity you can find a way like the tried and trusted method below.

If you are sending only a few seed packets to a client then you should use a CD or DVD case. Make sure that the case is not clear and has some cards on the front and back with a CD/DVD holder that is dark and not see-through. Unclip this holder from the case and place a white card on the back of the hole so that it is no longer see-through. Tape the seed packs onto the back of this holder and clip it back into the case again. Write some name down on the CD/DVD case so that it looks official. You may also want to heat seal the CD/DVD pack. You can also buy packaging boxes for CDs and DVDs to send the case in. These packages not only increase stealth but also prevent damage. Never use your correct return address when sending the package.

4 | COMPATIBLE BREEDING MODELS

PARENT COMPATIBILITY

Compatibility has a lot to do with the plant's species type and heritage. The first line of compatibility is cannabis itself. All cannabis plants on today's market are descended from cannabis stock. There are no trees or animals directly involved in the cannabis breeding process! Cannabis plants are compatible with each other and can be bred together no matter what the species or strain type.

Since all cannabis plants are compatible with one another we have achieved the first step of compatibility. However, our term *compatibility* has nothing really to do with the cannabis plant's ability to breed with other cannabis plants. It has to do with how the plants will retain an overall style with similar characteristics which breed true between different cannabis strains.

We know that there are three main species of cannabis plants: Indica, Sativa and Ruderalis. If a pure species is crossed with another plant of the same pure species type then it will retain a large degree of that pure specie's traits. So this is the first rule of compatibility.

If the strains being crossed to create the F1 hybrid seeds are from the same pure species type, then the parent plants are very compatible with each other and the types of variations will be limited in the offspring.

If both these parents share **homozygous** genotypes for certain traits then the results in the offspring will carry this homozygous genotype without any heterozygous properties for that trait. This means that the parents are very compatible and will breed true for these traits automatically without selective breeding.

This shows that there is a high degree of compatibility between plants of the same pure species types. This should clue you in to how difficult it is to actually breed strains from different species types. Let us treat the complete opposite of our statement above.

If a pure species is crossed with a different pure species then the offspring will have a lot of variations. This means that the parents are not very compatible.

If the strains being crossed to create the F1 hybrid seeds are from different pure species types then the parent plants will not be very compatible with each other and there will be many variations in the offspring.

Since these parents are from different species then they will not share many traits. We can see straightaway that a breeder's job is harder if he mixes cannabis species. Let's ask a new question from what we learned in the previous chapter: Is the Kushberry an easier strain to stabilize than the Masterkush or the Blueberry? To understand this we must look at Masterkush and Blueberry and their heritage.

Masterkush is a cross between two Kush strains. The two Kush strains it came from were both Pure Indica strains. This means that there was a high degree of compatibility throughout the breeding project. This would have made the breeder's job a little easier than say, creating a Mostly Indica plant.

Blueberry is a Mostly Indica strain but does have some Sativa in it. This means that the breeder had to work with traits that were not very compatible with one another. This would have made the breeder's job a bit harder than creating a pure species Indica plant.

Let's say that the breeder made both plants very homozygous for most of their traits, even enough to call each one an IBL. Kushberry would be a cross of a Pure Indica strain (Masterkush) and a Mostly Indica strain (Blueberry). This means that there is a good deal of compatibility BUT it will still not be as easy to work on as the Masterkush strain.

There is also another level of compatibility to consider. Two different strains may have a similar parent. If the parent has managed to produce similar homozygous traits in both strains then this trait will also breed true. This is much like the pure species compatibility level, but we are looking more at the breeder's traits and how they have been retained in different strains.

If you are new to breeding then working with two known stable plants from the same pure species type will help you to stabilize a strain quickly.

The same rule can be applied to the sub-species types. Most sub-species types— Indica/Sativa, Mostly Indica and Mostly Sativa—are hard to combine with one another. It is easier to combine a Mostly Indica with a Mostly Indica but combining a Mostly Indica with a Mostly Sativa or an Indica/Sativa is just as hard as combining two different pure species types.

What it really boils down too is Homozygous Dominant vs Homozygous Recessive vs Heterozygous. The more homozygous dominant traits a plant shares with another, the easier it is to true breed the traits that they do not have in common. Let's look at this in action.

We like the red pistil tips of the Masterkush and we do not like the white pistil tips of the Hindu Kush. They are both stable Kush strains. We may find that they share 90% of the same traits except for this red pistil tip phenotype. This means that we will have an easy time locking down the red pistil tip trait into the Hindu Kush because there is a large degree of compatibility with the two strains and our first F1 hybrid cross will probably retain a high percentage of the homozygous traits.

On the other hand if we used a Thai or a Haze strain they might have as little as 25% of their characteristics in common. The offspring will have very many variations.

In some breeding projects a breeder may find that he or she wants to inject another phenotype into a given plant. If he is going to do this then he will always want to try and find a compatible donor plant for the project to make his life easier. Sometimes you might find that the only donor plant around is not very compatible with your plant. Sometimes it is nice to take on a challenge like this, but you are better off having some experience with basic breeding procedures before you do.

SPECIES TYPE COMPATIBILITY TABLE

	Pure Indica	Mostly Indica	Indica/Sativa	Mostly Sativa	Pure Sativa
Pure Indica	1	2	3	4	5
Mostly Indica	2	3	3	4	4
Indica/Sativa	3	3	3	3	3
Mostly Sativa	4	4	3	3	2
Pure Sativa	5	4	3	2	1

1 = A high degree of compatibility, 2 = A good degree of compatibility, 3 = A medium amount of compatibility, 4 = Less than compatible, 5 = A high degree of incompatibility. Keep in mind that strains with similar parents will have better compatibility.

5 | PLANT CELLS, GROWTH AND HORMONES

THE CANNABIS PLANT'S GENETIC CODE is passed from the male parent's pollen to the ovule of the female parent. Pollen and ovules are referred to as *gametes* in plant botany. As we explained in chapter 2 both males and females contribute their sets of genes, which sort of look like the two sides of a zipper. When they combine they create the offspring's identity. We also know that each allele can either be of a recessive or dominant type.

When they combine they form what is known as the genotype. The genotype can either be Homozygous Dominant, Heterozygous or Homozygous Recessive. These results can be observed, smelt, tasted and experienced in the plant's phenotype.

We have discussed the breeding element of the combination of genes. However we should take a step back for the moment and look at how they contribute their genetic code to their own individual gametes.

BASIC PLANT CELL STRUCTURES AND THE BASICS OF MOLECULAR GENETICS

Cells are the basic structural and functional units of which living organisms and tissues are composed. They are microscopic and consist of cytoplasm bounded by a membrane, with genetic material (DNA) contained in a nucleus.

Animals and plants have cells and so do all other living things. Animal cells look very different from those of plants but are very similar in appearance when you look at them using an electron microscope. Both animal and plant cells have a nucleus, mitochondria, endoplasmic reticulum, ribosomes, Golgi bodies and lysosomes.

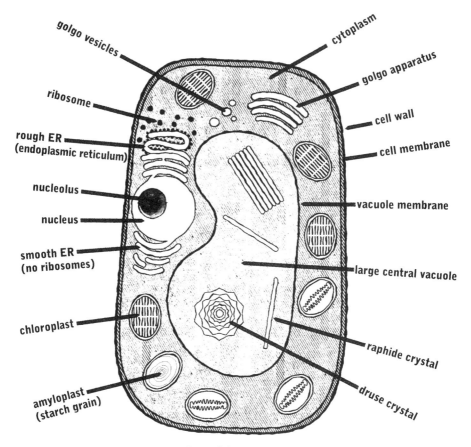

Parts of the plant cell.

If one were to take these individual parts away from both the animal cell and the plant cell it would be very difficult to tell what type of organism these components came from unless you had a great deal of experience studying both structures. But as a whole unit, both types of cell structures have some major differences that would automatically help you identify which organism the cell came from. For instance, plant cells do not have centrioles or intermediate filaments, which may be seen in animal cells.

So now we know that plant cells appear differently than animal cells. Obviously that appearance has a lot to do with how these cells work. Let's look briefly at how plant cells work.

Plant cells are eukaryotic, which means they are characterized by a discrete nucleus with a membrane, and other organelles. Plant cells have the following organelles.

- plasma membrane
- nucleus and nucleolus
- mitochondria
- ribosomes
- endoplasmic reticulum
- Golgi apparatus
- peroxisomes
- microtubules

Plant cells also have plastids, a cell wall and large vacuoles, which animal cells do not.

Chloroplasts
Chloroplasts are the most obvious plastids. They are usually round in shape and a typical cell has around 30, although there can be 10 more or less than that. Chloroplasts have a green pigment because they contain the chlorophyll that works with light during photosynthesis.

The Cell Wall
The cell wall is made of fibrils of cellulose, which are contained in polymers. The cellulose molecules work with intermolecular hydrogen bonding and build up this wall as a hard fibrils. There is a primary cell wall and a secondary cell wall.

1. The primary cell wall consists of the parenchyma and meristem. Both are roughly the same width. These primary walls are perforated to allow plasmodesmata to connect with nearby cells.
2. The secondary cell wall consists of a sclerenchyma, collenchyma and a xylem. They are basically supports to add stability to the cell.

Vacuoles
Vacuoles are encompassed by a membrane. Seedling plants contain lots of small vacuoles, but as the cells mature with age they come together to form a single large vacuole. Vacuoles store foods, wastes, acids and turgor. When your plant does not get enough water the turgor levels drop and the plant begins to wilt.

Plasma Membrane
The outer membrane of a cell is called the plasma membrane. The outer membrane contains other membranes within it. It is a thin, fluid, semipermeable lipid

bilayer that includes proteins that form structures within the cell.

It serves the function of interfacing the extracellular fluid that encompasses all the cells in the plant. When the plasma membrane is covered in a liquid its phospholipids control this by forming a phospholipid bilayer.

Also contained in the plasma membrane are the integral membrane proteins. These proteins are firmly connected to it and allow the membrane a certain degree of movement.

Nucleus
The nucleus is covered in a number of membranes which contain tiny perforations. The perforations allow molecules to transfer in and out of the nucleus. The nucleus is important for the breeder to know about because it contains the chromosomes of a given cell. Each chromosome contains a single molecule of DNA and proteins. The entire unit—nucleus, DNA and proteins—is called the chromatin. Basically, the nucleus is the brain inside the cell.

Mitochondria
The mitochondria are involved in the conversion of food energy into molecules for cellular respiration. Cellular respiration is the procedure of oxidizing food molecules such as sugars into carbon dioxide and water.

Mitochondria have an outside membrane that encompasses the whole structure. They also have an inner membrane that sandwiches fluids between the two membranes. This space is called the inter-membrane.

Ribosomes
Ribosomes are particles found in the cytoplasm (the material inside a cell other than the nucleus) of cells. They can be free or attached to the endoplasmic reticulum, which binds messenger RNA and transfers RNA to synthesize polypeptides and proteins.

Endoplasmic Reticulum
This is a fine network of fibers found within the cytoplasm of a cell. These fibers are involved in a process called protein kinesis. Protein kinesis is essentially the movement, division and transport of proteins in a cell to specific locations.

Golgi Apparatus
The Golgi Apparatus is a series of complex membranous vesicles in the cytoplasm. It is involved in secretion and intracellular transport and works with the

endoplasmic reticulum in protein kinesis.

Peroxisomes
A peroxisome is a cytoplasmic organelle that contains the reducing enzyme catalase. The Golgi apparatus manufactures peroxisomes and these are used in protein kinesis.

Microtubules
These are protein filaments found in the cytoskeleton and used mainly in cell motion, although they do provide some other smaller tasks.

These are the basic organelles and their components. Further discussion explaining exactly what kind of movement and protein kinesis goes on would be too complex for the nature of this book. If you want to learn more about plant cells then you may want to pick up a science book on the subject. What we've outlined above are some elements of the plant cell that are directly responsible for sharing the plant's genetic code. Here we briefly discussed the nucleus of the cell and how it contains the chromosomes that are the genetic material that we are manipulating. We will look more closely at chromosomes later.

PLANT GROWTH
It is easy for most growers to mistake plant height for an increase in growth. Although this may seem to be the case it actually is not quite as simple as this. To be more precise, plant growth actually corresponds to the increase of plant cell numbers which are, by their nature, irreversible without pruning or cutting the plant back. Areas of the plant which grow are called "Meristems." Meristems come in two types:

Apical Meristems
Apical Meristems are mostly found at the shoot and root tips. In their initial stages of development the cells are not specialized or designed to carry out specific tasks, but they gradually become elongated and go through vacuolation. After this they are specialized to carry out various tasks and become stable plant tissue.

Lateral Meristems
Lateral meristems are called lateral because they are found growing out from the side of the plant. They usually perform tasks like stem, branch and root thickening. They also form the phloem and xylem.

In order for meristems to be produced the plant must be growing in near optimal conditions for photosynthesis to occur. Nutrients will also contribute to their development. If the conditions are less than optimal, the production of meristems decreases or even stops. This is especially noticeable in cold growing conditions or where photosynthesis is not working. The lack of meristems being produced is more commonly known as "growth stunting."

Hormones
Hormones are organic compounds produced by plants that regulate growth and other physiological activities. Plants have five classes of hormones.

Auxins
Auxins promote stem cell elongation and have some function in controlling yields. Auxins are mainly produced in the stem, bud and roots. Auxins play an active part in **phototropism**. Phototropism occurs when a plant bends toward the light. Auxins also work with apical dominance. When auxins are present they prevent lateral growth. When you prune back the shoot tip of a plant auxins are no longer present to prevent lateral growth. This is known as apical dominance. Auxins also stimulate cell division in the cambium, stimulate differentiation of phloem and xylem, and stimulate root initiation on stem cuttings. Auxins also delay leaf aging and stimulate flowering. They are also known to promote females. Auxins can both inhibit and increase growth depending on how the plant uses them.

Barmac Auxinone is an auxin-based hormone that is available from most good grow stores. It is used to stimulate root growth.

SensaSpray is another auxin-based hormone and is used to promote females. It also contains ethylene (see below), another plant hormone.

Gibberellins
Gibberellins are very similar to auxins, however gibberellins do not seem to inhibit growth (unless introduced in large amounts) except possibly in root growth. Gibberellins promote cell division and stem elongation. They are also involved in the production of a seed's embryo and can help seeds to germinate faster. Gibberellins can speed up growth but they can also promote more males.

Bonza Bud is an anti-gibberellins-based hormone that is available from most good grow shops. It will help keep internode lengths short and promote female flowers.

Ozi Tonic contains tricantanol, gibberellic acid, propolis and vitamin B. The gibberellic acid can promote male growth, and females that grow from Ozi Tonic treated plants may have increased yields.

Cytokinins

Cytokinins promote cell division and leaf expansion, are responsible for morphogensis in tissue culture and are involved in the stimulation of chlorophyll synthesis. They are mostly produced at the tip of a shoot. They work very closely with auxins for plant growth.

Acadian Seaweed Extract is a common cytokinin product. It contains the cytokinin BAP and is used to prevent transplant shock.

Nitrozyme is another cytokinin product. It is easier to find than Acadian Seaweed Extract and is also used to treat transplant shock.

Abscisic Acid

Abscisic acid promotes seed dormancy by inhibiting cell growth. It helps seeds to synthesize storage proteins. It also slows down cell division and bud production. Abscisic acid inhibits shoot growth but does not seem to affect the roots. It is also involved in the processes of leaf wilt. Abscisic acid is an antagonist of gibberellic acid, auxine and cytokinine. It also plays a role in pathogen defense.

Ethylene

Ethylene is a gaseous hormone closely regulated by the plant. It stimulates shoot and root growth and promotes flowering maturation. It also controls leaf aging. For ethylene products see SensaSpray above.

HORMONE CHART

	Location	Function
Auxin	Embryo of seed, meristems of apical buds and new leaves	Cell elongation, phototropism, gravitropism, vascular differentiation, apical dominance and stimulation of ethylene synthesis
Gibberellins	Embryo of seed, meristems of apical buds and new leaves.	Shoot elongation and promotion of cell division
Cytokines	Synthesized in roots and transported to other organs	Promotes cell division and shoot growth, involved in leaf aging and sequencing
Abscisic Acid	Leaves and stems	Stimulates stomatal closure
Ethylene	Node regions and senescent leaves and flowers	Stimulates flowering maturation and leaf and flower senescence

ADDITIONAL HORMONE PRODUCTS

Here is a list of additional hormone products that we have not covered already.

Aminogro

Aminogrow contains L form amino acids and is used to help improve plant vigor and increase resistance to stress, pest attacks, mold and fungi.

Checking your bud for mold is important. Immediately clip away any moldy bud. Humidity promotes mold. Fresh air is the solution to mold problems. Prevention is better than using fungicides.

Ethrel

Ethrel contains ethlephon and is used to promote yields.

Formula 1

Formula 1 contains a broad range of hormones and is used to promote plant growth and also helps nitrogen-deficiency-related stress.

PowerBloom

PowerBloom also contains a broad range of hormones and is used to control plant height and internode lengths, and reduce branch growth. It also promotes flowering.

SensaSoak

SensaSoak is a germination solution that is used to encourage the production of females.

Superthrive

Superthrive contains the vitamin B1 (thiamine) and is used to help prevent transplant shock. It also promotes good growth and plant vigor. Superthrive is popular with cloning techniques.

Wood's Rooting Compound

Wood's Rooting Compound contains indole-3-butyric acid (IBA), 1-napthalene acetic acid (NAA) and is used to promote root growth in cuttings.

Remember when using hormones that you are directly affecting plant growth. Plants already produce their own hormones and sometimes adding hormones can have an adverse effect on your plants. Hormone treatment is mostly experimentation. The only hormone treatment that comes highly recommended is Superthrive (B1-thiamine), which is clinically proven to help cuttings root and plants survive transplant shock.

TROPISM

It is difficult to talk about hormones without talking a little about tropism. Tropism is the turning of an organism or part of an organism in a particular direction by growth, bending, or locomotion, in response to some special external stimulus. Hormones also regulate many tropisms. As a cannabis breeder there are three tropisms you should know about.

Geotropism

Geotropism is the sense of the direction of gravity. Seedlings use it to know which way they should grow after germination.

Gravitropism

Gravitropism is very similar to geotropism. Most cannabis branches curve upward. Auxin development causes the branch to curve upward due to cell expansion. The choice of where auxins develop is strategic for gravitropism to occur. Gravitropism causes roots to grow down.

Phototropism

Phototropism is a growth response toward the light caused by auxin stimulation of cells not exposed to light. An uneven distribution of auxins in the plant's stem causes phototropism. Auxins gather on the side of the stem that does not receive the most light. These auxins cause the stem to bend toward the light. When the light is received the auxins are eradicated and the bending process stops.

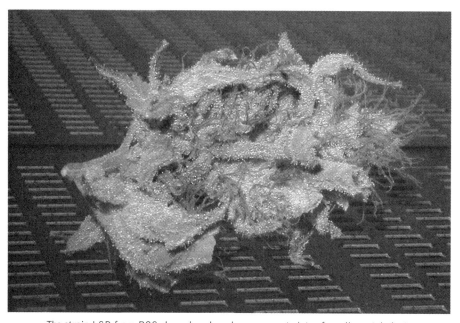

The strain LSD from BOG shows how breeders can create lots of small crystal plenty nuggets on one plant. The grower, BOG, was featured in The Cannabis Grow Bible before he became a breeder. If you have seen his plants in our previous book then you can understand why the market started demanding seeds from him.

6 | THE CODE OF LIFE

THE BASICS OF CHROMOSOMES

Chromosomes consist of a single molecule of DNA and are associated with histones. Histones are a group of simple basic water-soluble proteins that occur and are associated with DNA in the cell nuclei of eukaryotes. There are some non-histones present there too. They actually work on sorting out which parts of the DNA will be converted into RNA.

DNA are nucleic acids in which the sugar component is deoxyribose. It is a self-replicating material present in nearly all living organisms, especially in the case of chromosomes, as the carrier of genetic information and the determiner of protein synthesis. DNA stands for DeoxyriboNucleicAcid and RNA stands for RiboNucleicAcid.

Before we discuss more about chromosomes and what they are, let's look at the process of mitosis.

MITOSIS

Mitosis is the process of division by which a cell nucleus gives rise to two daughter nuclei identical to the parent in number and size of chromosomes.

Chromosome:
A threadlike structure of nucleic acids and protein which carries a set of linked genes and occurs singly in prokaryotes and in characteristic numbers, usually paired, in the cell nuclei of higher organisms.

In mitosis a eukaryotic cell divides into two. Each daughter or progeny cell will get:

1. A complete set of genes.
2. Some mitochondria and chloroplasts.
3. Some ribosomes, some of the endoplasmic reticulum, and maybe some other organelles.

Mitosis is simply genetic code reproduction within a cell. This is all you really need to know about mitosis for breeding purposes. The actual stages of mitosis are the prophase, prometaphase, metaphase, anaphase and telophase.

The interesting point about mitosis and genetic code reproduction within a cell is that some cells carry identical gene pairs to ensure that mitosis works and that the genetic code for a trait actually gets through to its destination. There are two main types of cells with regard to the reproduction of chromosomes that we need to know about for the time being: haploid cells and diploid cells.

Haploid cells are sometimes called monoploid cells. It means that the cell only has a single set of chromosomes. The notation symbol is - (n). When the cell divides it only reproduces one version of the chromosome at a time.

Diploid cells have two of each kind of chromosome except for the sex chromosomes. The notation is - (2n). When the cell divides it reproduces one version of each chromosome at a time but the resulting numbers are higher than a haploid cell.

Chromosomes are too small to be seen without expensive equipment. Before mitosis occurs each cell prepares itself for cell division. The duplicated chromosomes are called dyads and these can be seen with less expensive microscope equipment because the chromosome stretches itself out.

All information transmitted from the parent plant to the offspring generation must be contained in the pollen of the staminate parent and the ovule of the pistillate parent.

Fertilization unites these two sets of genetic information. A seed forms and a new generation begins. As we have seen, both pollen and ovules are known as *gametes,* and the transmitted units determining the expression of a character are known as *genes.* Individual plants have two identical sets of genes (2n) in every cell except the gametes, which through reduction and division have only one set of genes. Upon fertilization one set from each parent combines to form a seed (2n).

In cannabis the haploid number of chromosomes is 10 and the diploid is 20. The gametes are haploid.

POLYPLOIDY

There is an unnatural condition in cannabis called the polyploid state. This happens when a cell contains more than two homologous sets of chromosomes and may breed the condition through to other cannabis plants. It is possible that such a condition arose from mutations and that those mutant plants drifted in and out of different populations in the wild, but the problem is that the trait is not usually stable or sustainable through seed.

Polyploids have been noticed in the wild on rare occasions but are more than likely either the result of man-made interference with cannabis plants or an ancestral mutation that passed down the lines. Either way there is not enough information currently available on the polyploid status of the cannabis plant to know much about it. Some researchers, such as H.E Warmke, have suggested that polyploid cannabis plants have higher potency levels than normal. This does not appear to be case. Although there are known linkages in cannabis genes there is nothing to suggest that the polyploid condition is somehow linked to potency. Nor is there any evidence to suggest that the polyploid condition will affect potency. It is extremely hard to continue the polyploid trait in offspring because the parent plants usually end up sterile in the process. You need to have large selections in order to experiment with this condition.

There are many products on the market that will mutate cells. Colchicine is one such substance that actually promotes the polyploid condition. However colchicine is also a mutagen and mutations are not under the grower's control. It is more than probable that the potent polyploid condition was the result of separate mutations in Warmke's experiments. In the future we hope to see more research in this area.

7 | EVOLUTION AND MUTATIONS

GREGOR MENDEL AND EVOLUTION

The theory of evolution is just that—a theory. Although the theory itself, proposed by Darwin, contains much merit, and is very much applicable to cannabis species development, it is still very much a recent discovery and much of it is still an incomplete work. The reader is asked not to take evolution theory at face value but to consider the anomalies associated with evolution theory and maybe do a little research for him or herself before subscribing entirely to this area of scientific thought.

While we can look at principles like Hardy-Weinberg's Equilibrium and see set rules and know how and when those rules can be broken, the theory of evolution still has some problems that we have yet to clearly observe or discover answers to.

One of the most important elements to the theory of evolution is mutations. Since man, plants, fly and worm have all evolved from the same source, why are there no links found in fossils which prove this is so? It could be that we have not found such links yet, but as science dictates we clearly have no evidence to support the half-human/half-ape concept. There are no fossils of any such creature in any science lab or museum. All we have at our disposal is a theory coupled with all these different life-forms that we actually say are linked through evolution.

Some Problems to Consider

1. Gregor Mendel himself showed that the theory of evolution needs to be looked at more closely.
2. No mutations have ever been observed which are beneficial to an organism.
3. Mutations are not really controllable. They are random, without focus and can be extremely damaging to the organism and its offspring.

These are important points for the reader to consider if he or she believes the theory of evolution is a fact. It is not a fact, it is just an extremely good theory. The theory of organic evolution is unfounded in many aspects. Organic evolution has never been observed. Let's start at the beginning and work our way through this so that we get a better understanding of mutations.

Spontaneous generation of life from dead matter or nonliving matter has never been seen nor has it been performed. We cannot bring the dead back to life, nor do mountains full of every material known to man under every condition known to man produce from themselves living matter. Life appears to only come from other living things. A rock does not mutate into a living creature and neither does a jar full of dead animal tissue. Biogenetics is the actual study of this topic and is taught in universities.

The most famous experiment attempt to prove whether or not life could be created from chemicals was carried out in 1953 by Stanley L. Miller and Harold C. Urey, working at the University of Chicago. The experiment has since been known as the Miller/Urey experiment. Miller obtained molecules which were thought to be the major parts of the early Earth's atmosphere and put them into a closed system. The experiment produce amino acids and these are the basics of DNA. However there are still many questions that need to be asked and the Miller/Urey experiment is still a far cry from developing life from chemicals in a test tube. They did not create DNA nor has anyone managed to do so in the lab using these environmental experiments. At the moment we are still in the realm of biogenetics whereby life is producible only from other living organisms and not dead matter. However we do know that the possibility of DNA developing from amino acids MAY occur and this is how we currently explain the model of life evolving from dead matter, although we must remember that this has never been proven or observed in the lab.

Biogenetics also shows that acquired characteristics cannot be inherited. For example, an athlete does not pass on his marvelous long jumping skills to his or her child through inheritance. Darwin believed that this was possible and he has since been proven wrong.

Plants and animals can produce offspring that have traits for defense against certain environmental conditions. The traits are not new genetic traits (unless they are mutated genes which bring about the trait), but may be dormant genetic material that is suddenly turned on. This means that plant genetic material already contains traits that are needed to combat problems found in nature. It does not mean that the environment causes these new genes to be created.

Mendel discovered that genes are shuffled in the genetic combination of an individual, and if parents breed then new genetic recombination comes about, but these have laws attached to them and we have talked about these in chapter 2 (Hardy-Weinberg). This tells us that natural selection DOES NOT PRODUCE NEW GENES, but only selects genes for phenotype expression that are already present in a population.

This leaves us with the final conclusion that mutations are the only way an organism can generate NEW genetic material. However it appears that nearly all types of mutations are not controllable, but random.

If there was a nuclear fallout near a large plantation of various populations of cannabis plants, and the radiation caused mutations, the types of mutations would probably end up killing every single plant in those populations. The chances that a new gene would be hatched by a plant to defend itself against the very thing that caused the mutation in the first place is extremely unlikely.

What is more likely is that a plant might have awakened a pre-existing gene to combat the problem, but this gene would have been around before any mutation was induced by the radiation. The current scientific model for adaptability in evolution suggests that environmental factors may affect some of the plant's genes to make it resistant to the negative aspects of the growing environment (unproven and only a hypothesis). Essentially the plants that cannot survive the disadvantageous environment simply don't make it and thus do not contribute any of their genes to next gene pool. The ones that survive either already have the gene they need to survive or may have mutated, there and then, to adapt to that disadvantageous environment—however mutations are not controllable nor do they respond by actually setting out to create a gene that defeats the negative environmental influences. It must appear by accident—a 'one-off'—in order to fit the current scientific model of evolution.

There is no evidence in science that suggests that mutations can produce an organism that is more viable than its parents in the same environment. But we are also faced with the fact that plants have evolved to some degree through mutation.

So this method of evolution by mutation does happen, but it does not mean that the organism will:

1. Survive the mutation.
2. Be better than its parents.

In most cases mutations result in:

1. Nonviable organisms that produce nonviable offspring.
2. A serious disruption of genetic material that can cause death.
3. A new gene that is not viable or has no purpose.

However a mutation may:

1. Bring about new genetic material that is viable and was not present before.
2. Improve a feature of an organism.

Mutation control is a rapidly developing new technology and there are different costly procedures in place which can manipulate DNA, but for the purpose of the average cannabis breeder this is not accessible nor is it considered appropriate because of concerns over genetically modified (GM) crops.

A living cell is a very complex organ. A cell may have evolved through mutation to be what it is today, but the chances of that happening are very slim. One can imagine the analogy of a monkey hitting keys on a typewriter at random. It is possible that the monkey may spell a small three-letter word or may eventually type a six-letter word with enough time and random work. The monkey may even type a sentence if the duration of the experiment is long enough. This is what mathematicians call "probability". With an infinite amount of time and work the monkey can theoretically type a book or even type a book that has already been written, but the chances of this happening are extremely slim.

The point is that a living muscle or organ like the brain is not impossible to create via mutations of living cells, but we are reminded that the chances of this happening are nonexistent in our lifetime, or even in the same time as it took the Earth to form and get to where it is today. Scientists understand that there are many questions that need to be asked behind the actual foundation of mutation theory.

Neurophysicians understand that various organs in the human body are so complex that it would be hard to imagine mutations being responsible for their development. Also, we appear to have organs that are fully developed, not partially developed. Some may claim that the brain uses 1/16 of its capacity but it is more than likely that we do not yet understand what the other 15/16s does. We have made mistakes like this in the past, for instance saying that the human appendix has no function but maybe when we were apes we used them for some purpose. Now it is clear to scientists that the appendix helps develop antibodies for the intestines and protects part of the intestine from developing harmful growths such as cancer.

All of these questions must be looked at before we accept that evolution through mutation is the key to all the variations that we see in life today. More than likely it is not the only key.

MUTATIONS

In cannabis cells DNA undergoes chemical changes all the time, especially during mitosis. These changes are very quickly repaired, bringing the DNA back to its original format. There are circumstances where the chemical change will not undergo DNA repair because of a problem. This results in a mutation of the DNA.

In some cases there is a basic substitution of DNA during mutation. This is called "point mutation" or "transition" or "transversion," depending on the type of point mutation that takes place. Another type of mutation is the "mussense missense" mutation. This involves a new nucleotide altering the codon which in turn alters amino acids in the protein content of the DNA. The codon is a group of three consecutive nucleotides that together form a unit of the genetic code and determine which amino acid is added at a particular point in protein synthesis.

"Silent mutations" are another type of mutation, but they do not appear to change DNA and can only be seen in gene sequencing.

"Splice site mutations" occur when a mutation effects a nucleotide signal. If the signal is altered and translated wrongly then protein mutation will occur, which effects the DNA.

"Insertion mutations" and "deletion mutations" occur at the base protein level when a violent mutation causes a new gene to appear or one to be deleted. There can be a total and complete shift in the DNA sequence and this type of mutation can be quite disastrous to the organism if it affects a high number of genes. If it only affects one gene, then the mutation may be beneficial. If it affects more than one gene, then the chances of a beneficial mutation are decreased as the mutation will be 50% good and 50% bad at best. The 50% bad would be enough to cause severe problems with the organism.

"Duplication" is a doubling of part of the genome. A crossover between chromatids that are out of phase with each other can produce one chromatid with a duplicated gene and the other having two with deletions. This causes an imbalance in the gene and the mutant gene becomes dominant. This is also a problem for future offspring.

"Translocations" are another type of mutation, one that causes a gene to break, which simply obliterates it or causes it to become a hybrid gene.

What is even more interesting is that a huge percentage of genes in the cannabis plant do not appear to contribute anything to the phenotype of the plant. So if we think about this coupled with plant diversity and then couple that with mutation theory, it does make us ask a lot of questions about why we have so many different organisms on this planet in such a short space of time.

All of the above mutations result in two broad types of mutations. These are "somatic mutations" and "germline mutations".

A mutation that occurs in somatic cells can end up killing the cell or seriously damaging it. Germline mutations will be found in all the cells that came from the zygote. Every one of the offspring's cells will contain this mutation, passing it down from generation to generation where breeding permits it.

Now that you understand what a mutation is, let's move forward and see some environmental and growing factors that can cause mutations.

WHAT CAUSES A MUTATION

Mutations that are passed through from parent to offspring are called germline mutations. Germline mutations have traits that can be treated much like any other trait. We will find that the genotype of the mutant gene can be dominant homozygous, heterozygous or recessive homozygous.

Since there are many things found in nature that can cause a mutation, some man-made, some not, we would find it hard to list them all here. Here are a couple of factors that are known to breeders at this time and these are the ones that you should know about. There are five main factors as follows:

1. Stress.
2. Genotype.
3. Age.
4. The mutation of cuttings.
5. Transfer techniques.

Let's go through these one by one.

Stress

In *The Cannabis Grow Bible* we talked about plant stress and how it can effect optimal growth. What we did not mention was that stress factors can affect DNA repair. So anything that stresses a plant has the potential to create a mutation.

What causes stress? Anything that your plant does not like will stress it, such as: overfeeding, overwatering, heat, pest damage, accidents, pH problems, soil problems, root damage … the list can go on and on.

How much stress a plant must endure before it expresses a physical mutation is not clear, nor is this mutation controllable in any way via stress.

Genotype

If a weak plant is developed, with genotypes that are not very protective or don't help it to grow well then the plant is at risk of mutating under stressful conditions. It is doubtful that a plant would exist like this in nature because it would have died long ago.

However indoor breeding projects may bring such a plant about. Again a weakling plant will have trouble repairing DNA and more than likely over time develop a mutation or a number of mutations.

Age

As the plant gets older it will create new cells to replace older ones. Eventually the plant will die. Before the plant dies there will probably be a problem with chromosome division and this is one way that the plant knows that its work here is coming to an end. When this happens DNA repair may be affected, causing a mutation to occur. Taking a cutting from an old dying mother is never really a good idea because of this so keep cloning new mother plants every few grows.

The Mutation of Cuttings

Breeders have noticed that clones can change in phenotype expression over a long period of time after constant cloning from the same mother plant. This has led many growers and marijuana writers to inaccurately believe that clones lose some form of genetic integrity. Well-maintained clones will not lose any such thing. This mutation of cuttings is troublesome since a clone is supposed to be an exact genetic replication of the parent plant it came from.

It is not understood how many times the same plant must be cloned for this to happen, but the figure looks to be from well into the thousands to maybe tens of thousands, although it is possible that the mutation can occur through less cuttings. In theory and practice a clone should be able to reproduce its exact genetic code indefinitely.

Paradise Seeds generate a new population of clone mothers kept under fluorescent lights on moveable trays. These female clones will be pollinated for seed production.

Breeders who were trying to figure out why this was happening to their clones came to the conclusion that cloning can cause a plant mutation. We know that stress factors affect DNA repair. Since a cutting damages part of the cut area of the plant, then this area may have a problem with DNA repair and if a new shoot forms at this cut point (on the mother plant) then we may find ourselves dealing with a shoot that has some mutations. Likewise the clone may mutate because of the cutting procedure. This is actually very rare, but it does happen and is a contributing factor to clone variations.

This type of cutting mutation is most common with aged mother plants. Again we know that age can cause mutations. If we take cuttings from an aged mother plant or a plant that is dying, then we increase our chances of taking a cutting from an area of the plant that has undergone DNA repair malfunction. The cure for this is a simple one. Keep generating new mother plants by cloning and do not let the mother plant from which you are taking cuttings get too old.* Another way of preventing the mutation of cuttings is to try not to take repeated cuttings from the same cut zone. Repetitive "cut and grow" from the same zone of the mother plant may induce DNA repair malfunction in that zone. Again, the best solution to this problem is to keep generating new mother plants by cloning. This is a good practice to get into.

All variations in a clone are called "somaclonal" variation.

Transfer Techniques:
In cannabis propagation there are a number of techniques that can stress a plant to the point where DNA repair might fail. Cloning is one; another is transplantation.

During transplantation a plant is moved out of one growing medium and into another. During the transplant the roots may be disturbed, causing the plant to go into shock. Shock leads to stress and stress can contribute to the malfunctioning of DNA repair. One more propagation technique that can cause DNA repair to fail is tissue culture, which will be the focus of the next chapter.

CHEMICALS THAT CAUSE MUTATIONS (MUTAGENS)
It is a fact that cannabis plants do not mutate that easily through any of the risks we have mentioned above. Trying to deliberately induce a mutation using any of these causes is very difficult. If growers *want* to mutate their plants, they go the chemical route.

There are some chemical products on the market which can cause plants to mutate.

A good percentage of the elements on the periodic table will cause mutations in any living organism, however there are one or two products on the market that are used by cannabis growers and breeders that can mostly lead to mutations. The two products are "**Growth Hormones**" and "**Colchicine**".

---

*   Some clones are more than 20 years old, however cloning allows the mature clone to grow into a new plant again. Here we are talking about old growth and not the clones total age.

Basic Growth Hormones and Gibberellic Acid

We already know that hormones are numerous organic compounds produced by plants that regulate growth and other physiological activities. Hormones can be man-made as synthetic compounds and will have the same effect as normal natural hormones.

We mentioned gibberellic acid back in chapter 5 when we discussed selfing a plant. Gibberellic acid, or *GA,* is a compound derived from a fungus called *Gibberella fujikuroi.* This hormone is associated with growth development in plants and can sometimes speed up growth development to the point where cells may collapse under the hormone's influence.

One influence GA has is in the early development of the seedling stage in cannabis plants. If a plant is in vegetative growth GA application can promote early flowering, but GA will more than likely produce male flowers because of the way the hormone interacts with the cannabis plant. High levels can actually reverse the flowering process and bring the plant back around to vegetative growth again.

As a growth hormone, GA has the potential to mutate genetic material, so by using GA to play with a plant's growth cycle we may accidentally cause a mutation to occur. These mutations are not controllable by any means and the results can even cause plant death.

GA is available in most countries but in some countries such hormones are banned because of the effect that they may have on a plant's genetic material. It is not known if GA will cause problems in humans but so far there do not appear to be any problems with its use. You should always follow the instructions on the bottle carefully before using the substance.

As you work with a particular strain you will be able to deduce how much your concentration levels should be mixed at to get the desired results. GA as a hormone can increase bud mass by up to 50%, although the application amounts of GA to get this effect are variable from strain to strain. Also the major problem with GA is its propensity for promoting male flower growth from within the female bud, so you end up with a crop that is not sinsemilla if the pollen is viable. GA is good for working on mutations but it is not good for increasing your overall sinsemilla yields.

Never smoke the bud from a crop that has undergone the application GA for health reasons. Always grow out the offspring from the treated mother and use these instead.

Other types of growth hormones that do not promote male flower growth in female plants unless the hormone is incorrectly mixed or applied in doses that stress a plant are available on the market. One famous product used by growers around the world is Superthrive. It is proven to increase yields but may be banned in some countries. You can find out more about growth hormones if you visit your local grow store. They are hundreds of different brands and types to choose from.

Colchicine

This chemical compound is widely used to produce germline mutation in plants. It actually gives rise to the polyploid condition if you use it in larger quantities with lots of seeds (some breeders even go into the thousands of seeds when using this technique but a minimum of one hundred is recommended for best results). It is a toxic yellow alkaloid found in the Colchicum plant species. Basically it inhibits chromosome segregation to daughter cells and cell wall formation. This causes multiple chromosome sets to develop. Colchicine can be poisonous and plants that have been treated are rarely ever smoked. The offspring from the colchicine-treated plants are the ones the breeders are most interested in— although sometimes colchicine-treated plants are sterile and fail to reproduce. Colchicine should be used with extreme care.

Colchicine use is very unstable for producing viable seed numbers. Sometimes a minor percentage of seeds will germinate—1% to 4%—because of the effects that colchicine has on the individual seed's embryo. Any seeds that do pass through have a good chance of being polyploid and/or mutated. Colchicine mixtures are best used at less than 1%, 0.5% being the most common percentage used. Seeds are steeped in the mixture for 24 hours and then planted afterward. If none of the seeds germinate, then slowly reduce the time down to 6 hours. If still no seeds germinate then reduce the strength of your mixture.

From 100 seeds you may be able to produce one or two polyploids. Ideally you should undertake this process with 1000+ seeds to get better results. Remember though that colchicine is also a mutagen and so other mutations may arise aside from the polyploid condition.

Colchicine can be found in gout medicine, autumn crocus bulbs, winter crocus bulbs, meadow saffron or as raw colchicine. Garlic crushers can be used to juice the bulbs. The juice is then mixed with water.

Common polyploid mutation. This mutation is not exclusive to the polyploid condition.

The application of colchicine should be carefully investigated before you attempt it. Technically you are using a poison, which does affect human health, so make sure you read the instructions carefully before use. Wear rubber gloves and try not to get the stuff on your skin.

WHY MUTATE CANNABIS?

There is no need to use chemicals for mutating plants unless we have the money and equipment to study our findings. The home grower does not need to mutate the gene pool and neither do breeders. Cannabis breeders can develop very potent strains with good yields and great vigor by breeding alone. This is important to remember.

Mutations are odd factors that crop up in breeding programs. Experiment all you want but do not go flooding the gene pool with a great new strain that actually contains harmful genetic material. If you do mutate a plant do not release it onto the market unless you know more about it. This is essentially what we have been explaining all along.

Do not be confused about mutation somehow being related to potency. It never has been and all such related material is simply propaganda. The most potent strains that true breed for potency traits are the result of plants being selected for these traits that are found in large plant populations and not through a breeder forcing mutations.

Most modern (not to mention sudden) breakthroughs in the discovery of some highly desirable traits in cannabis are found in the phenotype of a hybrid through simple breeding practices. Any trait that you would like to find in cannabis is already probably there in the gene pool. There is an abundance of variation in flavor, smell, taste, looks and potency. You just need to go looking for these variations in large populations.

LOOKS CAN BE DECEIVING

Over the years I have seen breeders produce pictures of plants that are high-yielding monsters. The breeder introduces the strain to the market by advertising with pictures all over the place. Then they set about getting their friends to pretend that they have obtained these genetics and have grown them out for themselves with great results. The market takes notice and growers put up their dollars for this latest great strain. Then the growers find out the truth after wasting bulb life, electricity, nutrients, grow space and a lot of precious 'grow time.'

Hermies

Hermaphrodite strains can produce large bud quantities. Breeders can be very clever in the way that they present their hermaphrodite strains. They take a small pair of clippers and proceed to clip away any male flowers for the photographic presentation. In reality the strain will not provide a sinsemilla crop and any offspring from this strain will carry the same hermaphrodite trait.

If the hermaphrodite is introduced into someone's breeding project, then the hermaphrodite condition will probably breed into the offspring. This contaminates the gene pool and is a huge problem that the cannabis growing community is faced with. Be very careful when buying something new on the market. Sometimes the old saying "If it sounds too good to be true..." has a lot of merit.

Image Altering

Image altering is another huge problem that breeders and growers are faced with. Software packages like Adobe Photoshop can easily enhance an image, color buds and remove male flowers. Always keep this in mind. Photographs on the Internet and even in print can be fakes.

Perspective

Another problem with plant size is that some photographers can use perspective to make their plants look bigger than what they are. Their strain might only grow to 14" high but using perspective with proper location and lighting they can make their plant look 48″ high. Using Photoshop a grower or breeder can even reduce the size of a pencil or coin in the foreground of the picture, making the plant lying next to it look massive.

Knock-Offs

Something new may in fact be something that already exists. A breeder just might take another breeder's work and give it a new name. The plant is then distributed under this false name at maybe twice the price. People with experience in growing different strains might recognize the plant as being a knock-off but the average Joe will not know what this plant is. Always research a bit about the breeder's background before you purchase a strain.

Size and Potency Are Not Related

Size does not equal potency. Potency and size are two different traits in a plant, and are governed by different genes. You can have a plant that is 6′ tall but very low in potency and you can have a plant that is 1′ high but extremely potent.

PROPER NAMING OF STRAINS

At one time there existed a protocol for the proper naming of strains that has since been left behind, but you would do well to help reestablish this protocol. If you cross Northern Lights by Skunk#1 then the offspring will be known as Northern Lights x Skunk#1, but this does not tell us which one was the male parent and which one was the female parent.

The correct way to establish the hybrid parents is by using the female first followed by the male. So if the Northern Lights was male and the Skunk#1 was female then the correct protocol to use would be Skunk#1 x Northern Lights and not Northern Lights x Skunk#1.

However this rule does not hold steadfast any more as a lot of breeders have decided just to list the cross in alphabetical order. The old method provides more useful information.

8 | TISSUE CULTURE

TISSUE CULTURE IS A RELATIVELY NEW CLONING METHOD involving a certain degree of lab work. However this is the twenty-first century and this kind of lab equipment can cost as little as $40. What follows is a basic rundown of what tissue culture is and how it works.

A mother plant is selected and a leaf is clipped off a shoot. The leaf is then cleaned of any contaminating microorganisms, spores, dirt, insects or any other foreign bodies. A small sterile chamber is then used to cut the leaf into a number of very small segments. These are referred to as "explants."

The explants are then placed in a special chemical medium for tissue culture. This medium provides nutrients and hormones for the explants to grow. While in this medium the explants start to develop new cells and organs before finally developing small roots and shoots. The process takes between four to eight weeks. The new shoots will start to look like a small leaf with a stem. When big enough the explants can be taken from the solution and transferred to a propagation chamber. The process will result in a new plant that is identical to the mother plant.

Getting started in tissue culture is easy if you maintain a clean environment. The process of cleaning down the leaf is called "surface cleaning." A simple rinse with clean water is the first step. To get the best results use de-ionized water with some cleanser. Tween 20 is a popular brand of cleanser used in tissue culture. The idea behind the cleaning is to prevent any other cell tissues from growing other than the tissue you want to propagate. After the wash you need to prepare your leaf by dipping it in either ethanol, alcohol or sodium hypochlorite. After leaving for ten minutes the leaf is ready for the next stage of the tissue culture procedure. There is already a great product on the market called Clorox which serves this tissue culture cleaning purpose.

After completing this sterilization, place the leaf inside a unit called a "laminar flow hood." This hood is essentially your miniature clean room. Inside the hood you slice up your leaf into multiple little explants. Each of the explants can be placed into separate tissue culture mediums. The slices are made using a sterile scalpel.

The tissue culture is a semiliquid medium. The explants are placed on the surface of the medium. There are many tissue culture mediums available on the internet. Most of them contain the same ingredients, the most common being Agar. The mediums usually contain the elements N, P, K, Mg, S, Ca, Fe, Zn, B, I, Mn, Mo, Co, Cu with the vitamins thiamine, nicotinic acid, and riboflavin. Sugars are also present in the medium along with sugar alcohols. The final ingredients are hormones such as auxins, cytokinins, gibberellins, abscisic acid and ethylene. Some products may contain all of these or only some of these.

The medium must be prepared before use so after you have read the instructions and mixed up your medium on the tissue culture bottle you will have to take a pH reading to make sure that everything is okay. You should have a pH of about 5.5 to 6.0. It should not really change from this pH if you have mixed the tissue culture medium as directed on the bottles. Some tissue culture mediums only come in one bottle.

The medium is then placed in the tissue culture vessel, which has been cleansed much the same way as the leaf was. The vessel can be a test tube, a canning jar, a small glass jar or a special tissue culture jar. One widely used tissue culture jar is the Magenta Vessel which is widely advertised on the internet. All the vessels must be capped off with a gas permeable lid.

Now cannabis plants should form in the jar without much light at all although some light is needed to allow photosynthesis to occur when the explants start to grow. You will find that a window or very mild fluorescent light will provide enough light for your explants to grow under. Also keep the area cool, but not too cold. If you find that your tissue culture does not work too well then try starting the tissue culture in darkness for two or three weeks before transferring the explants to a light source.

There is fine line between which methods work for your strains and which do not. You may have to experiment with a couple of mixtures, temperatures and light sources before you will find the conditions that suit your strain the best. Tissue culture is a very easy method of sending other people clone material in the post but it does take a long time to propagate the explants and the recipient must know a little bit about tissue culture. Most cuttings only take two to three weeks to root. Tissue culture can take two months to form anything that can be considered a new plant. However you can only take a limited amount of clones at any one time from a plant. With tissue culture you can create up to 50 plants per leaf! So if you take one mother cannabis plant with 20 leaves then you can make 1000 clones from those leaves—sometimes even more!

This is why tissue culture is quickly becoming one of the most sought after methods of cloning propagation in the market today.

9 WHAT THE MARKET WANTS

SEED PRICING

The market wants cheap seeds that are high-yielding and very potent, or at least that is what most of the market is looking for. There are many strains on the market today that cost a pretty penny. Some of the more popular seed banks sell seeds that cost as high as $200USD for 10-16 seeds. When you see seeds at this price you can probably guess that the seed has won a prize in a Cannabis Cup competition. Generally when a strain wins a prize the price of that strain shoots up above the $100 mark. Supply and demand sets these prices.

Pure Sativa strains take quite some time to breed true because we are looking at an overall grow time of five to nine months. Indica strains can produce new seeds as early as three months from seed. It is actually quicker to breed an Indica plant than it is to breed a Sativa plant. Sativa strains, especially Haze strain, tend to be expensive. Some people can afford to spend $1000 on a couple of packets of seeds, but the new grower probably does not want to part with more than $100 for some seeds.

It is interesting to note that the majority of cannabis seed customers are new and are looking to spend no more than $30 for 10 seeds. There are many different fixed prices on strains but the following gives a basic rundown of what the seed banks charge for different types of strains.

This refers to all good hybrid or IBL strains. We are not talking about problematic unstable strains which can be bought as cheaply as $5. We also do not include feminized strains (selfed plants).

Afghani

Big Bud

California-Indica

Durban

Skunk

Hindu Kush

Haze Strains
The cheapest Haze strain on the market is priced at about $35. The most expensive Haze strain costs $150. The average price of a Haze strain is $80.

Kush Strain
The most expensive Kush strain on the market is $40. The cheapest is $20. The average price is about $30.

Skunk Strains
The most expensive strain is $60 while the cheapest is $15. The average price of a Skunk strain is about $30.

African Strains
They are all priced at around $60.

Proven High-Yielding Hybrid Strains
The strains have fancy names like Cindy 99, Matanuska Thunderfuck and AK-47, and are usually used in ScrOG and SOG grows. You are looking at an average cost of about $80 per strain. Some are even as expensive as $140.

High-Yielding Resinous Indica Strains
These plants are usually very resinous and so popular with hash makers. Afghani#1 and Black Domina are good examples of this type of strain. You are looking at prices between $40 and $80 for these strain types.

New Hybrid Strains
Anything that is new on the market (less than six years old) costs between $15 and $45. These strains are Mostly Indica and Mostly Sativa strains. Since they are new you can expect some or a lot of variations.

Some seed banks have taken advantage of new growers, selling new hybrids for $60 or more. This is a bad business practice and you should keep away from these strains.

IBL Strains
This is surprising. Some of the best IBL strains on the market are the cheapest. Let's list them here.

Afghani#1	$60	Big Bud	$70
Blueberry	$70	California Orange	$20
Durban Posion	$25	Hindu Kush	$40
Northern Lights	$120	Skunk#1	$30

So we have 4 out of the 8 strains under $40, 3 around the $70 and 1 above the $100. That is not bad considering that these strains are IBL.

As a breeder this may tell you a few things about your strain and how you can expect to price it. If you are looking at an entry cost of $30 for 10 seeds, being new to the market, then you really want to be shipping around 1000 seeds to make $3,000. One thousand seeds can be manufactured from ten good plants or less depending on the species type and bud volumes. Ten plants generating 100 seeds per plant is very achievable. So with 10 plants you can officially start a small seed business and be able to supply the consumer on demand. You could make up 100 seed packets with 10 seeds in each one. This means you need 100 customers to make your money back. Most good seed banks ship between 3000 and 100,000 seeds per month.

The best way to get good feedback from the market is to give away seeds on the major Internet Websites that allow growers to show their produce in a picture gallery. (Check the Websites' rules before you do this, since some do not encourage giveaways.) If you give away seeds then people will more than likely take you up on that offer. Make sure that you remind them to post some feedback on the Website about your strain.

BEST SELLERS

Most of the good seed banks release information on occasion about sales. There is no universal best-selling strain list but the seed banks do talk a little bit about their best sellers. I can give you an idea of what comes up every year in terms of best sellers.

1. Mysterious strains.
2. Easy strains for new growers.
3. The Cannabis-Cup-winning strain.
4. A high-yielding, potent indoor strain.
5. The latest 'buzz on the block' strain.
6. Presentation strains.
7. Historical strains.
8. A mix.
9. Cheaper knock-offs.
10. 'Free with order' strains.

Let's look at each one closely.

Mysterious Strains

You are probably asking, What is a mysterious strain? A mysterious strain is a strain that is good for a number of reasons but has a certain mystery attached to it. Some breeders might claim that the strain came from a secret government cannabis research lab or from a guru who lives in some unknown cave in the Himalayas. The strain is actually very good but the story is hardly ever proven to be the truth. People like a good story and will buy strains that have a mysterious edge. However it must be said that if your story falls apart then sadly your career as a breeder will go down the tubes. There is also no use in breeding a poor quality strain and saying that the mother plant was given to you by a great Ganja God in India. Even though cannabis users can be very spiritual people and will give you the benefit of the doubt, at least have a great strain to give them along with the story.

Examples: G-13, Chemo, Matanuska Valley Thunderfuck.

Easy Strains for New Growers

Every day seed banks get hundreds of letters from people who are new to growing. The seed bank wants to keep these customers for future sales, so the seed bank wants to give them a great cheap strain that will take a beating in the garden no matter what the grower does to it except maybe uprooting the plant.

There are a few great strains that provide this function and seed banks rely on these strains in order to get good feedback from new customers. These strains have been developed by growers so that they will perform well under nearly any conditions. As a breeder you should know that there are only four or five strains which fit this category at the moment.

Examples: Skunk#1, Afghani#1, Northern Lights.

The Cannabis-Cup-Winning Strain

Any Cannabis-Cup-winning strain will sell and that is why people from all over the world enter the Cannabis Cup. Winning the cup usually means that you can charge more for your strain. However this will only last for a year and then someone else wins the cup, but your strain will still be remembered.

Examples: Blueberry, AK-47.

A High-Yielding, Potent Indoor Strain

Some potent strains have very high yields and these are favored by the commercial grower. Since the strain performs well and produces large yields, the grower has more bud weight at the end of the day. These strains are always successful and make quite a good turnover.

Examples: Jack Herer, Great White Shark, Hindu Kush.

The high yielding strain 'Lifesaver' from BOG seeds.

The Latest 'Buzz on the Block' Strain

Negative incidents such as a public grow bust can boost a strain's sales. Sometimes we hear about very large commercial growers being caught and the officer in charge of the investigation mentions the strain name. This kind of advertising can send strain sales through the roof.

Also if there is a shortage of good bud around and someone grows out a good strain to supplement the drought, that brand name can take on a 'savior' image and sticks in people's heads. One famous case is BC Big Bud, which was developed in Canada. Across the border there was a drought in the United States and a few Canadians were caught smuggling the stuff over. Of course this hit the news and the power of television soon boosted BC Big Bud sales. Unfortunately there are no BC Big Bud seeds (it is a clone) so the developers were never able to sell the strain in seed format. Movies like *American Beauty* have boosted G-13 sales.

Presentation Strains

These strains are created more for presentation than for yield and potency. They usually have very colorful buds and lovely leaf patterns. The strains always look good in a photograph so many people are taken in by the looks and go buy them. It might not be one of the better strains around but they sure do look nice in your garden.

Examples: Blue Satellite, Flo.

Historical Strains

A historical strain is a strain that has been around since the '70s or early '80s. Hippie folktales are responsible for these sales. Skunk#1 is a very popular historical strain that nearly everyone in the cannabis community has heard about. Since historical strains seem to crop up in common everyday talk about cannabis plants, people remember the names and probably end up buying these strains at some time or another.

Examples: Afghani#1, Skunk#1, Neville's Haze.

A Mix

These are popular and cheap to buy but come with no guarantee and you do not know what it is you are getting. A breeder may have seven or eight strains on the market. During their harvest of seeds or seed packaging some of the seeds may fall on the floor or get mixed up. The breeder takes these seeds and just dumps them in a box somewhere. When the box is full the breeder will sometimes want to do something with these seeds so the breeder divides out the seeds at random and packages them as an indoor/outdoor mix. No one really has a clue how they will turn out but you will get some of the breeder's stock in with mix. The baggies of twenty seeds sell for about $20 and are popular because you may get lucky and only pay $20 for a strain that costs $120 from the same breeder. It is also fun to see what you get too. Sometimes you get lucky, sometimes you don't.

Cheaper Knock-Offs

Like anything else, last year's Cannabis Cup winner will most certainly undergo attempts by various parties to reproduce the strain. Since they will never reproduce the same strain you sort of get something that is different and will almost certainly have a large degree of variations in the pack. These seeds come cheap, sometimes 90% cheaper than the original, and are popular among growers who do not have that much money to spend on seeds but want something that is as good as the Cannabis-Cup-winning strain. As the man says—if you want a Rolex, buy a Rolex.

Free with Order Strains

Some seed banks, in an attempt to help promote a strain, give it away free with orders that exceed a specific amount of money. Since everyone who orders with that amount of money gets these other seeds for free they will probably try to grow them out. Since mass numbers of people will be growing them out these seeds tend to gain popularity with grow reports surfacing around the Internet. If the reports are good then people will go buy the strain.

The more you grow and listen to what people are growing the more you will understand the market and be able to focus your breeding projects in a direction that will bring about a certain degree of success for your brand name.

10 | QUARANTINING FOREIGN CUTTINGS

ONE SURE WAY OF DESTROYING your entire breeding project is to allow some form of pest infestation to take over your breeding room. Some pests are easily dealt with but others may require that you completely clean down your grow room and toss away your strains.

This is a major problem for breeders who have not taken the necessary precautions to ensure that their grow room stays free from pests and fungi. (Detailed information on pests and fungi can be found in chapter 12 of *The Cannabis Grow Bible*.) Can you imagine a bad spider mite attack on your breeding project? Chances are your project would not survive such an infestation if it got into the severe later stages and you would have to throw away your crop if your pesticides did not completely get rid of the attacker. Prevention is better than cure and so you should always take the utmost care in maintaining a clean growing environment.

As a breeder you may have cuttings passed on to you from another source. The danger with taking cuttings is that you may be receiving a cutting that has been contaminated in some way by a pest or fungus. The best way to deal with cuttings is to keep them in quarantine. This requires you to build a very small quarantine grow box.

The box just needs one 10-30W fluorescent light to keep the plant alive. The box should not be kept in your grow room but as far away from it as possible.

Basically the cutting must be kept there for up to three weeks. Every day the plant should be observed for any signs of pests or molds. The reason for keeping the plant in the same place for three weeks is that some pests incubate their eggs in the stems, leaves and branches. If any pests are about to show then they should do so within the three week period. If you do not find any pests or fungi in the quarantine box after three weeks then the cutting should be safe enough to move to your breeding room.

Quarantine room for cuttings. Photograph by Eco.

Some types of mold and fungi can also go unnoticed on cuttings in the early stages of infestation. Some types of mold and fungi travel in spores and these spores can lie dormant for a while before the problem shows itself.

If you do come across any pests, fungi or mold then the quarantine cuttings should be treated according to pest type. The cuttings should be treated until there are no signs of any pests, mold or fungi for at least three weeks. Go an extra fourth week if you need the assurance that no pests have laid their eggs in the soil, stems or leaves. Some breeders have several quarantine boxes and keep cloning the affected plant over and over to reduce the amount of bugs or disease and this makes eradication a lot more successful. Check your cuttings daily to ensure that the problem has not returned.

Mold problems can quickly fail new growth.

Mold typically can be found near old cut zones where the plant has been pruned.
These areas need your special attention.

11 | BREEDING TALK

TO GIVE YOU AN IDEA OF WHAT OTHER BREEDERS GET UP TO and the ways in which they think out breeding strategies let's hear an experienced breeder's advice. This breeder is a special friend of the author's who has created some admirable plants. Not all breeders play big on the market. Some just like to participate in the domestic rather than the commercial scene.

There are many countries and states which allow clones to be sold for medical use. This breeder told me that in the very near future, breeders will be able to create medical strains for specific medical problems. I tend to listen carefully to his advice and I advise you to do the same.

Being a breeder can be rewarding and fun but you must have patience or else you will not get good results. When I think in my head of putting something new together I have to remember what my resources are and where I can get good parent plants to start the project from. Luckily for me I have a number of people around the world that are willing to send me some seeds of the finest strains I can get.

I sometimes think of these strains like coffee or tea, each one with its own flavor, taste and stimulation. If I like a type of tea or coffee then I will probably like most of the teas or coffees that come from that part of the world. I also make sure that whatever selections are sent to me are the finest of the selections, so the person who brings me the seeds is as important as the seeds themselves. I trust these people because I know that they have an eye for detail or a good sense of what a nice parent plant should be like.

I can give you my own judgment on what a nice cannabis plant should be like but people have different tastes. This is why some people like strains from one breeder and not from another. You will find breeders who produce a type of strain that fits in with what they have produced before. As a breeder, try to stay away from stereotyping your image.

Back to what I like: a nice cannabis plant, regardless of species, should have a nice thick stem and short internodes.

If the strain is very Sativa dominant then I would not mind the long internodes as long as these nodes develop bud areas. If the strain does not flower well at the majority of its nodes then I do not choose that plant. I also look for nice flat leaves on a plant because I do not regard curling leaves or floppy leaves as healthy leaves. I want to see pointy fingers and strong veins supporting those leaves. The healthier the plant looks the better it will be for the breeding project.

I also like to see vigorous growth with no stunting under good growing conditions. I like a plant that can develop strong branches and a good thick base where the soil meets the plant.

Next up I need to make sure that the plant flowers according to the photoperiod. I do not want to see any Ruderalis auto-flowering responses in the plant. The plant must not be hermaphrodite.

Even before the breeding project begins I am spending maybe two or three years growing the selected plant or having others do this for me. The more numbers that we grow the better it is for me to be able to pick out a strain that fits the bill.

When I am happy that I have found a good solid plant that meets my satisfaction it becomes the skeleton for the breeding project. I usually go for a good male over a female plant because I am not interested in the flowers or the high at this point. I just want to see a good solid plant that will become my first donor in a breeding operation.

If my project is going to be a hybrid project then I need to get hold of another strain that I thought performed well under my standards. All breeders have different standards when it comes to choosing a parent but I think any breeder with a good chunk of experience will have similar standards.

When I have found a suitable strain I go for bud looks and potency. I want to see tight bud clusters, resin and a frosty look first. I will settle for two out of the three but never one. Once I see this I start to work on that strain to get the best potent plant I can find in it. If the plant is not potent or loses potency in a couple of grows then I will not choose it for the breeding project.

If I find a bunch of plants that I think are good and meet bud and potency requirements I will clone them out and begin the first phase of the breeding project which is about flowering characteristics and potency.

I take on five traits at a time for each of the above two strains. With the skeleton parent I watch the leaf shape, internodes, stem thickness, branch length and color. With the flowering female I watch bud color, taste, smell, flowering times and resin production. By doing test crosses I can determine the genotype of all these traits. I have not created a hybrid plant yet—I just want to determine the genotype of each of the phenotypes that I desire in my work. The next step is to breed each of these strains out separately to try and control the frequencies of each trait. I do this by backcrossing the strain with a mother that contained the phenotypes that I wanted. After a couple of backcrosses I will soon find that my offspring will contain a majority of the traits that I am looking for.

All this is done before I even make the first hybrid cross.

Once the 90% majority has been reached, I then perform my first hybrid cross. This is called the F1 generation of the plant that I am developing.

The F1 generation will have a mass of variations in the pack. But the variations will be limited to the traits that I choose and their recessive counterparts. The key here is to make multiple F1 offspring so that I have a better selection to work from. I then carefully observe the selection and try to find the hybrid that I am looking for. This hybrid will be the template for the new strain that I want to finish up with. If I do not find my desired plant in the offspring I will make an F2 generation of offspring by crossing a large selection of the F1 offspring. It is possible that she will be in F2. She should be in the F1 or F2 offspring but never more than that.

When I have found her I examine her traits very carefully to see that she contains everything that I am looking for. The traits should be a combination of both parents. They are: thick stem, nice flat leaves, short fingers, pointy leaves, strong veins, bud color, resin, frost, smell and taste.

Smell and taste are actually the last things I look for unless I am developing a strain that requires these elements. A Berry-type strain would almost certainly require me to work on taste and Skunky strains would have to smell Skunky to some extent to be categorized as a Skunk.

I have found the mother plant that contains all the traits that I am looking for. I will clone her out and see how she will perform in a Sea of Green setup. I like to be able to get people's opinions on taste and potency at this point in time so a good harvest is important. If the feedback I get is good then the real project begins. If not, then I will cancel everything.

You see, this is what breeding is all about. I do not want to spend lots of time developing an IBL that nobody will like. That would be a waste. I will gladly spend something between ten and fifteen years to IBL my strain if it is good. As you can guess I have at least five or six breeding projects under my belt at any one time so that at least one works out well with the public.

The IBL creation is no easy task. It requires me to true breed as many traits as I can find. Those traits can either be homozygous dominant or homozygous recessive. The idea is to knock out as many heterozygous traits as I can find. The more selections I make the better my chances of removing a heterozygous trait.

When I work on a breeding project I also must consider environmental influences on the phenotype. A population of plants might show some variations, but these variations may be environmental. It is very important for me to grow in a breeding room that has an even light, space, air and CO_2 distribution. The soil needs to be the same, the containers the same size and the nutrients of all the same dosage. A variation in bud color or stem color can be the result of a lack of a nutrients. Purple stems, leaves and bud can be caused by very cold conditions or a lack of K in the medium. This can be mistaken quickly for a recessive trait if you find only a few of these plants in your breeding room. Mistakes can be made this way so having a bit of growing experience under your belt helps.

I would also never recommend putting an IBL on the market unless you do not mind losing your hard work to money-hungry 'breeders' who will exploit your work and call it their own. An IBL will only produce IBL seeds with no variations so maybe you should only release F1 seed produce of your IBL.

As you can see, breeders have a style of breeding which is unique to themselves but uses more than one of our breeding techniques to achieve true breeding traits.

We have now explained a number of things in detail; let's quickly recap the major points before we move on. This is important because what we have covered so far is mostly basic genetics. Later on we will cover a more advanced area of genetics that concerns the cannabis plant and how to breed it.

So far we have a good awareness of why seeds are the goal of every breeder. We understand a bit about how the market works and we know that finding a logical reason for breeding a trait will result in a much better commercial plant.

You understand basic genetics and are competent enough to remember how not to make mistakes that most other breeders will make.

You can process compatibility data to plan your breeding project more efficiently. You understand enough of the cannabis cell structure to grasp mitosis, which is important in understanding how chromosomes are made.

We have explored mutations and what causes them so that you are aware of the issues involved. We have explained how this is done. Tissue culture is the new method of cloning that you will probably adopt because of its success with large numbers.

Storage issues should be clearer now, and you have also heard directly from breeders about how they conduct their breeding projects.

This kind of knowledge when applied in practice will help you to produce strains that have the edge on others'. It is more than possible to produce several highly desired lines. There are no perfect cannabis breeders because there are no perfect cannabis plants. You don't have to be the best—you just have to do your best. The market is growing and is in need of good breeders and strains to meet its demands.

Medical markets will be the new wave of cannabis breeding operations. Even though the end results may be synthesized in another format someone still has to find it first. Locate your nearest medical marijuana center and ask them how you can help. Most countries and states are becoming tolerant of cannabis medical research. Make sure you check your country's laws before exploring such avenues though.

12 HOW TO PROTECT YOUR WORK

AS WITH ANY OTHER AREA OF CREATIVE ENDEAVOR in life, if you create something original, then other people should ask your permission if they want to reproduce it. Ownership of strains is important but so is the fact that the herb is free.

If people are not making money out of your strains then let them pass on their offspring to other people. This is a great way to get your name into the public domain.

However you may find that a breeder has decided to recreate and sell your strain or brand name without your permission. This can be a problem because in most countries cannabis is still illegal. How do you take an illegal produce and copyright it? The answer is to find a country where cannabis is a legal product and that has copyright laws on plant produce. Countries like The Netherlands, Belgium, Canada and Switzerland are gaining more and more legal ground on the subject of copyrighting a cannabis strain (you can copyright strains right now in The Netherlands). That is the first step you could take, although it would be very hard to enforce the copyright across the seas.

The next thing you should do is to understand fully what the concept of IBLs, F1 and F2 seeds are and you should use this to inform your clients about the stability of knock-off strains. Let's recap for a moment what IBL, F1 and F2 offspring really are.

IBL, F1 and F2

If we release an IBL onto the market then we are going to be giving our clients a real treat. If we take an example trait such as purple bud color, and let us say that the trait is recessive (mm) and that the dominant side to that trait is white bud color (MM). What will the offspring produce if both parents are homozygous recessive for that trait?

	m	m
m	mm	mm
m	mm	mm

Look at that—all purple bud colors. That is very interesting because no matter what seeds you produce using these two parents (mm and mm) the grower will always get purple bud and will be happy with the results (no variations in bud color), but this trait is then very easy to knock off because the offspring when crossed with themselves or backcrossed to a parent plant will always produce purple bud. Now let's see what happens if only one of the parents is homozygous for that same trait. Here is the F1 produce.

	M	m
m	Mm	mm
m	Mm	mm

Fifty percent will have white buds and fifty percent will have purple buds. You can't really release that on the market can you? You will have some unhappy customers if they don't get the purple bud as advertised. What if we used the offspring for an F2 cross? What would we get? Well, this depends on the parent plants. Let's take the mm parent and an Mm parent and do both sets. The mm parent first crossed with the mm offspring.

	m	m
m	mm	mm
m	mm	mm

Good. That trait breeds true. Our clients will love it but it will be very easy to knock off.

	m	m
M	Mm	Mm
m	mm	mm

Fifty percent/fifty percent. We are still in the same boat if we use the mm parent. Client will be unhappy. Let's try the Mm parent instead.

	M	m
m	Mm	mm
m	Mm	mm

Same problem again. Let's try the heterozygous offspring next.

	M	m
M	MM	Mm
m	Mm	mm

Totally out of the question. We have a serious problem here. Only 1/4 of the off-spring will show the purple bud trait. Client will be unhappy. If you sell ten seeds then chances are two to three will have purple buds. Remember also that the male/female ratios are not set so what are the chances that those two to three will be female? Client will be very unhappy and may not get any purple bud at all. So the only way we can please the client is to release the true breeding trait for the purple phenotype......but all is not lost yet! We can still protect our plant from knock-offs.

When breeders release a strain onto the market they release the F1 produce. However they make sure that any homozygous recessive traits breed true in that F1 produce. This is the key if you have a strain that depends on a homozygous recessive trait. Our problem above was with the recessive trait that was dominant. Let's pretend for a moment that our strain is very potent and this trait plays a big part of our plant's mega-marketing plan. Potency is PP. If we release the true breeding trait for potency onto the market then we will only end up with all PP offspring and people will be able to knock off the potency trait very easily. But if we have a heterozygous trait in one of the parents then watch what happens in the offspring.

	P	P
P	PP	PP
p	Pp	Pp

Client is very happy. They will have all their offspring potent because the P is dominant. However 50% are heterozygous and 50% are homozygous. If people want to knock off your strain then they will have to do a test cross to discover the homozygous trait. That requires work on their part so you have made your strain harder to knock off. Let's see what happens when we use two heterozygous parents.

	P	p
P	PP	Pp
p	Pp	pp

Happy customer again. Three quarters will show the potency trait, only one quarter will show the recessive trait, plus ONLY one quarter is actually dominant homozygous for that trait. This makes it harder for the knock-off artist. However they can notice the pp because it will be different from the rest, so they can eliminate this from their breeding efforts.

So, both of these methods will help to prevent your strain from being stolen.

THE MORE HETEROZYGOUS TRAITS THAT CONTAIN THE DOMINANT ALLELE FOR THE TRAIT THAT YOU WHERE BREEDING FOR - THE BETTER THE CHANCES OF PROTECTING YOUR STRAIN AND KEEPING THE CLIENT HAPPY.

By keeping a heterozygous parent that shows the characteristics of your selected strain you can breed offspring that will meet your clients' demands and keep the knock-off artists at bay. The knock-off artist will have a tough time trying to reproduce your strain entirely.

Now you are in a position to warn your clients of the fake F2 produce on the market. By explaining what F2 produce is, you can help educate them. If the knock-off artist tries to copy your seeds from any of these F1 results...

	P	P
P	PP	PP
p	Pp	Pp

	P	p
P	PP	Pp
p	Pp	pp

...he's only going to produce some very non-uniform plants for that trait. The client will be buying an inferior product. This is what ratios are all about. In real life all the major breeders release F1 seeds onto the market. F1s are not IBL so there will be variations in the pack. Maybe you are asking, what degree of variations will I find in the pack? This depends on how many traits the breeder has tried to lock down or make true breeding.

The less true breeding traits that are in the strain the more non-uniform in growth the F1 results will be. If the breeder is a good breeder and has released a good F1 product line then you should find only minor variations in the pack.

There are some Sativa plants like Haze that are very unstable but have true breeding traits for flowering times, taste and potency. The plants may develop at different heights and have different leaf shapes but the breeder has created this plant for potency and taste. Unstable Sativa genetics are very common. Many breeders do not have the time to IBL a Sativa so they release a strain onto the market that is stable for only a few traits. Here is a list of what should be stable in a species before it can compete in the market.

	Indica	Sativa
POTENCY	✓	✓
TASTE	✓	✓
BUD COLOR	✓	✗
LEAF SHAPE	✓	✗
FLOWERING TIME	✓	✓
HEIGHT	✓	✗
RESIN PRODUCTION	✓	✗
SMELL	✓	✓
INTERNODES	✓	✗
BRANCHING NUMBERS	✓	✗
YIELDS	✓	✓

As we have previously noted, true breeding traits takes time. Since a Sativa has almost twice the flowering times of an Indica plant then it will take twice as long to develop the strain. Because of this, growers do not mind if they don't get a consistent bud color, leaf shape, height, resinous look, internodes or branching numbers with Sativa strains. They generally don't mind how the plant looks either. What a Sativa grower wants to see consistent is the potency, taste, flower times, smell and yields on the plant.

So which strain is easier to protect? Probably the Indica strain because it has eleven true breeding traits to knock off compared to the five of the Sativa.

In reality, protecting your work has to take both the customer and the knock-off artist into consideration. The customer should come first in terms of what you produce because he's the one who will critique your work and want to get his money's worth. If you release a strain with too many variations then you will not get good feedback from the consumer.

The only true way to protect your work is to make it known to people that you are the original creator of the strain and that they should only buy seeds from you or your authorized seed bank resellers. This goes a long way, because there are many growers out there who do not like knock-off artists and they will help pass along the message that you are the creator of a strain and buyers should accept no substitute. The one thing you should never do is tell anybody what traits you are selecting for. You can tell them about your plant's history, i.e., your parent plants and where they came from, but you should not tell people what traits you where selecting for. If you tell people that you were selecting a number of specific traits and describe those traits, then the knock-off artist may be able to reproduce a very similar strain by selecting for those same traits using similar parents. Also, make sure that you do not give your strain a name that could infringe on any trademarked names such as "Coca-Cola", or "Pepsi." That could land you in hot water very quickly.

A very interesting case is that of the Matanuska Valley Thunderfuck strain. To understand more about this strain, we should first have a look at its origins.

MATANUSKA VALLEY THUNDERFUCK

The Matanuska Valley in Alaska is a wonderful place to visit. Alaska became a very popular settlement for hippies who had left the cities in America and Canada to travel the world. Most of them wanted to grow pot when they got home from their tour of the globe and so Alaska seemed like an interesting place to settle down in. Today you will find that Alaska is home to a large cannabis community. It is very common to find whole villages and towns that like nothing better than to sit down and have a spliff. There are many people who live the hippie life in communes there or deep in the woods with their families in log cabins they have made. These people are not poor or neglected parts of the community. They are people who have chosen a more relaxing, natural and healthy way of life.

In the '70s, work began on a strain that could withstand the extreme climatic conditions of Alaskan cold weather. Since Sativa and Indica plants are rarely found growing naturally in the wild in countries that have a cold climate another species would have to be used. Ruderalis is a very popular species of cannabis found in cold climates. Ruderalis was used in the development of MTF because of its thick leaves and weather-proof sturdiness. The Alaskan people started to cross Ruderalis strains with high-yielding Indica plants. The result was a new strain of the Indica/Ruderalis species called MTF.

MTF is very popular in Canada and America because of its high-yielding produce and heavy stone effect. However the plant has auto-flowering values which do not make it very popular among all or most growers.

The other factor you should know about is that the original MTF is only available in clone format. There are no seeds because the original creator of this strain did not release seeds onto the market. The original creator of this strain probably found a good mother plant and did not true breed her traits because there was no need to do so if the clone format was the only release he or she was going to do. The original propagation of the strain took place in the Matanuska-Suisitna Valley, and was done in clone format. Since then many breeders have tried to replicate the strain by breeding more Indica into the plant. I have heard many people claim that there is now a version of MTF called MT on the market. I have seen this strain and it appears to be a new hybrid version of MTF. It is more Indica in appearance and contains no visible traces of Ruderalis, although it does have a hint of some auto-flowering properties.

This is nearly always the case with successful clones. Since clones do not require any homozygous breeding the breeder who wishes to continue the strain via cloning will have to work very hard to stabilize a hybrid strain of it. One possible way of doing this is to find one of the parent plants that the MTF came from. The parent could then be used in a backcross to create seeds that resemble the original MTF mother plant with some variations. The breeder could then try to lock down the traits that most represent the original clone mother. It appears that there are many breeders out there who are working on such clone strains. Some of the most famous clone plants known to growers around the world are:

Matanuska Valley Thunderfuck	Chemo	Champagne
Cali' O	G-13	Willem's Wonder
Humboldt	BC Big Bud	BC Hash Plant

Always be aware of the fact that when you buy bud from these strains and find seeds, these did not come from the clone's original father. The seeds will more than likely come from a hybrid version of the clone or even worse, the clone may have been selfed to produce hermaphrodite seeds.*

---

* The hermaphrodite condition should not pass onto the offspring in theory if the genes are not present in the parents. However as we will see later the sexual expression of the cannabis plant is a complex subject and although some selfing techniques will not produce hermaphrodites the risk is still high because of the way sexual expression occurs in cannabis. See chapter 15

13 | THE BREEDING LAB

A BREEDING LAB CAN BE BUILT just like a basic grow room, as discussed in *The Cannabis Grow Bible*. In order to grow out 100 offspring you will need provisions for this, such as an outdoor field or a very large basement. This can be hard to manage especially if you are working in small living quarters or do not have the funds to generate a proper breeding lab. You will have to work this out for yourself, but maybe you would be interested in learning how a commercial breeding lab is set up.

In order to create a laboratory that operates well you will need to take a few things into account. Safety is foremost, followed by cleanliness and the general setup. A correctly designed breeding lab will help you to maintain a cleaner breeding project and develop produce to meet high standards.

Always start small and work your way up. There is no need to spend vast sums of money on a lab that is not going to be used. Working double space is the best. If you have over 50 plants growing at any one time, then double that area to allow you room to work in. You may have to install walls to separate different areas. You are going to need a flowering room and a vegetative grow room. A simple shelf will work well for seedling propagation. You will also need a small clone cabinet and a storage area for your grow materials and tools.

Your breeding lab should be isolated from any popular avenues and no outside contamination should be able to enter the room. You should have sufficient electrical inputs and outputs, mounted and sealed and away from any wet areas. The room's temperature should be controlled with thermostats and the floor should have a drainage point for any spills that may occur. You will need a sink, a drain and some work lights for yourself. Ventilation should also be installed. Prefab constructions are very popular these days and you might want to invest your time looking at the various prefab construction options on the market. If you live in a country where marijuana cultivation is legal then there may be some health and safety regulations that you need to follow, especially with domestic electrical junction boxes and safety trip switches.

Indoor mother plant breeding room by Paradise Seeds.

The floor should be made from concrete, not wood. The concrete should be covered with white tiles so that dirt and dust can easily be seen. Windows should be properly sealed and only opened if there is no risk of contamination from external influences. Air-conditioning should be a major part of your design. Avoiding contamination is important because contamination, including pest contamination, causes 60% of all breeding project failures. 38% is caused by bad growing techniques and 2% is caused by genetic problems with the plants. Contamination can cost you money and time, so prevention is better than cure.

A complex ducting of air cooling tubes for three HID lights. Photograph by Alan.

Walls and floors should be regularly swept and cleaned. It's best to develop a cleaning routine and have a checklist that shows that you have been maintaining the cleaning standards on your schedule. Shoes should be removed before entering the breeding room. Walls are best painted using urethane epoxy wall paint or acrylic of the flat white type.

The entrance to your breeding lab should not be near the breeding project but rather closer to your tools and workbench. The breeding lab and grow room should be the furthest point away from the entrance and exit to this room to avoid contamination.

Fire safety is also a must, especially where grow lights and plants are concerned. You should have a fire extinguisher nearby and a fire blanket on standby. You may also need a temporary generator to supplement your breeding room with electricity during periods of blackouts or brownouts. A freezer will be an important tool if you choose to deep-freeze seeds and pollen.

Chemicals should be kept in a cool unit and away from any electrical items. They should be stored by following the guidelines on the bottles. All plant foods and chemicals should be thrown out when they reach their sell-by date.

Pyrex-type glass utensils are best purchased instead of glass materials because they are harder to break and easier to clean.

Outdoor mother plant breeding patch by Paradise Seeds.

Here are a few additional tips and pointers to help you out:

1. Always remove dead plant tissue that falls onto the floor or soil. Some people may leave it on the soil saying that it will work as compost. This is true, but it will always attract unwanted pests.
2. Watch out for hermaphrodite plants. Any male pollen sacks that develop on a female can potentially pollinate that female and others around it if the pollen is viable. The seeds will mostly be hermaphrodite with some females and possibly some males. This will seriously compromise your breeding project if it goes by unnoticed.
3. CO_2 enrichment will help produce better plants and higher yields. CO_2 comes in compressed tanks. Be careful when working with CO_2 and follow instructions about CO_2 storage carefully.

Paradise Seeds maintain several breeding rooms for different strains.

4. Label your plants, clones, seeds and tissue culture. Forgetting to label your work will only result in work data being lost. Make sure that you label everything.

5. Always make a routine of visiting your grow room everyday. Check your plants for bugs as often as you can. Pay visits to your plants because they like to be visited. Plants are living things and should be treated that way.

6. Always circulate fresh air into your breeding room whenever possible. Plants thrive in fresh air.

7. Tidy up loose ends. Your breeding room is not your garage or tool shed. Make sure that you clean out your pots after use and throw away soil that has already provided for a plant. Reusing soil is never a good idea because it is full of roots and minerals that you have added to your grow. Always start fresh with new soil for a new grow. Soil is generally the cheapest part of your grow.

8. Sterilize your equipment on a regular basis.

9. Keep logs of your work. You will always need to look back on your notes during your breeding program.

14 | PRODUCT TESTING AND THE CUSTOMER

THE TIME WILL COME WHEN YOU WILL HAVE TO TEST your product before you release it onto the market. Product testing is very easy to do and just requires a bit of logic and time on your part. A 90% germination rate is an acceptable level and one that the consumer wants. Anything lower than 70% and the consumer will not be happy because 1/4 of your produce did not work out. Out of 200 seeds, 10 or so may not be viable. If the germination rates are lower than this you must reconsider your seed production, harvesting and storage techniques.

When you produce a batch of seeds from a single female plant you should label the seeds to show which mother they came from. Out of 200 seeds you should test 10-15 of the seeds for yourself before releasing the others onto the market. If you achieve 90% germination rates then you are doing well. If you reach 80% then maybe your technique could be better. If you go below 70%, again, you have a problem. If the seeds do well then you should release them onto the market, but make sure that you keep track of each order and which female plant the seeds came from. If a customer complains you should take note of the complaint. If more than one customer complains then you should consider removing your stock and replacing it with newly tested stock. Even in today's market the top breeders sometimes make mistakes and have to pull their line from the market. Too much bad publicity will only inhibit your sales. It is best to pull the seeds from the market and replace them with new ones.

Before you pull your produce from the market you should always ask how the grower propagated the seeds. If the grower is new to growing then he may have done something wrong. You should not be held accountable for the grower's mistakes but you should not immediately fire back that he messed up and claim that it is not your problem. Be nice and inform the customer that his germination method was not the best, if that's the case, and maybe *recommend a good grower's guide, for instance, The Cannabis Grow Bible,* which explains several propagation techniques for seed germination. If a grower refuses to acknowledge having made any mistakes because of being a first-time grower, then simply say you're sorry and move on. Never get cross or try to defend yourself too adamantly because that will just look bad on you.

If the grower has some experience and seems to have been propagating the seeds correctly, then you should reconsider your harvest technique, or put it down to bad seeds. You should always reimburse the client by sending him another packet of free seeds of the same strain. Never give them a different strain, always give them the same one. If they continue to be pushy about getting different seeds, just terminate your communication, saying that you have already offered them new seeds of the same variety that they purchased.

Here are a number of complaints that you may come across, with suggestions from our experiences for how to deal with each one. Remember, choosing a seed bank to sell your stock will keep you out of the equation. The seed bank will have to deal with the client, not you. This is one of the better reasons to choose a seed bank. It will allow you to concentrate on your work rather than also having to deal directly with sales, marketing and complaints.

There are some things that you need to do before you engage in helping out your disgruntled clients.

1. Check to see that they actually bought your seeds.
Some people like to play games. If they have purchased seeds then you should be able to confirm this via a tracking order that you had for their purchase.

2. Ask them to resolve the dispute via emails or written communications, rather than using a public forum.
They should be under no obligation not to make this public but you do reserve the right to make this request. Tell them that you respond quicker to e-mails and letters than you do to public forums. If they make it public do not reply to the public debate. Resolve the matter in e-mails or letters.

3. Ask them for photographic evidence to support their case. Digital Cameras are popular among growers because they like to take pictures of their bud.

The grower is under no obligation to provide you with pictures. Pictures do help their case though, and you should inform them about that.

4. Ask them about any previous growing experience that they have had.
This will help you build up an idea of the skill level and experience behind the grower. The less grow experience growers have had the greater the chances are that they are not using the right germination techniques.

5. Ask them how they germinated the seeds.
This will help you identify whether the problem is with your stock or with their germination techniques.

ALWAYS BE POLITE. NEVER BE RUDE TO CUSTOMERS AND NEVER GET HOT-HEADED.

Here are some complaints that you may come across, with suggested solutions for you to reach a settlement with your clients. Make sure that you have first followed the previous steps.

Complaint: *My seeds did not germinate or I had bad germination rates.*

Response: Ask about their germination technique. Tell them that 80% and 90% germination rates are common in the industry. Tell them that nobody can guarantee 100% germination rates because you are dealing with a living organism. If they do not agree with this then you can always ask them to contact some seed-resellers to see if they will get guarantees on 100% germination rates. No one in the industry who is serious about his work will offer 100% germination rate guarantees on their stock. Once customers have found this out you can then go about examining their propagation techniques. If their technique does not seem sound then you may offer them an alternative solution. You should be able to help them to get better results next time round by recommending reading resources for them.

Complaint: *I have a good germination technique and my seeds did not germinate or I had bad germination rates.*

Response: Ask them about their grow, their history, and their germination technique. If it seems sound to you then you should offer them a new packet of seeds from the same strain. They may refuse to accept the packet of seeds and demand money. Do not give money back to them. Everyone should be aware that seeds are a living produce and you cannot guarantee success but you can help them to get more seeds.

If they still do not believe you then you should have a list of your clientele waiting to support your case. If you have given out free seeds then you should have had people give you feedback on your strain by posting their results on a public forum along with photographs. Supply the problematic client with proof that people are able to germinate and grow your seeds. The more people you have to back up your case the more it will seem to the client that he must not be doing it right. Never make your problem with the client public before he does. Always provide him with data using letter, e-mails or web URL links.

Complaint: *I ended up with all male plants or a high ratio of male to female plants.*

Response: Inform them that this is not under your control and that you cannot control the sex ratios in natural seeds. If they claim to have gotten all males, ask them for proof. You should in general send them out a new pack of seeds if they did get all males. You want to try and keep your clients, so at least try to help them see and smoke what your female produce is like. If they ask for money back, simply answer as above.

Complaint: *My seeds were crushed in the post.*

Response: Ask them to send the seeds back and replace their order. Your packaging should be better than to allow seeds to get crushed in the post. You must also examine the seeds to see if they were indeed from your batch (Your strain, if it's an IBL or very stable, should have a common seed shape and pattern and a reference number for that seed batch) and if they look crushed. Make sure that you get the seed pack back unopened.

Complaint: *My yield was small and not like the picture on your advertisement.*

Response: Ask about their growing techniques. Tell them that your picture was done under optimal growing conditions and that in order to get the same results they need to try and reach the same growing conditions that you have. Recommend good growing material for them to read, and do your best to get them access to information that will help them to get better yields.

Complaint: *Some of my plants look a bit different from others. Why is this?*

Response: Tell them that all the best breeders release F1 produce onto the market. Tell them that F1 produce may have some variations in the pack. If they complain that there are lots of variations then ask them about their grow method. You should be able identify environmental reasons for the variations if your strains are stable.

Complaint: *My plants were not potent.*

Response: If you claimed that your seeds were potent then you will have to back up your case. Ask them about when they harvested, how they harvested and how they cured their bud. Also ask them what they have been smoking recently. Sometimes people build up a tolerance level if they have been smoking stronger weed. Again, steer them toward information on good harvesting and curing techniques.

Complaint: *My plants were hermaphrodite.*

Response: If you do not have hermie or Ruderalis plants in your breeding project then it should not be a genetic problem. Inform the grower that stress such as irregular photoperiods can lead to the hermaphrodite condition, and recommend some reference materials.

Some breeders even deliberately stress out their plants to see what conditions will promote the hermaphrodite condition and how the plants express that condition. If your plants are very uniform and stable then the hermaphrodite condition should be similar in all the plants, including where the hermaphrodite condition starts and how it develops. You should also know if the male pollen in the hermaphrodite is viable or not. You should stress your plants out in different controlled stressful conditions such as: over-pruning, bad cloning techniques, irregular photoperiods, heat, irregular pH, overwatering, overfeeding, different stressful soil types (sand + clay only), forced flowering and even pest attacks. All of these can cause hermies. Try to find out what causes hermaphrodites in your strain.

Complaint: *My plants do not clone well.*

Response: You provide plants in seed format and not clone format. You are not responsible for cloning success rates. Some strains do clone more easily than others. Refer them to good background material on the subject.

Complaint: *My plants became burnt after I fed them using the exact concentration levels written on the bottle.*

Response: You never recommend feeding seedlings. That will kill them. Also you never recommend feeding cannabis at 100% strengths. Inform them that cannabis does not require 100% feeding strengths.

This seedling has been fed. Note the burnt look on the tips of the leaves. These burnt areas eventually crumble like ash in your hand if left untreated. This seedling needs to be flushed with water to clear it of nutrients. Do not feed seedlings. Picture by Growmaster420.

Complaint: *I got busted because you sent seeds to me in the post and it got intercepted by customs.*

Response: Direct them to the disclaimer on your order form, which they filled out and signed.

Complaint: *I got busted because you sent seeds to me in the post and it got intercepted by customs. They called around to the addresses and found my plants. I am going to tell people about this.*

Response: Wait until they make the public announcement and tell them again to have a look at the disclaimer on your order form. Also tell them in the public forum that it is a stupid idea to have seeds sent to the same address where they are growing. Ninety-nine percent of the growing community will agree with you.

Complaint: *These plants are knock-offs. I have grown something similar before!*

Response: Ask where they got the other plants from. Maybe someone else is knocking off your produce and this client got to them before you. Also explain that you have a breeding history and part of being a good breeder is never engaging in such an activity.

Complaint: *I grew these plants outdoors (when it said indoors on your product information) and they did not perform well!*

Response: If you advertised these plants as indoor plants then they should have followed that advice. You do not recommend that indoor plants be grown outdoors or that outdoor plants be grown indoors. Tell them that cannabis plants can grow indoors and outdoors but they should only follow the product's recommendations. You are not responsible for this problem but listen to their troubles and do your best to offer them good advice.

Complaint: *I bought your seeds and tried to smoke them. They did not get me high!*

Response: "You're supposed to grow them, not smoke them!"

When dealing with clients you should never presume that they have done something wrong. You may have to consider the fact that your produce was not the best or they just got some bad seeds. At the same time the competition does like to play games and sometimes you might find a single person constantly complaining about your produce no matter what you say or do. The only way to combat such a person is to support your case by using examples of people who have grown out your strain and have had good results.

The more growers and grow reports you have at your disposal the better your chances of the public also debating the legitimacy of someone's complaint that has been made public (usually the false disputant will repeatedly attempt to keep the debate in the public domain and will refuse to resolve the problem with you personally). Never get angry with them and never call them names no matter what they say or do to you. If they do call you a name or get very verbally aggressive, tell them politely that this is not the best way to continue communications with you. If they continue tell them that you cannot help them because they are being abusive and though you would like to resolve the situation, you do not like to be abused in this manner.

Always offer them the free bag of seeds if they have provided proof of purchase and show that they know what they are talking about. Only provide one bag of seeds per problem, never two. If they still have the same problem after you have sent them the new seeds then it will look like they are doing something wrong. At this point tell them that you have done everything that you can and that maybe they would like to try something else. Do not entertain their requests for more seeds or their money back.

Try to avoid involving yourself in a public verbal fracas with a client, another breeder or a seed bank representative. Don't enter an argument for the sake of creating a bit of publicity for yourself. Even though bad publicity can be good publicity it will still only get your named attached to the junk world of seed bank and breeders' wars. There are never any winners in these wars and everyone loses out because the public becomes divided. Always remain neutral and in control of your temper and words. Always offer apologies for making mistakes.

Sometimes you may be asked to make bulk shipments of seeds to a seed bank or customer. If you are sending in excess of 10,000 seeds it is best to send the client a sample of the produce first for testing. If the client approves of the test samples then you can send the 10,000 seeds knowing that the client will be satisfied with the results. Sending bulk orders out to somebody you are not familiar with can cause problems if the client does not like the seeds or the overall produce. Legal action may be taken against you because of the large quantities and monies involved. If you charge $40 for 10 seeds and the client buys 10,000 seeds from you, then they are going to be spending roughly $40,000 for the seeds, excluding whatever discounts you offer, and the markup price they will be adding to your costs of seeds per unit. It is best that you draw up a contract between yourself and the client before any exchanges are made. You should state clearly what you guarantee and what you do not. You should make it clear that you do not guarantee over 90% germination and that you do not guarantee male/female ratios. You may have to guarantee quality, quantity and shipping. If your seeds do not perform to the same standards as the test samples you sent out then you will have a problem. If the seeds are damaged then you may need insurance to cover this.

Paradise Seeds 12K HID cannabis mother plant breeding room. Photograph by Paradise Seeds.

Paradise Seeds started this population of clone mothers under fluorescent lights on moveable trays. These female clones are eventually pollinated, producing a generation of stable seeds. Photograph by Paradise Seeds.

New growth starts with the vertical growth of new leaf blades. As growth continues, the leaves open out horizontally making way for the next new node level to appear. Photograph by Kissie.

When the male pollen-bearing organs begin to bend on their stem (peduncle) it is a sign that they will open very soon. Photograph by Kissie.

One should start checking for calyx development at the top cola region (main terminal bud) first, moving onto the tips of the branches (secondary terminal bud sites) before finally checking node regions on the stem (lateral bud sites). Photograph by Kissie.

This single outdoor Sativa plant has produced as much bud as several indoor plants. Breeding for outdoor guerilla growing is important for those who do not have the use of an indoor grow room. Good guerilla strains are always in need. Photograph by Kissie.

This is a European black cannabis plant. Its population will always produce black buds if no foreign genes enter its gene pool. They don't get much blacker than this. Photograph by Kissie.

Breeding and growing high yielding outdoor cannabis plants is not exclusive to men only. Photograph by Kissie.

Producing a couple of pounds of bud for free is no small accomplishment. Small numbers of high yielding outdoor plants can keep a grower and their friends happy for over a year. Photograph by Kissie.

Paradise Seeds are showing themselves as a new 21st Century world leader in cannabis breeding. Just have a look at some of the goods on display here.

This Indica strain, Durga Mata, is a hybrid of two Shiva strains that was continued for its high THC content. Paradise Seeds even suggest breeding this model. Photograph by Paradise Seeds.

Paradise Seeds recommends Durga Mata for breeding. Photograph by Paradise Seeds.

You will find Nebula everywhere for obvious reasons. It is a nicely potent, mostly Sativa with a very sweet and hashy taste. Nebula means "starcloud." Bred by Paradise Seeds in 1996 and a Cannabis Cup winning strain. Photograph by Paradise Seeds.

A wonderful mostly Sativa variety, abundant in growth, with a mix of tropical fruit flavors. The branching pattern makes her ideal for pruning. Photograph by Paradise Seeds.

Observe the pinnacle of breeding with Sensi Star.
Photograph by Paradise Seeds.

Sensi Star is a great indoor plant, producing
powerful, resinous, and very compact buds.
Photograph by Paradise Seeds.

Sensi Star is an excellent choice for any breeder. Photograph by Paradise Seeds.

Named for the heroic woman in The Thousand and One Nights, Paradise's Shererazade will take considerably less time than the title implies, growing in about 56 nights. Photograph by Paradise Seeds.

Sheherazade reveals her Afghani-Kush traits in appearance and other growth indicators, but the one-quarter Sativa shines through in the quality of the high, which is dynamic and long lasting. Photograph by Paradise Seeds.

A tall plant of fine sativa quality, Dutch Dragon has superb yields from long sticky colas. Photograph by Paradise Seeds.

The aroma is very fruity and sweet, as is the taste. The buzz is a lasting high that increases an appetite for music and pleasure. Photograph by Paradise Seeds.

Outdoor fields of fat mother plant populations bask in the sunshine and cool off at dusk, flowering mostly at night. Photograph by Paradise Seeds.

When we talk about 'large selection' populations we mean something like the kind that Paradise Seeds work with. Photograph by Paradise Seeds.

Sagarmatha produces some of the most interesting varieties. Sagarmatha has some original choices that will certainly be shown-off by growers who want to try something alternative.

Bubbleberry

Type: Indica-Sativa, indoor and outdoor
Vegetate until: 4-7 internodes. Clip center cola for bushier plant.
Flowering time: 65 days
Average height: 0.7-1 meter
Yield: 300-325 grams/m²

This sturdy Bubbleberry plant produces larger buds with more strength and taste than original Bubblegum or Blueberry. Photograph by Sagarmatha.

Bubbleberry has been one of Sagarmatha's most satisfying varieties to date, creating a legend for herself in the grow rooms and neighborhoods of cannabis connoisseurs. Photograph by Sagarmatha.

Intense flavor, chocolaty aroma and potency in Matanuska Tundra have combined to form the densest variety Sagarmatha Seeds have had the pleasure of producing thus far. Photograph by Sagarmatha.

A glacier of THC crystals frosts Matanuska Tundra's colas. She packs more power than an icepack polar bear. Photograph by Sagarmatha.

The high Stonehedge possesses is soaring and overwhelming, providing the smoker with a lithographic outlook. Photograph by Sagarmatha.

Stimulating, cranial sensations are often followed by an upswing in altitude and attitude. Whether taken in the evening or after work, Stonehedge magic is well received. Photograph by Sagarmatha.

She is believed to have originated from Himalayas of Afghanistan and climatized in the mountains of Humbolt County California in the late 70's. Several generations later in the early 90's we were blessed with the seeds and then propagated them in Holland. Sagarmatha entered her in a Cannabis Cup and received an honorable mention. Photograph by Sagarmatha

Early Riser is Sagarmatha's first variety especially developed for outdoor production in northern climates. Several generations of select breeding - choosing individuals with the shortest flowering period combined with the highest density of cannabinoidal resin - have produced a wonderful example of botanical wizardry. Photograph by Sagarmatha.

The high is uplifting and motivational, releasing the sun's natural energy with every bowl. So let the sun shine in and don't get burnt. Photograph by Sagarmatha.

Yumbolt brings back that old-fashioned flavor from the fabled hills of Humboldt Co. California. Possessing a sedative stone with an outdoor aroma, she will often induce heavy eyelids with a satisfying smile, from the first toke till the last the taste remains. Photograph by Sagarmatha.

Watering during vegetative growth can be done either by feeding down low or sprinkling from a height as long as there is a tray to catch the falling water. Avoid getting water in contact with the lights if you do it this way. In flowering, you will probably want to water down low to avoid damaging flowering pistils from the spray.

A home grower can easily create a medium sized selection to choose a good mother plant.

As you can see this is a medical cannabis breeding project.

Sensi Seeds is the classic seed company that still continues to produce some of finest specimens. Some of these classics date back to the early 1970's with late 18th century landrace genes only a few generations away.

First Lady originated in the high valleys near Mazar-I-Sharif, Chitral, and Kandahar, in Afghanistan and Pakistan. This Indica cross will remind older growers of the good old days when the first ladies were introduced in the western world. Photograph by Sensi Seeds.

Mother's Finest is an Indica-Sativa cross, as funky as they come. Don't be fooled by the shorter flowering times and heavier yields — her Sativa breeding is evident from the first toke. Photograph by Sensi Seeds.

Sensi Seeds G-13 x Hashplant. Photograph by Sensi Seeds.

G-13 is Pure Indica crossed with the Hash Plant to produce one of the best indoor hybrids that Sensi Seeds has to offer. Photograph by Sagarmatha.

This is a Sensi Seeds Jack Herer hybrid with the flowering times reduced for a faster crop. Photograph by Sensi Seeds.

This multiple hybrid is the result of many years of selective breeding, — combining 3 of the strongest known varieties — Skunk#1 X Northern Lights#5 X Haze. Photograph by Sensi Seeds.

One of the most famous cuttings from the Northwest USA, Hash Plant is named for its hashy-tasting, highly resinous buds. Photograph by Sensi Seeds.

This cross of 25% NL#1 and 75% Hash Plant produces some of the strongest specimens. Even experienced Dutch smokers have trouble finishing a joint. Very good for resin extraction. Photograph by Sensi Seeds.

This is a 4-way hybrid of Sensi's best indoor strains. Although somewhat variable in growth pattern, all tested plants were fast flowering and of very high quality. This hybrid has some of the sweetest, most balanced tastes and highs that Sensi have yet produced. Photograph by Sensi Seeds.

The Mexican Sativa is a hybrid containing a Mexican Oahakan, a Pakistani hashplant and Durban. A great mix of international flavors from the fusion cuisine of The Cannabis Castle. Photograph by Sensi Seeds.

This Afghani with its penetrating Indica aroma is one of the better yielders in the Sensi collection. It has a very pleasant and smooth taste. Photograph by Sensi Seeds.

Shiva Shanti II is a 3-way hybrid which consists mostly an Afghani strain that Sensi call Garlic Bud because of its characteristic aroma. Photograph by Sensi Seeds.

Spot the difference. Variations in a population can sometimes be stunning.
This purple trait came out of nowhere.

Displaying their related genetic attributes, stable
and uniform in growth, two sister plants in tandem
alike in their perfections and flaws.

A 1K HID is used to light a 4 x 4 breeding space.
A 3.5 x 3.5 is more suited to a 600W, a 400W for
3 x 3 and less than this is for the 250W range.

Yet more professional breeding against which to measure one's own goals. This is a mass of resin-full trichomes with a cannabis plant growing out of them! – Ha ha. The strain is called Nebula. Very popular. Photograph by Paradise Seeds.

This female was pollinated 16 days ago and yet the calyxes are swollen with seed production. Photograph by Paradise Seeds.

Of course as a breeder who manufactures seeds you should be on the right side of the law when you do this. Make sure that you check with your country's laws before setting up a seed breeding business so that you know your rights and clearly understand the business risks associated with such a venture. Getting good legal advice is always recommended.

Here are some things to bring up in your discussions with a seed bank you're thinking of working with. Negotiating with seed banks is always important.

- Ask the seed bank to collect the bulk seeds from you. You do not have to do this in person. Simply have a drop point near where you live. Most seed banks have enough cash flow to arrange pick-up and delivery themselves.
- Ask to be paid half in advance and half when your strain has been sold. If you are a new breeder on the scene you will probably not be able to make a deal like this but ask for it anyway (you are providing the product, remember). If you give away a generous amount to the seed bank for free then that trust might be able to get you more money up front for your seeds. Seed banks mostly pay breeders a commission after the seeds are sold, but some well known and good breeders get money up front for their produce. You should aim for money up front because it is more secure and gives you a more immediate cash flow to continue your breeding projects.
- Find out about any applicable sales tax. Always pay your taxes on seed sales in some shape or form. Seed bank owners will be able to advise you on this.
- As part of your deal with the seed bank, request that they enter your strain in competitions.
- Reserve the proper rights to photos that you have taken of your plant. Seed banks do sell picture rights to companies that print these pictures up on lighters, books, roach books/filter packs, pipes, rolling papers and all sorts of other cannabis-related merchandising.
- Create a logo for your image. You have the right to use a logo with your strain. Most logos contain the breeder's name or nickname.
- Ask about what publications the seed bank advertises in.
- Ask to be shown copies of any media (like catalogues) that has your strain in it.
- Negotiate to be sure there is language in the contract that specifies what steps you or the seed bank must take to terminate your business relationship at any time.

15 | GENDER AND SEX-INHERITED TRAITS

QUESTIONS ABOUT CANNABIS GENDER

Probably one of the most hotly contested subjects in the cannabis breeding world is that of cannabis gender and the relationship between the genotype for sex and final expression of that 'set' gender in the phenotype. We know that the predetermination of the plant's sex can be linked directly to the genes in the embryo of the seed, but the environment also plays an important part in the way the plant's gender is finally expressed. In this chapter we will try to explain the relation between gender genes and their phenotypic expression.

FEMINIZED SEEDS AND PLANT GENDER

We have already looked at feminized seeds in chapter 2, Basic Breeding. Feminized seeds have proven that sex in not just an inherited trait. During the feminized seed process an XX female is selected and stressed to make seeds that will only produce female plants and sometimes hermaphrodites. Still, a tiny percentage of male plants may appear in the feminized offspring. The reason for this is that the environment and growing conditions appear to influence the feminized plant's sex. In fact standard seeds are also influenced by the environment and growing factors alongside their genotype for sex.

This is a very important concept to grasp: a set genotype can have a different phenotype because of environmental conditions.

We have already stated that in breeding projects you must take growing factors into consideration when you judge genotypes in a test cross. Your recessive homozygous genotypes might in fact be dominant homozygous and the environment has effected the actual final presentation of the genotype in its phenotype.

There appears to be a strong connection between the hermaphrodite trait and male plants. Female plants tend to develop in optimal growing conditions while male and hermaphrodite plants occur in less optimal conditions. This is not 100% accurate but it does seem to be the case. Let's look at the conditions that can cause more males to form than females.

Standard Seeds, Feminized Seeds and Producing More Females

Most growers believe that the cannabis seed is genetically predisposed to its sexual orientation as soon as fertilization of the ovule takes place. This means that if you acquire a solitary female plant and produce seeds from her, the offspring will naturally produce males and females because of their genetic predisposition to do so.

Imagine if you will that a gender recognition analysis could be performed on the seeds. We would be more than able to remove the males from the females even before we start propagation. Such a device would allow breeders to create packs of all female seeds without having to feminize the parent plants. This theory has flaws, however.

Feminized seeds are very expensive. Seed banks charge almost twice the price for feminized seeds. Their sellers claim to provide the grower with all female seeds. But in fact growers experience variable results with feminized seeds. They find females, hermaphrodites and males in the feminized seed population. Some growers may not find any males, but along with the females some hermaphrodites. Most good growers will only see females. So what is it that is causing growers to see different plant genders from feminized seeds? Why is it that good growers see females and others growers see males and hermaphrodites? The answer lies in the term *"good growers"*.

Feminized seeds perform on the foundation that there is a genetic predisposition for the seed to produce only females because of the unique treatment that the XX female parent plant was subjected to. We discussed this treatment of an XX female in chapter 2 and you may want to refer back to that material again.

Under optimal growing conditions, which all good growers should have, the feminized seeds will produce only females. Feminized seeds appear to produce only females in growing conditions that are well maintained. In growing environments that are less than optimal, or in situations where the plants are stressed, males and hermaphrodites tend to show up in populations. This shows that sexual expression is not governed by the plant's genes alone and that the environment plays an active roll in the final expression of the plant's gender.

Seed banks cannot be responsible for bad female to male ratios. Can they be held responsible for feminized seeds turning male? Since this is very much dependent on the growing environment, the answer is no, they should not be held responsible.*

You may be interested to know that the breeder/seed bank Dutch Passion released a statement of male and female ratios. This was because Dutch Passion were among the first breeders to release feminized seeds onto the market. Here is what they had to say:

Feminized Cannabis Seeds Courtesy of Dutch Passion

In November 1998 we introduced our "Female Cannabis Seed." We did this after our own experiments showed that from female seed, we acquired almost 100% female offspring.

In the meantime we are six months further on. We have received a lot of feedback from our customers. The reactions are mostly positive, from clients who have successfully produced almost 100% female offspring. However there have been reactions from customers who found a few hermaphrodites or males plants. Apparently environmental influences affect the sex of the female seeds as well. Because of the fact that female seeds do not grow into female plants under all circumstances, we changed the name from "Female Cannabis Seeds" to "Feminized Cannabis Seeds."

From literature and from our own findings it appears that the growth of a male or a female plant from seed, except for the predisposition in the gender chromosomes, also depends on various environmental factors. Not only the origination of entirely male or female plants is partly affected by these environmental factors, the number of male and female flowers on a hermaphrodite plant is affected as well. The environmental factors that influence the sex of the plant (or the flower in the case of hermaphrodites), are, among other things:

* *the quantity of nitrogen and potassium of the seedbed*
* *humidity and moistness of the seedbed*
* *level of temperatures*
* *color of the light used*
* *length of daylight*

Stress, any form of stress, causes more male individuals to originate from seed.

---

* Note that the seeds are called "Feminized" and not "Female". If they were called "Female" you may have a case.

Even the taking of cuttings from female plants may produce male or hermaphrodite cuttings.

To optimize the result, changes in one or more of the above-mentioned environmental factors for a certain period during growth, may be applied. During this time these environmental factors will deviate from the standard growing system for maximum harvest and quality, as described in nursery literature. The desired change(s) in the environmental factor(s) are started from the moment that the seedling has three pairs of real leaves (not counting the seed-lobes). This is the moment that male and/or female predisposition in florescence is being formed. After approximately two weeks the standard growing system can be reconverted to.

Of the five above-mentioned environmental factors the first three are the most practical:

1. *Level of nitrogen and potassium of the seedbed: a heightening of the standard level of nitrogen makes for more female plants originating from the seeds. A lowering of the nitrogen level shows more male plants. A heightening of the level of potassium tends to show more male plants, while a lowering of the potassium level shows more female plants. A combination of a higher nitrogen level for the period of a week or two and a lowering of the potassium level is recommended.*
2. *Humidity and moistness of the seedbed: a higher humidity makes for an increase in the number of female plants from seed, a lowering for an increase in male plants. The same is valid for the moistness of the seedbed.*
3. *Level of temperatures: lower temperatures make for a larger number of female plants, higher temperatures for more male plants.*
4. *Color of the light used: more blue light makes for female plants from seed, more red light makes for more male plants.*
5. *Length of daylight: few hours of daylight (e.g., 14 hours) makes for more female individuals, a long day (e.g., 18 hours) makes for more male plants.*

Most good growers choose standard seeds over feminized seeds for a number of reasons. Feminized seeds are expensive and are more likely to produce hermaphrodites as a result of stress than do standard seeds that are stressed. Since the hermaphrodite condition is not considered advantageous by growers who wish to produce a sinsemilla crop they will generally stick with standard seeds as opposed to feminized seeds, which have a propensity to herm if they go through a little stress.

With standard seeds the hermaphrodite condition is still realizable through stress but is very strain-dependant. There are two main very stressful conditions which promote the hermaphrodite trait in both standard and feminized seeds: first, an irregular flowering photoperiod and second, heat stress.

Heat Stress, obvious with the non-uniform bleaching and curling of the upper leaves.

During the later stages of the vegetative phase of growth the cannabis plants seem to have more of a predisposition to the manipulation of their sexual expression during flowering. This period occurs during sexual maturity, which is about a week or two before initial calyx development begins. Plants that are subjected to stress before calyx development tend to produce more males and hermaphrodites when they flower. Plants that are not subjected to stress before and during calyx development generally show more females in optimal growing conditions.

This stage of growth should be very interesting to growers who wish to try and promote more females than males in their gardens, although plant stress after sexual maturity can cause hermaphrodites to show.

Sinsemilla* crops may also show hermaphrodites during the final few weeks or days of flowering before their harvest time. This appears to be a natural condition with some

* The very nature of sinsemilla is somewhat stressful for the plant.

strains and generally the hermaphrodites are few and the pollen is sometimes nonviable.

It appears that the critical time for sexual expression occurs shortly before initial calyx development. Some growers like to force flower their plants before calyx development and this type of force flowering by photoperiod manipulation is prone to creating more males than females and even some hermaphrodites. This appears to be a very important area of plant growth in dictating the expression of the plant's sex. Plant populations that are free from stress before calyx development will show an increase in females.

Keeping plants free of stress will help increase your chances of producing females and some slightly stressful situations that are part of any good propagation program may influence sexual expression. Transplants, topping and pruning are all important parts of cultivation but can be stressful and may influence the final sexual expression of the plant. On the other side, pest attacks, fungi attacks, mold problems, pH fluctuations, underwatering, overwatering, small pots, nutrient deficiencies and inappropriate soil mixtures can also have an adverse effect on sexual expression.

Some bottle-sized colas getting thick. Photograph by Alan.

Here are some ways we can improve on Dutch Passions' methods for promoting females.

Nutrients
By using the right nutrients in the right ratios we can influence sexual expression. Nutrient formulas that are equal in N, P and K will help promote more females, but if the N levels decrease and P levels increase during vegetative growth we may see more

males than females. It is wiser to have more N than P and K amounts for this reason and this ratio is quite suitable for cannabis plants in vegetative growth anyway. This is especially important during the phase before initial calyx development occurs.

Watering

Before initial calyx development you should ensure that your plants are properly watered and are neither over- nor underwatered. Allowing the soil to completely dry out is never a good idea. Careful watering will help improve your chances of developing females.

Humidity

Higher humidity levels encourage cannabis-related diseases like mold and fungi. The best way to help solve these problems is to reduce the humidity levels in your growing environment. However an rH of 70 is considered a very good humidity level to promote females in the population. Cannabis disease thrives in these rH levels and so extra care must be paid to your plants in order to ensure that mold and fungi do not form. Mold and fungi will only stress your plants and this will lead to less females.

Temperatures and the Photoperiod

There are two main photoperiods that the grower can use in the vegetative phase of the plant's growth. These are 24/0 and 18/6. The 24/0 photoperiod should create a consistent temperature level in the grow room, whereas the 18/6 will not because there are 6 hours of darkness and during this period the heat from the grow bulb will not contribute to the temperature of the grow room. Special attention must be paid to preventing your grow room from getting too cold during this period of darkness if you use the 18/6 vegetative photoperiod.

To promote female growth, temperatures before calyx development should be between 65 and 75 degrees. Going below 65 to 55 will only promote average male to female ratios. Below 55 and you will stunt growth considerably, and cause more males and hermaphrodites to develop. Between 75 and 85 you will promote average amounts of male to female ratios. Again, this is very subjective but growers who stick between 65 and 75 degrees tend to see more females. Some strains can grow well in temperatures above 85, especially if they are of the equatorial variety.

Lighting

If you use MH (metal halide) lights in vegetative growth and HPS (high pressure sodium) in flowering you will see more females. Most growers who can only afford one light choose a HPS because it is more suitable for flowering than the MH, but MH users see more females after using this bulb type during vegetative growth.

This is a very good reason to use both MH and HPS lights to grow cannabis.

All the indications are that the plant chooses its sexual phenotypical expression just before pre-flowering, at about two to three weeks into vegetative growth. After pre-flowering some females may be forced to produce male flowers if exposed to stress factors, like heat or photoperiod manipulation, but if the plant is not stressed then the gender will remain consistent until harvest. However it must also be noted that this is very genetic dependent and not all strains of cannabis are environmentally influenced with regard to sex or more specifically not all of the offspring of a cross may be environmentally influenced to produce a certain sexual type. There may well be some members of a population who will display the sex set in the seed because of another gene that negates environmental influences on the sexual expression of the plant. Some strains or hybrids may be more prone to environmentally influenced phenotype gender expressions than others. However any good gardener will tell you that a good healthy grow room coupled with good genetics and an experienced green thumb will produce more females than males. You have to get all the above right before you start seeing the benefits. However, we should look at how sex is set in the seed a bit more.

X AND Y

As we have seen, cannabis gender can be affected by the environment but initially sex is inherited. Being diploid, cannabis chromosomes are paired. Cannabis has 10 pairs of chromosomes (n=10), for a total of 20 chromosomes (2n=20).

A single pair of chromosomes are responsible for the predetermination of the seed's sex. The female is X and male is Y, but since they combine as chromosome pairs the genders are set as follows: XX is female, XY is male. There is no YY because the female always contributes an X. The male can either contribute an X or a Y to make up the final pair, XY or XX.

We know that XX means female and XY means male so we should end up with a 50/50 chance of each in the seed produce. However this is not a basis for thinking that all our seeds will be 50% male and 50% female from some seeded bud. Each seed that is being developed has a 50/50 chance, not the overall seeded bud. You could very well produce 99% male seeds. Chances are this will not happen though, and you will probably end up with 50/50, 40/60 or 30/70 amounts.

So seeds can be set genetically with a sexual expression for the plant that will grow from the seed. However we must look more closely at chromosome inheritance to see how the final sexual expression can change from what appears to be set in its genes.

SEX-LINKED TRAITS

Cytology is the science of the structure and functions of the cells of organisms. Two men by the name of Walter Sutton and Theodor Boveri, who worked in this field of study, noticed the comparable factors between Mendel's work and the chromosome functions. They developed the theory of chromosome inheritance.

A Columbia University researcher named Thomas Hunt Morgan performed experiments that proved that inheritable factors can be sex linked. Morgan chose the fruit fly in his experiments and noted that the fruit fly has only four pairs of chromosomes. Three of these pairs were autosomes (a chromosome other than a sex chromosome) and one pair were sex chromosomes. After years of breeding the flies he noticed a unique male fly in the offspring that had white eyes when all the others had red eyes. He considered that the white eyes were an act of mutation so he decided to breed this male fly.

Morgan bred this white-eyed male with a red-eyed sister and found that white-colored eyes are sex linked. In the first generation of flies there were only red-eyed offspring, which suggested that the red eye color was dominant and that white eye color was recessive. To prove this Morgan carried on with an F2 generation. With the use of Mendel's notes he expected that there would be an equal number of males and females with white eyes but this did not happen. All the females had red eyes and only the males had white eyes. Morgan discovered that the white eye color was not only recessive but was also linked in some way to sex.

Morgan knew that a male must inherit the X chromosome from the mother and a Y from the father, so he proposed a connection between the sex chromosomes and the trait for eye color. When the mother was homozygous and had two copies of the gene for red eyes, the male offspring had red eyes, even if the male donor had white eyes. But when the mother had white eyes, the male offspring had white eyes too, even if the father's eyes were red. In distinction, a female fly gets one X chromosome from each of the parents and if one of the parents passes along an X chromosome with a gene for red eyes the offspring will have red eyes because this allele for color is dominant over white. Only when both parents gave her an X chromosome with a gene for white eyes did she display the recessive trait. Morgan was able to prove that the gene for eye color must reside on the X chromosome that also governs sex. This is a relationship between a specific trait and a specific chromosome. In our case it is called a sex-linked trait.

This is very important to remember in your breeding projects—that traits can be linked together and not only just with sex but with other different genotypes and their expressed phenotypes. Smell and taste may be linked. Bud color and potency may be linked. There are a number of elements that may be linked. It is not understood yet which cannabis traits are linked but maybe in a few years' time and with a bit more research we can help determine what traits are linked and what traits are not.

DIOECIOUS AND MONOECIOUS PLANTS

Dioecious: Having male and female flowers on different plants.
Monoecious: Having male and female flowers on the same plant.

Most cannabis plants are dioecious, which means that they generate male and female flowers on different plants. This plant type falls into the XX and XY set.

The hermaphrodite condition can be caused by growing conditions and the environment, but there are also types of hermaphrodites that are called monoecious hermaphrodites. These plants are hermie prone and all their offspring show the hermaphrodite trait. They are still mostly diploid plants but the plant's genes cause the plant to display both sex organs. In this case the hermaphrodite condition can attributed directly to the plant's genetics and not the environment's impact.

Apart from haploid or diploid chromosome types there are also triploid and tetraploid sex chromosomes in some plants (which are both polyploid types). These may occur in nature but mostly develop through mutations. The three most common types are:

    XXY - triploid.
    XXYY - tetraploid.
    XXXY - tetraploid.

There are two types of sex-linked traits you should know about. There are "sex limited" linked traits and "sex influenced" linked traits. Sometimes autosomal genes will affect the trait and this is called a sex limited trait. The opposite situation is when sex affects the autosomal genes. This is called a sex influenced trait.

REVERSING THE SEXUAL EXPRESSION OF FEMALES USING SILVER THIOSULFATE SOLUTION

We have already shown you methods of turning male plants into females. Here is a method of inducing the sexual reversal of female to male plants. Always use

Dutch Passion force a female to turn almost full blown male.

care when handling these chemicals. Avoid inhaling them by using a dust mask. Always ventilate when using this procedure.

1. Distill some water.
2. Obtain 0.5 grams of Silver Nitrate.
3. Obtain 2.5 grams of Sodium Thiosulfate (Anhydrous).
4. Stir the 0.5 grams of Silver Nitrate into 500ml of the distilled water.
5. Stir the 2.5 grams of Sodium Thiosulfate (Anhydrous) into 500ml of distilled water.
6. Wait 60 seconds for both solutions to dissolve properly. Stir well.

7. Add the Silver Nitrate water solution directly to the Sodium Thiosulfate water solution while stirring rapidly. This produces the Silver Thiosulfate Solution stock.
8. To use this stock on your female plants mix 1 part of the stock to 9 parts water (1:9 ratio).
9. Take this stock mix and put it into a spray can.
10. Spray the entire female plant until the solution appears to be dripping from the plant. Do not do this under lights because bulb heat may alter the chemicals and burn your plant. Do it away from a light source.
11. Let plant dry.
12. As soon as the treated female plant is dry take it back to the grow room and continue 12/12.
13. Store all stock materials and solutions in a fridge.
14. The female will eventually produce male sex organs during flowering. The female organs should not grow anymore, but you may still find some female sexual organs being produced.

Use the sexually reversed female to make feminized seeds or a male donor for females that can only be obtained in clone format. Results may vary from strain to strain. Sometimes plant nutrient deficiency problems may appear such as yellowing on the leaves. This appears to be normal for these treated plants. The plant may also stunt growth initially after treatment for a week or two. Treated plants should not be smoked, eaten or processed in any way. They are simply sexually reversed female plants that can now donate pollen. Never use the spray bottle for anything else other than this treatment.

16 | CHROMOSOME MODIFICATIONS IN CANNABIS

AN INTRODUCTION TO CHROMOSOME MODIFICATIONS

The map of the human genome has been completed but the genetic mapping of cannabis is still in the early days yet. We know that if certain chromosomes are altered in plants the effect can be a mutation, but we also know more about what certain chromosome alterations will result in. What follows is a description of some cannabis plant characteristics that have managed to survive in the gene pool with a common noticeable mutated trait.

ANEUPLOIDY

Nondisjunction is a type of mutation that occurs when the chromatids fail to separate. This results in only one gamete receiving two of the same type of chromosome and another gamete receiving no copy. Nondisjunction can result in a number of different mutations. Aneuploidy means "not euploid." Euploid means "an equal number of all the chromosomes of the haploid set." Aneuploidy is therefore a condition where abnormal numbers of certain chromosomes are present in an organism. Aneuploid plants result from a normal plant bred with another that has nondisjunction problems. Some aneuploid cell results may even triplicate that chromosome. The aneuploid cell will normally transfer this condition when bred with other normal plants causing serious problems with the offspring's health and appearance.

We know that this type of condition will affect the plant's offspring on a large scale while other types of mutations like deletion and translocation are subject to which chromosomes were deleted or how the translocation was newly arranged. Remember that some parts of plant DNA are just in a dormant state and do not appear to do anything while in that dormant state. However we do know that if the effect is not subtle, it may have a profound effect on the plant and its offspring. Sometimes we do not even get to see the effects in the offspring because it renders the plant sterile.

LEAF SPLITTING

Splitting is a very common mutation which results in the splitting of leaves and branches. At the tip of a branch a leaf may develop and then suddenly split into another leaf. The effect looks much like a leaf growing out from another leaf. If you look at the underside of the leaf you will see where the stem and veins have split. This is a common mutation found in Skunk and equatorial cannabis varieties.

On the left, leaf-fusion by EnergyTurtle and on the right a leaf split by strawdog.

TRILATERAL BRANCHING

Trilateral branching is common with South American Sativa strains. Instead of two branches—one at each side of the stem, 180 degrees apart—a third branch develops at the same region but the stem does not split or top itself. The third branch may be on one side or the other, or the three branches may be 120 degrees apart from one another. This popular mutation has picked up the name *whorled phylotaxy* coming from the words *whorl: an arrangement of three or more similar parts or organs at the same level about an axis* and *phylotaxy: The arrangement of leaves or other lateral members on an axis or stem.*

Trilaterial Branching (Whorled Phylotaxy) by Mr. Webb.

This warping of the leaf is permanent and is a mutation
that can be bred true in the offspring. Warped leaf by Growmaster420.

TWINNING

Twining is another common mutation that has passed into the gene pool. Some seeds germinate to produce two seedlings from the same seed. One seedling rarely ever makes it because of the competition and being root-bound. The twins will not share the same roots and stem and will not be Siamese, but if you have any more information on this please be sure to visit us at www.cannabisbook.com.

WARPING

Warping is another common mutation that is found in in-bred lines and clones that have been propagated through cuttings for a long time. The warping is usually seen in the leaves that curl sideways like a hook instead of up or down as they do when there's a nutrient problem. The stem may also be warped or bent with large blister-like surface points developing on the sides.

AUTO-TOPPING

Auto-topping is not very common and is usually the result of a mutation lower down in the plant that has caused the plant to automatically split into two stems. A whorled phylotaxy seems to cause this condition. So if you got a whorled phylotaxy then chances are your plant will auto-top itself.

POLYPLOIDS

The polyploid condition, as discussed before, appears as a result of a mutation.

A severely mutated polyploid cannabis plant. Photographs by HombredelMonte.

LEAF BUDS (BULBILS)

Another very strange mutation is flowers developing on the leaf. Where the branch meets the leaf a node may form and from the node a calyx and flower will grow. These types of mutations have been found in plants that grow around Nepal and the Himalayas. It is quite possible that this type of mutation is a translocation mutation. It does crop up in some hybrid plants now and again. It does not appear to affect the plant in any way.

Leaf buds that have developed on several petioles.
Photograph by Kryptonite.

A large percentage of chromosome mutations do nothing to the plant but sometimes these mutations may add up with other smaller mutations over a long period of time to cause an effect on the plant. As we have seen, cloning through constant cuttings can do this. Another large percentage of chromosome mutations render a plant sterile or can cause a female to abort seed production or to produce nonviable seeds.

This is the case with many of the mutations mentioned above. They do not appear to harm the plant in any way, but the plant will also try and compensate for some of the problems. For example splitting and warping of a leaf or branch will result in the extra node above working harder to produce a new leaf and branch. The plant may even try and produce a new leaf or branch at the very same node as the mutation. A noticeable way to see this is with fan leaf mutations. If a fan leaf suffers from a mutation or warping the node may develop a new fan leaf or the next node above will develop a new fan leaf. The cannabis plant rarely fails to produce a new fan leaf if one is mutated or even if it is just cut away. In fact, if you prune a fan leaf early on, a new fan leaf will develop on the next node level. However, it has been noted that the higher up the fan leaf tries to develop, the more it looks like a hybrid between a fan and the trim leaves.

Single-bladed leaves may also develop. Single-blade leaves are not really a mutation *per se*. Single blade leaves are developed naturally by the plant as it tries to gather as much light as quickly as possible for photosynthesis. If a warping or splitting occurs then the next node level above may produce a single blade leaf in order to access light as quickly as possible because the warped leaf is not doing

On the left a clone is developing single-bladed leaves. Photograph by strawdog.
On the right a clone has continued to produce single bladed leaves all over. Photograph by Kryptonite.

its job correctly or efficiently. You will notice this with clones. If you take a clone and root it, the clone will probably develop several single-blade leaves to try and receive light as soon as possible. I have even seen plants that have grown three feet high with single-bladed leaves all over. It is not a mutation, just a natural act of self-preservation.

17 | EVOLUTIONARY CONDUIT OF CANNABIS

THE REPRODUCTIVE ASSURANCE OF CANNABIS PLANTS

When we deal with nonrandom mating between related individual plants, including selfing (also called **autogamy**; the opposite normal condition of cross pollinating between separate male and female plants is called **allogamy**), we can see problems in a population with regard to the fitness of the progeny. Darwin noted that the progeny of inbred plants were not as vigorous as outcrosses. Nature does not seem to produce mostly hermaphrodite cannabis populations but they can still be found in small pockets in the wild. Because dioecious plants are more common we assume that the hermaphrodite condition is not suited to most of the environments in which cannabis is found. But this assumption needs to be debated, because inbreeding can make a strain more suitable for a specific environment and man has played a role in both hermaphrodite and dioecious cannabis plant propagation. The small pockets of wild hermaphrodite cannabis plants around the world also seem to indicate that the trait is not entirely unsuitable for the cannabis family.

In 1941, Ronald Alymer Fisher proposed the "automatic transmission advantage." Fisher's papers can be read on-line at http://www.library.adelaide.edu.au/digitised/fisher/index.html.

Fisher discovered that there was an automatic selection advantage during selfing. A selfed plant will contribute both the ovule and the pollen, as a single hermaphrodite parent, to offspring that it will create. In populations that are not selfed the males contributes pollen to separate female plants. The selfed plants however will contain an allele encouraging the hermaphrodite trait (selfing) and

Fisher found that this allele has a 3:2 transmission advantage over plants that do not self. This means that selfed plants will usually contain the allele for spreading the selfed trait to further populations unless equilibrium is not maintained and the gene is deleted from the gene pool. In short, selfed plants appear to have natural selective pressures to stay hermaphrodite and to spread the condition to its offspring, however it does not mean that a selfed hermaphrodite population cannot eventually become a dioecious population that does not self.

Cannabis seeds are heavy. Although they can travel over longer distances via animals or birds, in most cases seeds are going to grow in close proximity to the mother plant that they came from. Gravity is responsible for this. The vast majority of mother cannabis plants terminate their lives before the offspring can mature and so there is a low chance of any natural backcrossing occurring. However, if she does survive, the chances of a wild backcross are much higher.

We know that cannabis wants to prevent this because it is an annual plant and a high percentage of cannabis strains show traits that prevent natural backcrossing. We know that sometimes the plant will abort the seed or not use the pollen if selfed. This is called "homomorphic incompatibility" or "cryptic self-incompatibility".

Anthesis is the time when a flower opens or becomes sexually functional—the time and process of budding and unfolding of blossoms. Male and female plants show a clear difference in anthesis times. The male produces faster than the female, usually before the female even starts to flower. The hermaphrodite condition reproduces itself mostly in the flowering phase of the female plant. If pollen is already available from another male flowering plant before hermaphrodites appear in a population, then the pollen that is most readily available will be used by the females in the population. A 'seeded' female will rarely ever start to hermaphrodite after receiving pollen unless it goes through very stressful growing conditions after being pollinated.

So what are the benefits for which evolution has allowed the hermaphrodite trait to continue? It simply boils down to variations in strains promoting higher chances of adaptability and fitness in the offspring.

If you want reproductive assurance, you've got it with selfing. If a strain suits an environment without any problems, you might wonder why it doesn't just settle down and concentrate on reproduction by selfing? Selfing is mostly recognized as a process of self-preservation where stress has put the plant into a crisis bid to reproduce itself. But even in a cozy environment, wouldn't it also be in the plant's best interest to settle down and reproduce itself by autogamy? We are back to the same problem again. Is the hermaphrodite trait an extreme of both of these conditions? This does tell us that this mating system is strongly related to inbreeding.

Since inbreeding has a depression (which we will explain in a moment) in the variation possibilities and overall adaptability of a plant we can compare this with the offspring of the same strain that has not been involved in autogamy or selective breeding processes. The formula is expressed as:

$$1 - (Ws/W0)$$

Ws is the measured vigor of the selfed offspring and $W0$ is the measured vigor of non-selfed offspring. Vigor is measured by traits for nearly every stage of the plant's development and how well it copes with the environment. The reason for a depression can be found in strains that have higher amounts of homozygous traits in a population.

The best place to look for inbreeding depression is with pure lines. If two unre-lated purebred lines meet they will produce the first F1 hybrid offspring, which should have some vigorous characteristics in the population. **Heterosis** is the ten-dency of a crossbred individual, a hybrid, to show qualities superior to those of both parents. It is also called "hybrid vigor."

Inbreeding increases homozygosity and crossbreeding maximizes heterozygosity. Crossbreeding takes advantage of hybrid vigor, which results in bursts of fertility and growth. The differences between the two parents are what result in hybrid vigor. In a large population where unrelated breeds of a species mate, the off-spring in the first generation will be intermediate in characteristics to the par-ents and some will express the dominant phenotypes of both strains. Population means are deduced from the differences in gene frequencies among populations. We will have a look at these intermediate characteristics and how they can com-bine to produce hybrid vigor in a moment.

HYBRID VIGOR

Heterosis is a function of the square of the difference in gene frequency multi-plied by the dominance deviation. This hypothesis states that heterosis is caused by a superior manifestation of "deleterious genes" when homozygosity is amplified and the heterozygote terminated somewhere in between the two corresponding homozygotes. It can also be supposed that heterosis occurs because of the termination of deleterious recessives contributed by one of the parents in the heterozygous F1 cross. All of this will make more sense in a moment when we see the possible combinations of genes in a population with our hybrid vigor model.

So what is a deleterious recessive condition? Deleterious alleles reduce the likelihood of an individual's survival while safe alleles (non-deleterious) increase the chances of an individual's survival (basically bad traits versus good traits that have an impact on the plant's survival). If the recessive trait is a weak trait then fewer offspring will be produced to contribute to the population. Plants with deleterious alleles are usually eliminated quicker than healthier individuals.

Deleterious alleles exist and increase in a non-uniform population because of non-random mating factors. A deleterious recessive trait will generally cause a plant to use more resources in an effort to balance out the problem. Sometimes a deleterious recessive trait may cause a plant to grow taller with long internodes, naturally causing it to receive more light and it may dominate the smaller plants which have less non-deleterious recessive alleles. So in effect the deleterious gene has dominated the non-deleterious gene by default of its other dominant values. However this is rare and in most cases the number of deleterious alleles is kept low by a process of natural selection.

Breeders have been able to sustain plants that should not have survived in the wild because of their deleterious genes. This depends on what we consider a deleterious allele. Bad resistance to a certain type of pest can be treated as deleterious, yet indoors an IBL line may not encounter this pest and so the deleterious trait goes unnoticed. If this plant population were to exist in a locale where the pest is also present then the deleterious trait would be a disadvantage to the population and it might not continue. The deleterious allele will usually burden the plant in a population and it will use more energy and resources to survive. It uses more resources than plants with the non-deleterious genes for that trait and so is considered a waste of sorts in comparison. But plants with a deleterious allele may prove successful in dealing with a problem that a strain encounters. Again, variations are more adaptable. Recessive alleles are not classed as harmful or beneficial. The same goes for dominant alleles.

If we can understand these points and remember what we have learned about the recombination of cannabis genetic material then we should be able to understand hybrid vigor in the model below.

```
       aa      bb      CC      DD      ee
AA   AaAa
BB           BbBb
cc                   CcCc
dd                           DdDd
EE                                   EeEe
```

The most important element here is the consideration of a plant that is AaBbCcDdEe. Notice that none of the parents have this exact combination. The parents are AABBccddEE and aabbCCDDee. The first parent, AABBccddEE, has two recessives (cc, dd). The second parent, aabbCCDDee, has three recessives (aa,bb,ee). The offspring that has Aa,Bb,Cc,Dd, Ee is dominant for A,B,C,D and E. These A B C D E alleles are all present in this offspring and their dominance will be displayed in their respective phenotypes, which gives the plant its impression of hybrid vigor. This offspring is unique! Please remember, though, that we are using this model in the context of recessive and partially recessive deleterious alleles in respect to hybrid vigor.* You can see how a superior plant can emerge in a population via natural selection in hybrids. This is why it is important to grow large populations for selections when you are looking for that special mother plant that does better than all the rest. Usually the special mother can be attributed to hybrid vigor.

There is a lot of controversy about hybrid vigor because there is a back element to it that says that maybe the dominant allele is not the best allele for a new breeding environment. By breeding nonselectively in your environment you should help influence traits that suit that environment, with the subsequent removal of the deleterious alleles that do not suit your environment. The adaptable vigor of the F1 hybrid cross will decrease as we inbreed more.

"Over-dominance" is a term also used to explain hybrid vigor. True over-dominance occurs when there are multiple alleles for the same trait brought to the table in numbers of more than two. If nonrandom mating occurs then exceptional multiple hybrid variations for the same trait may be produced. As you can guess the more hybrids that are created the more recombinations will occur and the greater the chances of producing a vigorous plant that is seeking resolution in its environment.

---

* A combination of dominant and recessive traits can produce that special mother – the vigorous hybrid.

.

In short, breeders develop new and better cannabis genetics by reshuffling the genetic code rather than inbreeding. Inbreeding stabilizes a strain by locking down homozygous traits.

AN INTRODUCTION
TO THE SEXUAL EVOLUTION OF CANNABIS

Selfed plants usually produce more seeds because of selective pressures. Having pollen readily available is part of reproductive assurance.

In 1932 John Burton Haldane published "The Causes of Evolution." Haldane made the discovery that there was a higher probability of encouraging a fixation of beneficial alleles for adaptability in selfing rather than outcrosses because there is a greater forwarding of these alleles to the overall selection process. This process, known as Haldane's Sieve, also has negative effects because it forfeits long-term adaptability in favor of short-term advantages. This argument is known as "adaptedness," from the adaptability hypothesis founded by S. K. Jain in 1976 in his publication "The Evolution of Inbreeding in Plants."

In 1957 Dr. G. Ledyard Stebbins published "Regularities of Transformation in the Flower," "Self-Fertilization and Population Variability in the Higher Plants," and "The Inviability, Weakness and Sterility of Inter-Specific Hybrids" among many other important botany papers that year. Stebbins suggests that the evolution of selfing is an amalgamation of preliminary reproductive assurances followed by adaptability. Stebbins discovered that it is beneficial for a species to preserve well-adapted genotypes over long periods of time if the environment suits the population.

We have seen both advantages and disadvantages to selfing. In short, selfing increases reproductive assurance but can decrease long-term success (As a note, we are no longer considering the fact that sinsemilla crops from non-selfed populations are what the cannabis grower is looking for. Here, rather, we are considering the evolutionary processes of the dioecious and monoecious conditions in cannabis). In their 1985 publication "The Evolution of Self-Fertilization and Inbreeding Depression in Plants," R. Lande and D. W. Schemske found that there is actually a disorderly selection for selfing rates in wild plant populations which prevents the hermaphrodite condition from being more widespread. Both selfing (autogamy) and normal reproduction (allogamy) are styles of mating practices and are dependent on the fitness of the plant. Self-fertilization in mostly out-crossed populations will cause high levels of inbreeding depression because of higher genotype frequencies of recessive homozygotes which, in the absence of strong inbreeding, will not be purged. Thus, inbreeding in mostly outcrossed populations will tend to promote the maintenance of outcrossed systems and not selfing.

In 1996 M. Schierup and F.B. Christiansen in their publication "Inbreeding and Outbreeding in Plants" and in 1997 M. Fischer and D. Matthies in their publication "Mating Structure, and Inbreeding and Outbreeding Depression in the Rare Plant Gentianella Germanica (Gentianaceae)" considered that in contrast if we look at mostly selfing populations, the plants are highly adapted to their particular forte. Outcrossing, either with plants from another population by migration or from within the same population, can cause "Outbreeding Depression" where the offspring of the outcrosses are less fit than the offspring of selfing. Thus selfing rates are dependent on plant fitness.

Inbreeding can affect a plant's mating system and this is called "the evolution of mating systems" and can be seen in the difference between monoecious and dioecious types. **Dioecious plants actually appear to be a development of monoecious plants.**

The development of a dioecious plant is a two-step process. The initial step in the development of a dioecious plant is the "single gene male sterility mutation" which stops pollen production. The condition is known as "Gynodioecy" and the only reproductive parts that are functional in these monoecious plants are the female flowers. In this type of population there are female plants with sterile male sex organs and hermaphrodite plants. The male sterility gene will spread once a male sterility mutation combines with the population.

Cannabis in Androdioecy becoming male, cannabis in Gynodioecy becoming female and the original primordial hermaphrodite cannabis plant template.

"Androdioecy" is the related condition where a species has both male flowers with sterile *female* sex organs and hermaphrodite flowers, but this is a rare condition.

The next step in dioecious development is where a mutation of the pollen production at this locus occurs in the non-gynodioecious plants. The plants will try to stabilize this increase of males and in turn will reduce ovule production. As the modification takes place there is an equalized decrease in ovule production of the hermaphrodites over all the females. If hermaphrodites with increasing male function are selected, this gene will spread in the population. The resulting offspring will be females (with nonfunctional male organs) and males (with nonfunctional female organs). As time goes by the sex organs will evolve into either male or female sex organs and this is where the plants split into discrete sex types, which are dioecious. That is quite interesting isn't it? It also goes some way to explaining why the sexual inheritance in cannabis and the expression of that sex is a complex subject.

Inbred lines have an adaptive value that can be seen in both the wild and in breeding labs. Inbreeding can result in populations that have higher levels of fitness because they are more suited to the environment that they have been inbreeding in.

Selfing has reproductive advantage and also resembles the inbred lines' adaptive values. Although inbreeding results in a depression, that depression is only expressed if the inbred line's environment is compromised or equilibrium has been altered. In order to be fit for such a problem a species will adapt through the chances of hybrid vigor when foreign genes enter the pool. We must also remember that inbreeding does not necessarily mean that deleterious genes will be fully eradicated. Homozygosity is increased and deleterious recessive alleles can be homozygous. To be realistic, the only time that deleterious genes will be removed is when these alleles are flushed from the population through the pressures of selection.

Note that there are two very distinct types of hermaphrodites. Permanent hermaphrodites are capable of producing both ova and spermatozoa at the same time, while 'Protandrous hermaphrodites' male gametes mature and are shed before female gametes mature. As you can guess the combinations that can lead to dioecious development are many. Each has its own scenario that can be played out and, more importantly, reversed. This can lead to a breakthrough in creating dioecious strains from strains that have hermaphrodite problems! Breeders take note of this and remember the various sexual reversal experiments.

The aim of this chapter has been to explain a bit about the 'evolutionary conduit', or the evolutionary development, of the dioecious plant and the outcome of inbreeding depression. Each is relative to our growing environment. Since most of us want uniform plants for growing reasons, we are looking for inbred lines even though the line will be depressed. We are also looking for dioecious plants because we want a sinsemilla crop and if we want to add a genetic boost to our crop we should take advantage of hybrid vigor. On top of this we have covered the more advanced aspects of understanding cannabis gender types, how the genders evolved in cannabis and how it can be manipulated by the breeder. It is wise to try and keep all cannabis sex reversal experimentations away from contaminating the gene pool. You can however experiment on your own models to see if you can eliminate hermaphrodites from a known hermie population. This is a very good breeding project to try out especially with high yielding and potent hermaphrodite strains that nobody wants to work with because they can never produce a sinsemilla crop with it.

18 | MORPHOLOGY AND BREEDING TRAITS

AN INTRODUCTION TO CANNABIS PLANT MORPHOLOGY

"Cannabis plant morphology" is about the cannabis species as a whole and the various strains' relationships with one another. "Plant morphology" is a wider area of study focused on the relationships between different plant families, orders and classes. We will be dealing only with cannabis plant morphology here, relative to the topic of cannabis breeding. There are two major sections of cannabis morphology: cannabis vegetative characteristics and cannabis floral characteristics.

Cannabis Vegetative Characteristics

There are a few types of obvious vegetative characteristics that we need to look at. These are: leaf and branch arrangements, leaf shapes, leaf types, leaf venation, roots, stem habits and buds (not flowering bud, but vegetative buds).

Basic Structure

Cannabis is an erect plant with tough bast fibers. It grows upward and sideways. Side branching has a tendency to curve upward although this may not be apparent during the latter stages of flowering growth because of flowering weight on these branches. During germination of the plant, cannabis also has a straight **hypocotyl** (embryonic stem). The **cotyledons** (the seedling's first set of leaves) appear single-bladed and close to one another. As the seedling grows it develops petioles, branches and more leaves. After a few weeks it begins to look more like a cannabis plant.

Leaf/Branch Arrangements

The leaf/branch arrangement for cannabis is known as an "opposite" arrangement (decussate) because branching develops in pairs at the same levels on the

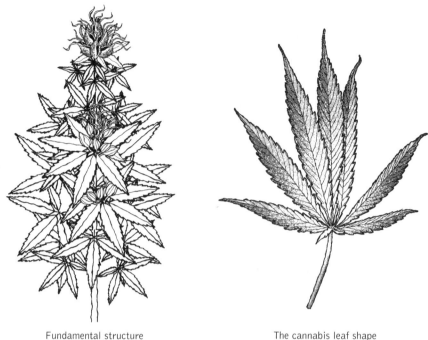

Fundamental structure
of the cannabis plant.

The cannabis leaf shape
(Indica/Sativa hybrid).

stem or branch. If more than a single pair of branches develops at the same level on the stem then, as discussed in chapter 17, the arrangement is referred to as a "whorled" arrangement. If the branches develop one above the other it is known as an "alternate (staggered)" arrangement.

A single cannabis plant can possess all of these arrangement types. Whorling is the rarest of the three. The alternate leaf/branch arrangement is the second most common type and usually occurs during flowering and/or after pruning; however it may also occur naturally without flowering or pruning

Leaf Shapes

Leaf shape is divided into the main leaf shape, the apices (narrowed or pointed end) and the base. The main leaf shape of the cannabis plant is "palmately-compound." (having veins or leaflets arranged like the fingers on a hand). The apices of the leaf is of the "aristate" type because of the fine long point that it comes to at the top of each linear blade. The base of each blade is "acuminate" because of its uniform slender closure. In some strains this base is "acute," in which case it comes to a very sharp close with a noticeable distance between the closure and opening out of the blade width. The leaflets are coarse-toothed which makes them "serrated."

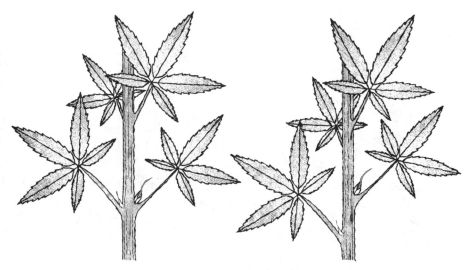

"Opposite and Alternate cannabis plant branching arrangements.

Cannabis blade shape and venation.

Leaf Venation

You would presume the palmately-compound leaf trait would indicate the palmately veined venation trait, but this is not so. Cannabis is in fact pinnately-veined, That is, there is a main vein running from the base to the tip of each finger. Along each main vein are smaller veins that branch off in a somewhat even fashion to touch the sides of each blade.

Roots

The cannabis plant roots are the "Taproot." type but are often short and stubby except for that of very large Sativa varieties that can grow a very long taproot. In general the taproot is poor in size and the plant depends largely on a more fibrous root system that branches from the taproot in many multiples. This fibrous route trait can also have "Prop root" properties where the roots that are very close to the soil's surface act like supports for the plant. This can be seen in long-flowering Sativa strains. The root type is classed as primary and cannabis roots grow most vigorously during vegetative growth and less so in flowering. If you transplant during vegetative growth you may notice with smaller strains of the

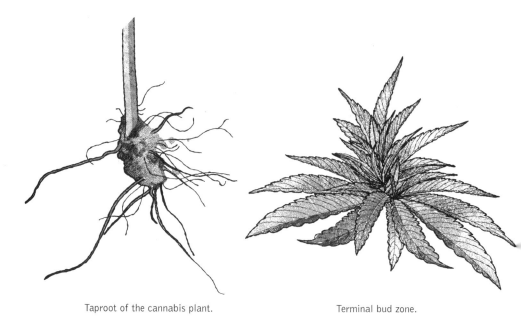

Taproot of the cannabis plant.   Terminal bud zone.

Indica species type that the roots have reached the outer edge of the soil even in large three gallon containers. After harvest you may notice that the roots do not appear to have reached the outer edge of soil in the larger container they were transplanted into. This is because roots do the majority of their growing in the vegetative stage. It is more than possible to produce several gallons of a root mass from a single cannabis plant when growing in hydroponics systems.

Stem Habits
The stem habit is a straightforward "ascending" stem characteristic. The most other straightforward trait is that the stem is of the above ground type.

Buds (Node Buds Not Flowering Buds)
There are two types of buds found on the cannabis plant, separated only by their location. They are the "stalked/lateral" bud type which is found on the node points and the "terminal" bud, which we find only at the very head of a stem or at the head of a number of stems. The most impressive terminal bud location of the cannabis plant is the "top cola".

All of these morphological elements are the cannabis plant's core vegetative attributes and are the most common physical aspects of the plant that you will be working on during your breeding projects. Even though cannabis has a set template for each of these shapes you can still control how that shape is expressed in size, numbers, color, location and spacing to a certain degree. For example: cannabis plants express the palmately-compound leaf type but Sativa leaves are very different from Indica leaves in their size, numbers, color and spacing.

There can also be multiple expressions of each classification. While the roots are of the taproot category, they can also fall into the fibrous root category. Though they do not appear to grow from the stem, sometimes low down on a plant the roots can increase in size and break the surface, giving the appearance of being "adventitious" and growing from something other than root tissue.

Buds (of the node type) are compressed undeveloped shoots and are either stalked/lateral or terminal. They are found at the nodes, which are points on the stem where leaf, branch, stem, calyx and flowers are created. The space between two nodes is called the "internode." The internode mostly refers to the space between stems on the main stem, but it can also describe the space between node regions on a branch. "Leaf scar" is a place on the stalk left where a leaf was previously attached. "Bud scale scar" is a mark on the stem where a bud was previously attached.

When the terminal bud grows small growth rings are formed on the stem. Sometimes these scar marks can be clearly seen.

Cannabis is treated as an Herb because it does not appear to have too much woody tissue on the stem. Woody tissue plants are normally referred to as shrubs, trees and vines. The cannabis plant is an annual plant that lives for one year or season, reproduces, and then dies—however if there is not a harsh winter or the plants are looked after with care, they can continue growing for a number of years, especially if the grower chooses rejuvenation (CGB, p. 172). Biennial plants live for two years or seasons, reproduce and then die. Perennial plants live for several to many years or seasons. The important thing to note is that cannabis can also be perennial if the given environmental conditions allow it to survive.

The "petiole" is the stalk of a leaf that connects to the branch or stem. The "blade" is the term used to describe the flat, wide portion of the leaf. Cannabis plants have several blades on each leaf and these can range in length, width and thickness between species and strains.

The leaf is not a simple one, so it falls into the "compound" leaf category. It is neither "once pinnately compound" or "twice pinnately compound", but "palmately compound," the difference being that palmately compound leaflets arise from one point at the base of the leaf. What we are looking at is the projection and division of a cannabis leaf. This area is correctly called the "lobe". There are only two basic categories of lobes and these are "pinnate lobes," which have a main mid-vein along with secondary veins arising from it at intervals, and "palmate lobes," where the main veins all arise from one point at the base of the leaf.

The structures we have looked at here can be changed on a very wide level as long as cannabis continues to breed with cannabis. You will also find some discrepancies between biologists noting the different types of morphology that the cannabis plant expresses, however this is not uncommon for a plant family so diverse in variations as cannabis is.

Breeding the Morphology

Cannabis is cannabis, whatever way you look at it. If you stand back and look at several different strains for different cannabis species types you will see variations and similarities. You can spot a cannabis species and strain type a mile away if you know what to look for. Many experienced growers can separate species into strain classifications like Kush, Skunk and Berry by looking at (or trying) the expressed phenotypes of each plant. We may find a group of strains from a species such as Kush strains, Haze strains, Skunk strains and Jack Herer strains. Through experience we can group strains like this together by their appearance. They all share common traits that make up the overall shape but those traits may contain variations. A good breeder knows and understands different strains. When breeders work on cannabis strains they do not need to change the way they think about the different cannabis species as whole. They might have to take certain factors into consideration but they are working with the same template each time. That template is Cannabis.

Here is a list of traits that we need to take into account when working on a strain. Floral traits, which will be covered further on, take other elements into consideration, like taste and smell.

- adaptableness/adaptability
- calyx/leaf ratio
- curing and manicuring
- floral traits
- maturity (including flowering times)
- size
- yield
- branching
- color
- disease resistance (including pests)
- leaf traits
- seed characteristics
- vigor

Vigorous pistil production is a good sign that an outdoor plant is adapting
well to the environment. Photograph by Anton

Adaptableness/Adaptability

Some strains are not very adaptable. For instance, Sativa strains are not very
adaptable to indoor growing environments without vigorous pruning or breeding.
Sometimes the genetic minimum internode lengths are so long that even 6-node-
level-tall plants are over six feet high, pushing the limits of what the grow room
is designed for. At the same time a breeder who creates the perfect ScrOG strain
is not going to be making an adaptable plant to suit other growing conditions, like
outdoor growing.

If you want to create an all-round adaptable plant then you need to work on a
strain that is easy to grow in warm/cool conditions, indoor/outdoor/greenhouse
and can be controlled by the grower via pruning. The only way you can do this is
to test the strain out yourself under these different conditions to see if you make
the strain more adaptable.

Generally, the less variations strains have the less adaptable they will be.
Unstable hybrid strains tend to be more adaptable than true-breeding stable

strains, depending on the environment. Remember hybrid vigor? Adaptable plants grow to suit the environment. Inflexible plants grow better in an environment that suits them.

Since the market is changing and breeders are creating more and more specialized strains, you can expect to find less adaptable plants on the market. Is there a niche in the market for adaptable plants? Well, most Sativa strains and pure Haze strains carry a lot of variations and these are expressed in the phenotypes. Unstable Sativa strains can produce fine mother plants during the selection process. The best way to create adaptable plants is by creating new hybrids with lots of variations.

Most grow books have erroneously suggested that varieties that perform well under artificial lights will also perform well outside or in a glass house under natural sunlight and that outdoor plants do not do well indoors. Although the later part of this statement is true, certainly the first part is not correct.

Yes, it is true that all cannabis strains can be grown indoors, outdoors or in greenhouses. It is also true that if we are looking for the best results we should stick to what the breeder recommended. It is a mistake to assume that indoor breeding projects can produce good outdoor plants. Outdoor maturity dates and outdoor flowering times are not selected for when breeding for an indoor environment. Indoor breeding programs also do not select for outdoor sexual maturation or the plant's response to the outdoor photoperiod. The outdoor environment also has a very different impact on the plant's final expressed phenotype when compared to plants grown under artificial lights indoors. The outdoor environment, and sunlight, will cause variations in the expressed phenotype of the plant. This can be identified in traits like smell and taste. Pests should not be found indoors in a sterile breeding room. Outdoors, pests can be everywhere and of multiple types. Sterile breeding rooms may leave a breeding project open later to problems like mold, fungi and pest attack. We will look at how to solve this later on.

The bottom line here is that stable lines are not very adaptable and growers want stable lines. In short, most breeders do not breed for adaptability. If you want to breed for adaptability then simply keep producing F1 hybrids using nonrandom mating programs in various different environments. The more variations a plant has the more adaptable it can be.

Branching
Branching is first determined by node levels and then sub-branching. Branches

add weight to the plant and can also stress the stem. Branching can be controlled by pruning, but every strain has:

- a genetically set branching limit during vegetative growth,
- a genetically set branching limit after vegetative growth.

Sometimes branches get so top cola heavy that they need to be tied together. Photograph by Kissie.

Sativa strains tend to have lots of branches that are spaced out between long internodes and node regions. This makes Sativa strains more loose than Indica plants. Indica plants have shorter internodes and that makes the species more compact than Sativa plants. Through breeding we have been able to totally control this and swap the traits around.

When working on branching traits we must also consider how productive the branches will be and how they will help boost yields. Each node is a potential bud

A nice squat and compact Indica/Sativa plant. Breeder
BOG has kept the internodes short on this one.

site and each branch will take up some amount of space. We must also consider
the fact that if we grow outdoors and it rains then each branch and leaf will be
covered in some rain drops. Rain drops do add weight to the plant and I have seen
some strains bend completely over during vegetative growth and snap at the stem
because of heavy rainfall. (It is not uncommon to find outdoor plants with colas
lying in dirt contracting mold and other plant diseases because of the added
weight of a recent rainfall and the fact that the bud mass could not be support-
ed by the branch. This condition is solved by tying up the branches or breeding
stronger branches into the strain.)

During flowering the branches are a bit stronger and the stem is thicker to support bud growth, but it can still snap or bend severely during rain if the branch
is not strong enough. Many indoor strains are not bred for outdoor use and many
of these strains can collapse under rainy conditions. Wind is important to consider as well. Some strains are better suited for the wind than others. A strong
gust can topple strains that were devised for indoor use.

When breeding an outdoor strain make sure that you create a sturdy plant that
can cope with all weather conditions. You must test your strains and breeding
projects in these conditions.

Skunk#1 is a very interesting plant to look at. Low down, the bottom branches
tend to curve upward with long internode gaps that do not produce much bud at
the internodes except for the tips, which produce above-average size colas. These
branches tend to bend over with the weight of the buds (a trait that is common
with many other strains of cannabis). As the branch bends the light-to-bud dis-

Note the breeding traits involved in various bud production areas
of a branch. Notice how flowering distribution and branching support play
major roles in how well the plant can handle the weight of each.

tance increases and this is the plant's own natural way of preventing itself from
being overburdened with bud weight that can effectively snap the branch or stem.
The less light these branches receive, the less the rate of photosynthesis will be
and the result will be less bud production. All strains tend to do this to some
degree when the flowers are getting too heavy for the plant to manage. This grav-
itational response to unmanageable yields is usually countered by the grower, who
ties up the branches to keep the plant producing high yields. With some strains,
during harvest when the branches are untied, the colas will flop down to the sides,
almost hitting the floor.

The way to counteract this problem is through breeding for shorter internodes. This
has been done to some degree for Skunk#1 with variations like Super Skunk and
Mazar. By breeding for shorter internode development the branches have fewer
gaps. Also the breeder will try to produce bud at most of the node regions, through
breeding, to cover these gaps with flowers. That way the bud amounts are more

Compact buds are nice and dense, but also top heavy. This
Bogbubble plant from breeder BOG sure can bend.

evenly distributed across the entire branch instead of ending up as one whole flowering mass at the growing tip.* This prevents the branch from bending too much,
however some indoor strains are designed to have high cola bud concentration
amounts with the anticipation that the grower will tie the branches up. For this reason breeders must also take into account that some growers like to prune, top and
train their plants. This has an impact on branching numbers and final yields. You
should experiment with your strain to see how well it responds to these plant care
techniques. Sometimes a pruned, topped or trained plant can produce much lower
yields, sometimes much greater. The only way you can know how well your strain
reacts to these branching control techniques is to prune, top and train your strains.
Sometimes breeders recommend pruning with their strains because it can increase
yields, however some growers make the mistake of thinking that this applies across
the board to all cannabis strains. Your 2-pound-producing monster plant can quickly become a 1-ounce-producing average cannabis strain because of pruning.

Plants have a genetic threshold for bud production and the distribution of these bud
amounts across the plant also depends on branch production. To be more accurate,
we are talking about node development here. New branch formations create new
node regions. All node regions are potential bud areas. We will look more closely at
the relationship between branch numbers, node regions and yields in a moment.

Calyx/Leaf Ratio

This is something that breeders have noticed over the years. If you look at a flowering cannabis plant you will see that each node should be developing bud. A node
occurs at a junction point where a new branch or new stem is produced. Calyxes

---

* SOG breeds are typically top-heavy.

This Ladybird beetle is hunting Aphids on the top cola. Note
that this strain has a very low calyx/leaf ratio. Photograph by Kissie.

mainly develop at the node regions. This is especially true during the early days of
calyx development. For every node region there is at least one branch developing
above or beyond it with at least one leaf at the tip of the branch that the node is
located on. Thus if you count the leaves on your plant, you should have a minimum
node/leaf ratio of roughly 1:1. Since a calyx will develop at the node region there
should also be a calyx/leaf ratio of 1:1 during the early stages of calyx development.
As the plant increases calyx development the ratio should rise to 2:1 and beyond.

This cannot be said for all plants. Some nodes do not develop a calyx and thus do
not flower. In cases like this the 1:1 ratio can drop down to 1:2 or even as low as
1:6 or 1:10. Plants that have a low calyx/leaf ratio such as 1:3 or 1:4 are inef-
ficient for a grower's purposes unless the quantity of bud created at the other
calyx sites compensates for these invalid node regions. This is the first thing we
need to know with regard to the calyx/leaf ratios.

The main focus of our calyx/leaf ratio scrutiny are the colas, which in most cases is
just a single top cola. (You may have pruned your plant, though, and this would lead
to multiple cola heads, or possibly your plant has naturally produced more than one
top cola). If you look at any top cola you will see that tiny branches are created to
support node development, calyx and flowers. This is especially observable during and

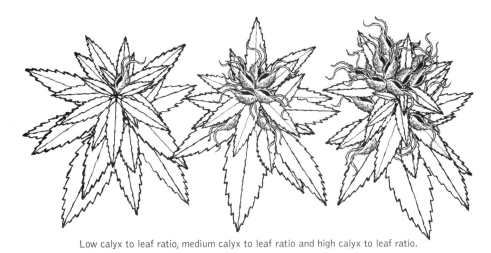

Low calyx to leaf ratio, medium calyx to leaf ratio and high calyx to leaf ratio.

after manicuring or after breaking up your bud from the branch after curing. These branches are usually tightly packed together, giving the top cola its density. If you look closely at a plant that has been bred well for a good calyx/leaf ratio, you may find 20 or more calyx areas with only one leaf supporting the branch but several calyx organs developing at these nodes. In general when a breeder refers to calyx/leaf ratio, he is talking about the top cola's calyx/leaf ratio. A poor top cola calyx/leaf ratio is 1:1, while the normal will be around 2:1. A good calyx ratio is around 4:1 or 5:1. An excellent calyx/leaf ratio would be 7:1 or even 10:1 and beyond.

Calyx development means more bud sites, but may not mean higher yields. Even a calyx/leaf ratio of 20:1 may produce low yields (a good example is the strain 'Flo'). If you are not going to be putting on the bud weight then what is the point to having a high calyx/leaf ratio? Again, breeding is interlinked in so many ways. Most breeders trying to develop high calyx/leaf ratios will also try to develop high bud quantities. Generally in growing terminology a high calyx/leaf ratio is expected to mean that the strain is capable of high yields. High calyx/leaf ratios are also easier to manicure. Plants with high yields but low calyx/leaf ratios are harder to manicure because more leaves must be trimmed. Calyx/leaf ratios are not related to potency.

Color
In general cannabis is a green plant. Sometimes hues of purple or red may crop up in a healthy individual but overall the plants should still display a lot of green. It is not recommended that you try and change the green color and it is also highly unlikely that you will succeed without using chemicals. Cannabis plants are green because they reflect green light that they do not need for photosynthesis. If they are any other color then they will absorb green light, which will not be bene-

ficial or used in photosynthesis and they may reflect a color that they need. Sick plants can change all sorts of different colors from black to blue to yellow to red, but we are not interested in breeding sick plants; we are interested in working with healthy ones. Cannabis flowers can vary in color but are mostly green too.

Chlorophyll is the compound in cannabis plants that gives it the green look because chlorophyll in the leaves reflects the green light, but during the flowering period, especially toward the end of flowering, chlorophyll may break down and reveal other pigments that it is hiding. This can produce all sorts of different-colored buds. Purple bud color is due to the anthocyanin pigments in the plant that are allowed to express through the degraded chlorophyll. But this has to be a trait in the plant in order for it to occur. If the plant does not have a colorful trait for anthocyanin pigment to come through after chlorophyll degradation then it will not be observed. It is a genetic trait. There are various parts of the plant's physiology that contribute to color.

It's incorrect to see color as something like a varnish on the plant. Color has a lot to do with the actual chemical makeup of the plant and the various parts they inhabit or move through. Pigments are the natural coloring matter in plant tissue, chlorophyll being the most predominant.

Carotenoids are a class of mainly yellow or red pigments of wide natural occurrence having the conjugated molecular structure typified by carotene. Carotene is an orange or red hydrocarbon ($C_{40}H56$) of which there are several isomers (common in carrots and many other plants and a precursor of vitamin A). Isomers consist of two or more compounds, or of one compound in relation to another, composed of the same elements in the same proportions, and having the same molecular weight, but forming substances with different properties owing to the different grouping or arrangement of the constituent atoms. In the actual formation of the substances a color is allocated to it. If you look at carotenoids that are red and yellow you'd see that red and yellow combine to create other colors and these give off different hues associated with carotenoids, such as brown and orange, which are very common on floral parts of the cannabis plant.

There are many ways to breed a plant so that when chlorophyll degrades the green is either totally transparent, revealing the color below, or it only loses a percentage of its color or tone which mixes with the color underneath. Chlorophyll amounts can be controlled in harvest by removing as much N as possible at the end of flowering. Also removing K will help reveal the underlying color. Remember though that nutrient removal will also affect plant health and yields.

The way you grow your plant and what lights you use are just as important in revealing your breeding colors as breeding itself. Generally a flowering plant that has high levels of N in the medium during flowering time will not reveal much of your color work. In most cases flower color will develop from one shade to another so the breeder should take those variations into account. A black budded plant may start off with red or orange or even white

When breeding for color try to work with strains that have a propensity to display lots of various colors so that you have a large selection of hues and their respective combinations to choose from. By creating hybrids and then true breeding specific color traits you will be able to locate, mix and lock down traits for color expression. It is great to see some breeders produce plants with dark green/purple leaves and great big black buds. There are so many different color types out there; experiment a bit with different strains before you find a beauty you can work with.

A resin thick, high calyx to leaf ratio, Black Domina strain from Sensi Seeds. Photograph by Mikal.

Curing and Manicuring

Before curing begins we need to manicure our bud and after we have cured our bud we may further manicure it. Manicuring includes the separation of the leaf and the branch material from the stem while leaving the flowering clusters attached. The calyx to leaf ratio is important here because plants that have a higher calyx to leaf ratio require less manicuring per flowering cluster. If a plant has a 1:1 calyx/leaf ratio then there is at least one leaf per calyx to clip off, while a 5:1 would mean there is only one leaf per 5 calyxes to manicure. Also leaf size and petiole length are important here. It is far easier to remove larger leaves on long petioles than it is to remove smaller ones on short petioles. However, smaller leaves allow light to penetrate more bud regions underneath and generally shorter petioles of the leaves on the flowering clusters can develop lots of trichomes at the base of the leaf. To make manicuring easier and more rewarding, try to develop a strain with a higher calyx to leaf ratio.

Curing is the length of time it takes for your bud to dry properly, which is generally between one to four weeks. You may find that some strains cure better and quicker than other strains grown under similar conditions. This has to do with a combination of the following factors.

- cannabinoid content.   • bud density.

We will look at these factors later on. "Bag seed"* is a term used to describe seed that is found in street weed. Street weed tends to come from countries or growers that like a quick turnover in their produce and so their plants are bred for quicker drying and curing processes, not to mention ease of manicuring. Bag seed tends to have the following problems:

- hermaphrodite   • non-uniform in growth
- not very potent   • bred for outdoor performance only
- lacks resin content   • lacks vigor
- lacks flavor   • lacks quantity

But most bag seed does have the shortest curing times (the cultivators want a quick turnover), not to mention resistance to disease and pests. However the hermaphrodite nature of the plant makes it absolutely dangerous to include in any breeding project. This is very dependent on where the bag seed came from. If it came from an excellent specimen then the strain might be very good.

Different domesticated landrace strains from various countries cure better and quicker than others. Through experimentation you will be able to find strains that have different rates of curing. Most Indica and Sativa strains on the market today

---

* We are talking about imported brick weed here.

A spider mite pest attack has caused this plant to develop dark
hues and unhealthy leaves. Photograph by Kissie.

have a curing time between three and eight weeks. (For full information on harvesting and curing, see chapter 14 of *The Cannabis Grow Bible.*)

Disease Resistance (Including Pests)
By taking any population of plants and infecting them with a disease you may find that a good percentage of the plants fail while others can live through the crisis. By applying the 'Survival of the Fittest' from the theory of evolution we can select offspring that we think have resistance to specific diseases and pests. We can run cross tests to see if we can breed the trait true and thus create a population of plants that are good at fighting disease and pests. The more different diseases and pests we introduce to the resistant population the better our chances of creating a strain that is hardy in these conditions.

There are two ways that a plant can deal with pest attacks and disease:

• prevention   • recovery

How well plants deal with these is called resistance. Resistance does not mean that the plant can recover well or prevent further attacks. Resistance is the length of time that a plant can survive an attack and complete the grow cycle. Low resistance would mean that the plant failed to regenerate itself quickly (basically not replacing damage at a faster rate than that at which the damage is occurring) or live through the attack. Plants with a strong resistance to pest and disease attacks can help a grower who is nearing harvest time but has a pest/disease problem to deal with. If the plant is able to resist the attack it may complete its maturation and thus be harvested. Plants that have a low resistance to pest and disease attacks may fail before floral maturity is complete. In many growers' eyes it is better to have something at the end of harvest rather than nothing all. A plant may have a low resistance to an attack and the attack effects plant health and the final yields but at least it produces something rather than failing completely. Just because the plant is growing in less than optimal conditions because of a pest attack should not mean that the plant fails altogether. Breeders should try and adopt some resistance to common pest and disease attacks with their strains, especially if creating a strain for the outdoor market.

There are many different pests and diseases to deal with, but a very common pest attack problem such as spider mite infestation (which can reduce a plant to trash in a couple of days), might be a useful one to try for our breeding resistance project. By introducing spider mites to a crop at flowering time we will find out which plants last longer than others.

A single grasshopper causes no harm, but in greater numbers
they can quickly do massive damage to a crop.

Prevention involves a defense against pest attack. Resin and smell are both associated with pest defense. Some smells can attract unwanted pests while other
smells will repel certain pests. We may notice that in a flowering crop of hybrid
plants, pests are attracted to some of the hybrids and not others. The ones that
are left alone may have a smell or an aroma that repels the pests.* Resin also
helps to prevent insect attack because some insects find resin too sticky to inhabit. Also the insect may find the cannabinoid content of the resin unpleasant.

---

* At the same time the pests just might prefer the other plants so individual testing is important.

Recovery is the plant's ability to regenerate itself during and/or after a pest/disease attack. Some plants can recover more quickly than others. If leaves are removed because of pest/disease destruction then new leaves might be generated just as quickly.

Locusts are a very interesting pest because in small numbers they will not harm a plant very much. They may spend a few days working on one leaf or remove a number of leaves over a long period of time. The plants can deal with this and regenerate new leaves very quickly. But a swarm of locusts can reduce the plant to just stems, roots and branches in a few hours. There is a threshold level at which the plant can reproduce leaves as quickly as they have been removed. The stress, coupled with lack of energy (no leaves = no photosynthesis = no energy) can kill a plant quickly.

Mold and fungi can also be tested on strains that you want to breed resistance into. Mold and fungi thrive in hot, humid and aged air conditions. Fresh air in the open deals well with aged air problems but indoor grows may suffer from heat, humidity and air-conditioning problems and thus be more susceptible to mold and fungi. This also helps to curb mold problems in the curing process.

Floral Traits
This is such a large topic that we will deal with it separately in the following chapter.

Leaf Traits
Most pure species have very obvious leaf traits such as the low blade number/broad stubby Indica leaf trait and the high blade number/long thin Sativa leaf trait. These are the first elements of plant species identification that a breeder would look out for when determining the species type of a strain.

Observation of height, internodes, branching, flowering times and high type would also help in deducing the species type. Once you have seen the pure species types you will be able to identify other different pure species types again elsewhere. Cross species such as Mostly Indica or Mostly Sativa or Indica/Sativa can have leaves different from the traditional pure species leaf trait. Indica tends to be darker than Sativa but some Indica/Sativa crosses can result in dark Sativa leaves or pale Indica leaves. Sativa leaves can have anywhere between five and twelve blades on each leaf while Indica leaves do not usually go above six or seven. Cross-species types can produce Indica leaves with more than six blades per leaf and Sativa strains can be bred to produce five blades or less.

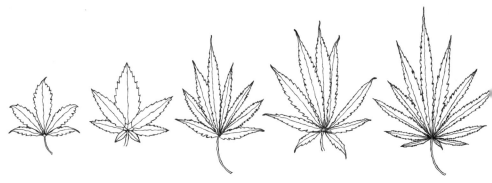

Leaf traits: Pure Indica, Mostly Indica, Indica/Sativa, Mostly Sativa and Pure Sativa.

There has been a lot of debate as to whether or not some leaf shapes can be passed down to future offspring. This is because cannabis observation in the past has uncovered some very strange leaf patterns and shapes produced through cross-species breeding projects. Most of the observations have been attributed to environmental factors influencing phenotypes, while other strange anomalies are thought to be the result of a mutation. (Remember the single-bladed leaf produced by some clones we discussed in chapter 17)

Environmental factors heavily influence the phenotype of cannabis leaves and sometimes it is hard, even under optimal growing conditions, to keep a plant's leaf trait very uniform. Some Mostly Indica species cannot help producing very dominant Sativa-shaped leaves around the top colas or even fan-type leaves very close to the top of the plant.

Whenever there is competition a healthy strong plant will try and outgrow the others to receive more light, producing strange leaf shapes and traits. A clone may produce single blade leaves for a couple of weeks in order to receive as much light as possible and sustain itself. This again amplifies the necessity of understanding that *the genotype is expressed in the phenotype, which is under the influence of the environment.*

When breeding for leaf traits it is best to observe the population very carefully and note the patterns of leaf growth and shape on every branch. You are trying to achieve uniformity but not at the expense of other characteristics. Because the leaf is the plant's primary tool for energy gathering it must be treated with extreme importance but never manipulated to the extent that it causes the plant to perform weakly in its intended environment. A large plant can survive with many thin Sativa leaves but never with only a few average sized or even large Indica-type leaves.

A healthy cannabis plant develops lateral branches with outstretched leaves that look as if they are enjoying the light, not too bushy, not too sparse, but even in distribution for optimal performance.

Everything in breeding is relative and you will be able to find this out for yourself when you experiment with leaf traits by creating hybrids between Sativa plants and Indica plants. Lots of variations will be present in the population and you will be able to see the different results in leaf traits via random mating without any selective breeding pressures.

Maturity (Including Flowering Times)

There are different levels of maturity that a plant will grow through and it will display different properties during each phase. The three main phases of maturity are:

- seedling maturity
- flowering maturity
- vegetative maturity

Although these phases are linear from seedling to flowering, you must remember that some strains can be rejuvenated and cloning is part of cannabis cultivation. Maturity is generally used to describe the end of a phase of growth and not the start of that phase although many growers do use the term "flowering maturity" to describe the action of calyx development. In truth flowering maturity occurs when the plant is ready for harvest. Here we will use maturity to describe the end of a phase of growth.

Seedling maturity is reached when secondary branching begins to develop. If you look at the branches on a seedling that have developed four or more leaves you may notice tiny leaves developing at the stem's node points (the start of lateral branching). This can take two to three weeks from when the seedling started to grow to occur under good growing conditions. As soon as you see these new leaves your plant is mature enough to start vegetative growth.

Vegetative maturity is reached when the nodes develop a calyx. Initial calyx development is an indication that the plant has reached vegetative maturity and is now ready to go into flowering.

Flowering maturity is reached when the flowers are fully developed and ready for harvest. Pollinated bud that is not sinsemilla should also be ready for collection.

Each of these phases is controlled by time and growing conditions. Under optimal growing conditions a very uniform strain should reach each point at equal times in the population, but plant gender will cause flowering growth and timing to be paced in their own respective ways. Male plants will grow a bit faster than the females and will in general pre-flower and flower more quickly than females. Note that clones carry the same age and maturity as the parent plant they came from and are never to be treated as plants without any maturity levels. A clone taken from a flowering mother can be flowered soon after the rooting period is over.

Different species and strains have different maturation times. Flowering maturity, seen in the ripeness of the buds, can take anywhere between four weeks and nine months depending on the strain type. Some Haze strains and Pure Sativa strains can take up to nine months to finish correctly. Other Indica plants may only take four to five weeks to complete. When breeding plants you will be able to control maturity times. If you want to keep the flowering times short in your strains then you need to introduce what is known as an "early" strain into the breeding project. "Late" strains are the opposite of this. Note, though, that late strains are also associated with an up cerebral high, while early strains provide more of a couch-lock type high. An Indica/Sativa plant should carry a mean of both high types and have a flowering time that would be roughly the mean of the Sativa and Indica parents.

In general the following flowering times are very common with regard to species type.

SPECIES TYPE	FLOWERING TIMES
Indica	5 to 8 weeks
Mostly Indica	7 to 9 weeks
Indica/Sativa	7 to 11 weeks
Mostly Sativa	9 to 14 weeks
Sativa	10 to 16 weeks or more

Breeders have noted that there is probably no specific gene for flowering times and that it is more than likely the result of a number of gene combinations. Figuring the mean between the parents' flowering times is the best way to guess flowering times in the offspring. If the offspring lean more in the direction of one parent's physiognomy, then it is quite likely that the flowering time will stray from the mean in that direction too. (For best results, refer to the expert harvest indication in chapter 14 of *The Cannabis Grow Bible*.)

Maturation is thus controlled by more than one gene and these genes influence maturity in conjunction with the environment, which will also have an effect on the expressed phenotypes of the maturation process. Obviously unstable offspring will show variations in maturation times.

Seed Characteristics

Seed characteristics are inherited. If you come across a very stable strain then you should find that any seeds created from two stable parents from the same strain will have the same seed shape and markings. The most common sizes are about 2-3mm in length but they can be as small as 0.5mm or as large as 5mm. Markings range from dark black to brown to light brown and even white. White seeds are usually a sign of immaturity but some white seeds actually are this color because it is a trait of the seed. Patterns range from stripes to spots to curved lines. The shape is very similar to that of apple seeds, but fatter and with a rougher texture. They also feel very dry. The more uniform your plants are the more uniform the seeds will be.

Shape

We already know that cannabis has a distinct shape and that different species of cannabis plants have their own unique cannabis features. Shape is also determined by environmental factors and the way you grow your plants. Shape is created as the result of a number of phenotypes combined. It should be clear to you by now that shape is the sum of your breeding attributes, so when you breed your plants keep in mind the individual characteristics—leaf size and number, branch length, internode lengths, height—that are going to add to the overall shape of your plant. Short squat plants will generally be more Indica influenced with lots of lateral branch growth. Single cola short plants will probably have a little Sativa in the mix, with longer internodes, less branch development and a higher concentration of bud growth on the main cola. High yielding plants will generally be taller with a mix of Indica and Sativa in the breed, which has average internode sizes; lots of branching with plenty of flowers while connoisseur Sativa bud will generally be derived from very tall Sativa plants with less than average yields, minimum branching but with quality resin production. How your strain will shape will depend on the environment you have selected the strain to grow in and the various cannabis traits that you manipulate. Almost any combination is possible..

Size

Size is determined by your growing conditions and strain type. Plants that have a gene for long internodes will in general grow very tall. Haze strains and any other Pure Sativa species are good examples of this. The length of the internodes can be controlled via breeding with plants that have shorter internodes. Skunk#1 has long internode development and these have been cut down in various Skunk#1 breeding projects like Sensi Skunk, Super Skunk and Mazar.

Bushy strains branch a lot. These bushy strains, such as Kush strains, push plenty of side branching outward without pruning. Kush strains do not grow very tall in general but can be bred with Sativa plants to gain extra height.

Stem thickness is also a trait that can be controlled by breeding. Some strains have thicker stems than others and can support a very tall plant with lots of branches. A good example of a strain with a very thick stem is Bubblegum from Serious Seeds. Some growers even say that stem thickness means larger colas. This is not completely true but does hold some water because stem thickness is a general characteristic of plants that produce high bud quantities.

Vigor

When we talk about vigor we are talking about the liveliness and activity of the plant. A good vigorous plant will flourish but only in an environment that meets its requirements.

The other aspect of vigor is in the plant's ability to adapt. Again, this is not important with uniform strains that are created to suit a specific environment but instead applies to hybrids that show variations in the population. Those variations will display various types of vigor when they try to adapt and compete in an environment.

Yield

Yield amounts are genetic and do have a threshold so it is up to you, the breeder, to get the most out of your strain before you can determine if a strain is high yielding or not. Growing conditions are of prime concern when trying to reach the plant's yield level. There is no evidence as of yet to suggest that calyx/leaf ratios, internodes, branch numbers or plant heights are genetically linked to final yield results although they are very important in reaching the maximum yield threshold. This can be seen in stable genetics that have heterozygous genotypes for yield. The variations in this sort of population will produce plants that are uniform in growth for all characteristics except yield. There is no other visible difference except for the overall yield quantities per plant.

This type of analysis clearly indicates to the breeder that yield is a genetic quantity but there is more than likely some unknown linkage to other genes that contribute to the yield's phenotype. Although all genes interact to some degree with one another to express the final phenotype coupled with environmental influences, a plant with a trait for high yield capabilities can pass this trait on. Yield is a trait that can be inherited.

Every trait can be altered through breeding to suit your environment. The key to breeding for these traits is to find suitable donor parents for each trait that you want to stabilize in your breeding project.

19 | ADVANCED FLORAL TRAITS

FLORAL TRAITS ARE BY THE FAR the most important aspect of any breeding project because this is exactly what the market is after. Some strains may look extremely ugly during vegetative growth but when they flower the plants show their true worth. Some Berry strains such as Blueberry are noted as not having the most beautiful stem development, branching or leaf traits but when it comes to producing buds and flowers they put on quite a display.

Overall floral traits are governed by their respective parts and those parts can be influenced by the breeder to create stunning results. We won't be focusing on staminate floral clusters of the male plant because these aren't really what growers want to see (although you can breed for these if you wish). Instead we will concentrate on the floral clusters of the female plants, the area that concerns breeders and growers the most.

STAGES OF FLORAL DEVELOPMENT

Floral traits develop in stages, from pre-flowering to maturity, and each stage may display many different attributes. The basic shape of the flowering cluster is determined by calyx numbers, the size of the pistils produced and how those pistil clusters develop.

The distance between calyx development and the number of calyxes per node region will also determine the density of the floral clusters. This distance is referred to as the "internodes flowering distance" because inside the bud cluster the main floral axis will have multiple branches on a very small scale. You will see these branches if you manicure your bud. Buds that are not closely packed are referred to as "airy." Pure Sativa plants tend to be more airy and

Look at the donkey ears on this top cola. Strain is American Dream by Sensi Seeds.

Indica plants tend to be dense, although a breeder can swap these traits. Carbon dioxide used in the grow room can also make buds more airy than usual so carbon dioxide + airy buds can equal extremely airy buds. Also keep in mind that a plant that needs to stretch to compete for light will increase length in its floral internodes.

BOG breeding nuggets so dense that the frost is falling off in chunks.
This strain is called 'Blue Moon Rocks' for that very reason.

"Donkey ears" may also turn up in strains that have dense floral clusters and long internodes. That trait can be seen where a main cola develops spikes of floral clusters at its top or sides that are almost like miniature colas. They develop toward the end of the flowering cycle and are very noticeable a few days before harvest. Donkey ears are generally a sign of a good yielding strain. Jack Herer is famous for producing lots of donkey ears.

Calyx development occurs throughout the flowering period but will stop short between a few days and two weeks before harvest. During this time the profiles of the floral clusters will approach their final shapes. Calyx size is another trait to watch. A mature calyx can sometimes be as big 1/4 of an inch and even less than 1mm in size. As the plant goes through flowering, calyx development will continue in clusters. Sometimes the calyx development can be so large and clustered that it pushes leaves aside. This is a good sign of a strain that has a high calyx/leaf ratio. Sometimes a low calyx/leaf ratio will produce very fat and large calyx sizes that compensate for the leafiness of the bud, but these strains are in low numbers. This trait is generally found in very psychoactive Mostly Sativa strains and Indica/Sativa strains. Some strains have even mutated to produce abnormal or fused calyx development. It must also be noted that not all calyxes may be viable and produce pistils. Some plants produce very few pistils and instead produce an abundance of resinous and trichomes-covered calyxes. Other plants may produce very few calyxes with lots of resinous pistils, but either type can also be devoid of the presence of trichomes or resin because of breeding (something we do not want).

TRICHOMES AND BREEDING FOR CANNABINOID LEVELS

The same rules apply to flowers in regard to color as those discussed in the previous chapter, only note that the flower must not be treated as a whole—each individual part has its own color attributes. The "adaxial" (facing towards the stem) and "abaxial" (facing away from the stem) flowering parts, including the petioles, have different color attributes that can be crossed and stabilized because they are hereditary traits.

Cannabinoid levels refer mainly to the amounts of THC in the flowers (there are many other cannabinoid types, but THC is the one we are primarily concerned with as breeders). It is known that cannabinoid levels are very intricate and can vary a great deal even within stable strains. It is also known that hybrid results between strains of different cannabinoid quantities and types will produce a mean between the two, but this mean will be open to fluctuation because of the non-uniformity of a hybrid strain. The problem with cannabinoid level is that it is controlled by different genes and each one of the genes needs to be locked down in order to produce a strain that is uniform in cannabinoid production. The biggest problem in selecting for high type is the introduction of the 'right' male for the job. Since this is technically a 'blind' approach in breeding you will only be able to select a proper male parent for this trait through trial and error, but more controllably through test crossing.

When we are breeding for floral traits we need to use a male in the process that contributes to the traits we are really looking to carry through in the offspring. Since this is a hit or miss type of breeding, careful observation of the offspring must be made in order to know if the male you selected is the one that you need. Remember that a strain that is homozygous for a trait you are trying to perpetuate will also have that homozygous trait in both the male and female plants. The key is to find the homozygous male for that trait. This can only be done properly in a test cross, so when you are breeding for floral traits, be prepared to undertake quite a number of test crosses in your breeding project. You cannot depend on male leaf smoke for testing results because of possible placebo effects and the fact that female is what we want to really test.

Breeder BOG bends a monster plant to reveal the fallen bud areas underneath. Those areas weigh a few ounces together. Top cola on the other end is about the size of an American football. In between the two ends is enough to keep you going for a long time. All from one plant. Optimal growth can be achieved by adopting the conditions set forth in *The Cannnabis Grow Bible*.

Obvious linked traits are taste and smell. These traits are not totally linked, but they do have much in common. A strain that smells skunky is going to taste skunky and a strain that smells fruity is going to taste fruity. What does change is the actual strength of each. We may have a very fruity smelling strain but the taste is masked by other traits in the bud's chemical constituents. You may have a great smelling strain that does not have any taste. The smell trait is produced by the **terpenoids** (any of a class of volatile aromatic hydrocarbons with the formula c10h16 and typically of isoprenoid structure, many of which occur in essential plant oils), which are located in the resin secreted by the trichomes. The actual aroma we smell is caused when resin comes in contact with the air as a result of trichome fissuring on the surface of a pistil or a calyx.

There are well over 100 terpenoids that we can now readily identify in most cannabis strains and there are probably many more. This means that we have virtually unlimited space for aroma and taste development in cannabis plants. This is an area of breeding that is also very specialized and absolutely subtle. You must have very keen senses of smell and taste to be able to work with these traits.

Trichomes also come in different types. They can be observed with a cheap 25x microscope, although stronger microscopes will give you better detail. The main type is the "glandular" trichome and this is subdivided down into "bulbous" tri-

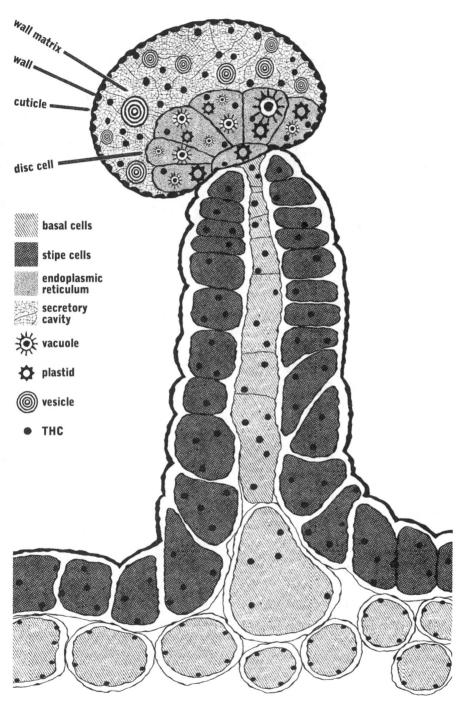

Anatomy of the cannabis trichome.

chomes, "capitate sessile" trichomes, "capitate stalked" trichomes and "simple" trichomes. Bulbous trichomes have a totally swollen look to them even at the start of their development. Capitate sessile trichomes do not appear to have a stalk but are rounded, extremely flat and closely clustered. Capitate stalked trichomes are the type most commonly found on cannabis plants. The trichome has three sections: the head, the stalk and the base. The effect is that of a rod with a bulb on the head, or as some might say, the mushroom look. Simple trichomes, which do not appear to have a head on the tip, generally do not produce much resin at all and are commonly found in low-resin-producing plants. There is a debate as to whether simple trichomes are in fact dysfunctional capitate stalked trichomes, but the trait can still be inherited and can produce good amounts of resin because resin production is not completely linked to trichome type and is a trait that can be bred through to future offspring. Trichome types can also be bred for vigor and strength, which is important for outdoor strains that may have to deal with harsh weather conditions. The flower may also terminate calyx development very early on. This type of termination is due to a trait that can be also be isolated by the breeder and bred much the same way we breed for flowering times. In general a mean is introduced between two strains that differ for this trait. Some strains like Afghani produce dense clusters of pistils that roll into balls as calyx development terminates. The remaining flowering time will concentrate mostly on resin production and pistil growth. The result is a rich content of resin being produced within the clusters. If a high resin production trait is not bred into this population then the remaining flowering time will just concentrate on pistil growth.

There are many theories as to why cannabis plants have trichomes and we can still only really guess why they are there. Probably the most obvious reason for trichome development is cannabinoid production. Man seems to enjoy the cannabis plant and has continued its propagation in many parts of the world, so man plays a major role in trichome development. Certainly mankind is an effective reason why the plant has kept producing trichomes and cannabinoids. Many insects and animals do not like cannabinoids. They find that the flowering female is too sticky to be near or the scent and taste puts them off—although there are still many other common insects and animals that thrive on cannabis. Cannabinoids appear to actually act as a good fungicide, preventing certain types of fungi and diseases from spreading too rapidly or occurring at all. A possible reason for cannabinoid development and trichomes can be found in the production of seeds. Even growers find it hard to remove the seeds from fresh bud without letting it dry out first, so trichomes offer a protective defense for the plant's seeds. Trichomes are also very suitable pollen catchers. Female cannabis has been known to catch pollen from males that exist over a mile away. In the final stages of flowering, trichomes tend to catch more on fabrics. Growers have often walked into their grow rooms only to walk away with little pieces of seeded bud stuck to the tail end of their sweaters. This suggests that animals can trek over long distances with seeds attached to their coats.

There are many variations in floral presentation and the combinations are far from limited. Floral traits are the final expression of the overall quality of a cannabis plant. By the manipulation of colors, types, textures, flowering times, calyx production, resin production, aroma and taste we can create amazing floral displays that have a bite as well.

We have covered an intermediate description of cannabis anatomy. If you would like an advanced description of cannabis anatomy, you might want to pursue the study of full plant anatomy and its classification systems in depth.

20 ADVANCED BREEDING PRINCIPLES

WE HAVE DISCUSSED WHAT PLANT BREEDING IS, a bit about the relationship of plant breeding to other sciences, Darwinian evolution and evolution under domestication. We have focused on the mating systems of plants and their respective modes of reproduction. Genotype, phenotype, and the environment have been discussed, along with inheritance and heritability. Molecular genetics has been discussed on the basic level. We have included genetic diversity in this material including the breeding of self-pollinated plants. We have discussed pedigree methods of breeding as in the case of IBL development and the creation of hybrid strains.

You may still be wondering how all of this fits together. If you are still having trouble understanding, this chapter should help you to make sense of it all. If you have grasped the concepts that you have learned so far then this section will help to improve that knowledge and also stimulate some ideas of your own.

Plant breeding has evolved because it can be a science and or an art or even both. It is also important because humans are dependent on plants. We need plants in order to survive. One of the principle goals of plant breeding is to increase yields for our consumption. The second goal of breeding is quality.

"Cultivar" is a term used to describe a cultivated variety of a crop. Most domestic cannabis plants are cultivars. "Biotechnology" is the combination of science and technology to make use of our facts about living systems for realistic applications.

We have not seen much of the effects of biotechnology on a cannabis cultivar yet but undoubtedly someone soon will say that they will do it or have done it. Maybe genetically modified cannabis exists already in the market but we do not know about.

Genetically modified cannabis has not appeared on the scene at this time of writing.

Advancing plant genetics is just one part of improving crop productivity but we know that other factors contribute to our overall productivity. These include:

- genotype
- pest management
- seed condition
- nutrition
- soil condition
- water

We also know that evolution may have caused changes in the hereditary characteristics of groups of organisms over the course of generations. Along with this we have seen the consequences of chance, coincidence, and chaos with regard to wild cannabis plant populations. Wild cannabis does not overrun the planet because:

- many plants are killed by predators;
- some plants are faster and more vigorous than cannabis.

The reproductive potential of cannabis is massive but the wild cannabis populations tend to remain steady in size because:

- cannabis populations suffer from high mortality in the wild;
- Wild individuals usually have variations within populations and this leads to unstable survival rates for some individuals in that population.

This should give you a clearer understanding of why and how species evolve and also how domestication has influenced the evolution of the cannabis plant.

FILIAL GENERATIONS

In breeding we use the following symbols to denote certain circumstances surrounding an offspring's appearance.

F = "filial." It designates the offspring of a cross.

F1 = the offspring result of the mating of two parent plants. F1 seed gives rise to F1 plants. These produce F2 seed, which creates F2 plants. These produce F3 seed, which gives rise to F3 plants, and so on.

F2:3 = an F3 line that was derived from an F2 line by a process of selection.

F4:5 = an F5 derived line in the F4 by a process of selection.

Let's recap what we've learned about inheritance and expand on it.

ADVANCED PRINCIPLES OF INHERITANCES

The chart below illustrates the Inheritance of two independent genes where YYBB = Large, Blue Bud and yybb = small, black bud.

	yb	yb
YB	YyBb	YyBb
YB	YyBb	YyBb

The genotypes of F1 are all heterozygous -> YyBb. Phenotypes of F1 are all Large and Blue Bud.

The F2:

	YB	Yb	yB	yb
YB	YYBB	YYBb	YyBB	YyBb
Yb	YYBb	YYbb	YyBb	Yybb
yB	YyBB	YyBb	yyBB	yyBb
yb	YyBb	Yybb	yyBb	yybb

In the F2 the genotypic results and ratios are 9 Large, Blue buds (1 - YYBB, 2 - YYBb, 2 - YyBB, 4- YyBb) : 3 Large, Black buds (1 - YYbb, 2 - Yybb) : 3 small, blue buds (1 - yyBB, 2 - yyBb) : 1 small, black bud (1 - yybb).

Gene interaction can also control the same character. A gene that masks the effects of another is said to be "epistatic" to the gene. Here are some types of gene interaction.

Complementary Genes

This occurs when a dominant allele is present at two different loci. Both gene Y and gene B must be present for expression.

	YB	Yb	yB	yb
YB	YYBB	YYBb	YyBB	YyBb
Yb	YYBb	YYbb	YyBb	Yybb
yB	YyBB	YyBb	yyBB	yyBb
yb	YyBb	Yybb	yyBb	yybb

The underlined combinations in this Punnet square convey this while the remainder do not. This F2 phenotypic ratio is 9:7.

Additive Genes

This situation occurs when the concentration of a character is amplified by the interaction of two genes.

	YB	Yb	yB	yb
YB	YYBB	YYBb	YyBB	YyBb
Yb	YYBb	(YYbb)	YyBb	(Yybb)
yB	YyBB	YyBb	(yyBB)	(yyBb)
yb	YyBb	(yYbb)	(yyBb)	+yybb+

The 9 underlined combinations have expressed this completely. The 6 combinations in brackets have partial expression of the trait. The homozygous recessive with + and + in-between it does not. The F2 phenotype ratio is 9: 6: 1.

Duplicate Genes

This occurs when 2 genes have the same expression.

	YB	Yb	yB	yb
YB	YYBB	YYBb	YyBB	YyBb
Yb	YYBb	YYbb	YyBb	Yybb
yB	YyBB	YyBb	yyBB	yyBb
yb	YyBb	yYbb	yyBb	yybb

The F2 have the same phenotype, except for the homozygous recessive, which does not express the gene. The F2 phenotype ratio is 15:1.

Suppressor Genes

These occur when a dominant gene's dominant expression is inhibited by another gene that is also dominant. For instance - Y dominates B.

	YB	Yb	yB	yb
YB	YYBB	YYBb	YyBB	YyBb
Yb	YYBb	YYbb	YyBb	Yybb
yB	YyBB	YyBb	yyBB	yyBb
yb	YyBb	yYbb	yyBb	+yybb+

12 underlined boxes show where Y is superior to B. In the homozygous recessive between the ++ indicators, B is also not expressed. There are 3 genotypes that allow B to be expressed. The F2 phenotype ratio is 13:3.

Dominant Epistasis

This occurs when Y dominates B and B is only expressed when no dominant Y allele is present.

	YB	Yb	yB	yb
YB	YYBB	YYBb	YyBB	YyBb
Yb	YYBb	YYbb	YyBb	Yybb
yB	YyBB	YyBb	yyBB	yyBb
yb	YyBb	yYbb	yyBb	+yybb+

Gene Y is expressed 12 times; 3 times gene B is expressed. The homozygous recessive in between the ++ does not express the gene. The F2 phenotype ratio is 12:3:1.

Modifying Genes

This occurs if gene Y dominates gene B, yet gene B intensifies expression of Y. Gene B also has no expression of the trait on its own.

	YB	Yb	yB	yb
YB	YYBB	YYBb	YyBB	YyBb
Yb	YYBb	(YYbb)	YyBb	(Yybb)
yB	YyBB	YyBb	yyBB	yyBb
yb	YyBb	(yYbb)	yyBb	yybb

9 of the underlined indicators express an exaggerated outcome of gene Y; 3 of the genes marked inside the brackets allow Y to be expressed but not as exaggerated. In the 4 remaining indicators Y is not expressed. The F2 phenotype ratio is 9:3:1.

Linked Genes

These occur when two or more genes in adjacent proximity on a chromosome cause a combining genotype.

CUBING

Cubing is a type of selective breeding that has gained some popularity among breeders but has disadvantages in that it does not selectively stabilize traits or make a strain more uniform in growth.* Cubing involves a certain amount of random mating and is used mainly to create desirable females or mothers plants in populations that are too small to be adequate for proper selections. Smaller breeding outfits will probably use cubing to find sought-after mother plants.

---

* Except by accident.

In the F1 offspring all the pollen from the males are extracted and put into one container. All of the male pollen is then used in a backcross with the mother plant to produce the first backcross progeny. In the offspring you should find a good clone mother or in future offspring by repeating this methodology - cubing. The problem is that the male that contributes to this clone mother female is unknown and so the process can not be repeated. The procedure is as follows:

In the F1 select a female that is desirable and backcross this female with her farther to create the offspring. Collect all the pollen from the males in this offspring and use all of this pollen to pollinate the mother plant that contributed to this offspring. Grow out the offspring and keep repeating the process until a very desirable female is found.

Obviously cubing is not really breeding and anything that you hear about cubing being able to stabilize traits is false (it can happen that a trait is stabilized, or a number of traits are stabilized, through cubing, but this occurs by accident and is not selective breeding). Cubing is just a way to generate mother plants in small populations.

A myth has been going around that cubing can create male parents for popular clones that do not have a male version. This is false and is just a sales gimmick. Cubing does not create males from a popular clone nor can cubing be used to create a standard seed format strain that is somewhat like 75% to 90% of the popular clone. It simply doesn't do that.

21 | CANNABIS PHOTOSYNTHESI CHEMISTRY

TWO TYPES OF CHLOROPHYLL ARE FOUND in plants - chlorophyll 'a' and chlorophyll 'b'.

In the chloroplast both types work with integral membrane proteins. Due to the chemical arrangement of chlorophyll, and how it is bonded, a special property is created that allows light to be absorbed at the molecular level.

Because a plant is green from chlorophyll does not mean that it absorbs green light!

If you grow a plant under a green bulb the plant will reflect all the green light. Plants are not very interested in green light and that is why they appear green to our eyes because they are *reflecting green light!*

Chlorophyll is a magnesium-containing green pigment. When we cure bud we attempt to get rid off chlorophyll. The reason for this is that magnesium burns the throat when hot. This is why poorly cured bud tastes harsh. Some growers choose to flush their plants of nutrients at least a week before harvest. The idea here is that it prevents the plants from creating anymore chlorophyll so that the bud will cure quicker. The side effect of flushing is less bud quantities because the plant is growing in less than optimal conditions before harvest.

Photosynthesis is a process in plants by which carbon dioxide is converted into organic compounds using the energy in light absorbed by the chlorophyll. It is essentially any photochemical synthesis of a chemical compound. CO_2 generators are very helpful in breeding labs.

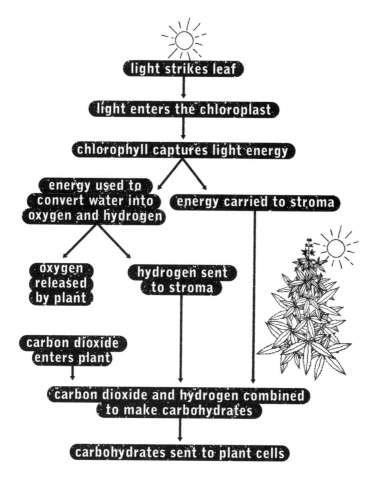

The plant photosynthesis flow chart

It is important for us to understand the basics of photosynthesis because it is at the heart of the cannabis plant's energy system. Green plants have the necessary ability to bio-chemically *make up* complex substances within themselves for themselves. This process is known as photosynthesis.

THE PROCESS OF PHOTOSYNTHESIS

Photosynthesis means *'combining with light'*. Photosynthesis is a "reactant - product" process which occurs wherever chlorophyll is found in the plant, which is mostly in the leaves. The symbolic equation for photosynthesis is:

$6\ CO_2 + 6\ H_2O$ - sunlight & chlorophyll - $C_6H_{12}O_6 + 6\ O_2$

If there is no light then there is no photosynthesis. At night plants cease photosynthesis. If there is not enough nutrients then chlorophyll will not be produced by the plant and photosynthesis will cease. Temperatures are also important for photosynthesis. If the temperatures go out of the normal range for good cannabis plant health then photosynthesis will slow down or even stop. (See chapter 6 of *The Cannabis Grow Bible* for a more detailed discussion.)

Cannabis does not need a dark period for photosynthesising—although other types of plants do. Cannabis will photosynthesise without problems under the 24/0 or 18/6 vegetative photoperiods.

22 | SCIENTIFIC CLASSIFICATION OF CANNABIS

THE CHART BELOW SHOWS THE STANDARD template for cannabis that we find in many botany books, although there may be some deviations from these standards.

KINGDOM: PLANTAE (PLANTS)
SUBKINGDOM: TRACHEOBIONTA – VASCULAR
SUPERDIVISION: SPERMATOPHYTA - SEED
DIVISION: MAGNOLIOPHYTA - FLOWERING
CLASS: MAGNOLIOPSIDA – DICOTYLEDONS
SUBCLASS: HAMAMELIDAE
ORDER: URTICALES
FAMILY: CANNABACEAE (HEMP or sometimes called MORACEAE)
SCIENTIFIC NAME: CANNABIS SATIVA
AUTHORITY: L.

BASICS OF CANNABINOIDS

Cannabis contains more than 400 active chemicals. When these chemicals are vaporized or ignited they can create over 2,000 chemicals. It would be beyond the scope of this book to go into detail about every cannabinoid and the other active chemicals found in cannabis, but in the meantime let's look at the more commonly known types of cannabinoids and chemicals found in cannabis.

Cannabis contains what is known as "isometric tetrahydrocannabinol." Cannabis also contains cannabiols and cannabidiols. Most of these types of compounds can produce psychoactive effects.

The cannabis plant is the only known plant on that planet that produces cannabinoids.

Non-cannabinoid precursor

CBG
(cannabigerol)

CBD
(cannabidiol)

THC
(tetrahydro-cannabinol)

CBN
(cannabinol)

Light strikes leaf
Cannabinoid receptor binding molecules

THC
(tetrahydro-cannabinol)

CP 55940

Anandamide

Cannabinoids and their respective molecular structures and processes.

THC, or *delta-9 tetrahydrocannabinol,* is the most important psychoactive chemical in cannabis. It can range in content anywhere between 0.1% and 30%. Unusual samples taken have recorded above 50% but these are more than likely rare variations in a large population. The trait for the 50% THC is undoubtedly unstable in the wild and cannot be attributed to the myth of cannabis being stronger than it used to be that is being put forward today by many politicians and anti-cannabis campaigners. The most potent strains of today are still the same potent strains that were available in the '70s. Any seed bank that sells potent strains knows that the most potent strains are the Haze strains, which have been around for decades

Cultivated industrial hemp has less than 0.3% THC. Most commercial varieties contain between 9% and 25% THC. As mentioned, wild cannabis plants can go as high as the 50% mark. Good cannabinoid research is still somewhat stifled because of cannabis laws and political bureaucracy.

THE MAJOR CANNABINOID LIST

The cannabis high type is mostly due to delta-9 tetrahydrocannabinol. Delta-9 THC can make up anywhere between 40% and 100% of the psychoactive effect of using cannabis. In some not very potent strains this percentage can go as low as 1%.

Delta-8 tetrahydrocannabinol is another psychoactive ingredient found in cannabis but it comes in much lower doses. It is not thought to be as psychoactive as delta-9 THC.

Normally when chemists, cannabis growers and users refer to THC they are actually referring to both delta-9 THC and delta-8 THC.

CBD is also known as cannabidiol. CBD is found in nearly all psychoactive cannabis strains. It can be present in very small or very large doses. CBD is not thought to be psychoactive on its own, but when mixed with THC it may affect and change the high type depending on the ratio of THC to CBD. CBD contributes to the onset and duration of the high type, although its effects are less substantial than was previously thought.

CBN, or cannabinol, occurs during the breakdown of THC in the curing process. CBN is psychoactive but is considered to be less than 1/5 the strength of THC. CBN may also contribute to the high type depending on its ratios to THC and CBD.

CBC, or cannabichromene, is found in similar low doses to those of CBD and CBN. It may also contribute to high type but is considered to be non-psychoactive. It is believed to be a precursor to THC.

CBG, or cannabigerol, is thought to be non-psychoactive. It is also believed to be a precursor to THC.

THCV, or tetrahydrocannabivarin, is psychoactive but the onset is quick and the duration is short. It is related to THC and is termed a "propyl cannabinoid." CBD and CBN also have their own propyl cannabinoids. These are CBDV and CBV respectively.

In total there are roughly 66 known cannabinoids from 10 groups and some miscellaneous ones. Each of the 10 groups has some variations. This is still an area of study under investigation so many things that we know about cannabinoids are subject to change.

Cannabinoid Categorization	Common Acronym	Number of Variations in Each Category
9-tetrahydrocannabinol	Δ9-THC	9
8-tetrahydrocannabinol	Δ8-THC	2
cannabidiol	CBD	7
cannabinol	CBN	3
cannabichromene	CBC	5
cannabielsoin	CBE	5
cannabigerol	CBG	6
cannabinidiol	CBND	2
cannabicyclol	CBL	3
cannabitriol	CBT	9
miscellaneous types		11
TOTAL		66

CANNABINOID RECEPTORS

In the '60s and '70s cannabis researchers hypothesized that THC and other cannabinoids work on the brain by targeting exclusive chemical receptors. This hypothesis suggested that cannabinoids belonged to a unique set of molecules that worked across the membranes of cells without disturbing them using a receptor system.

In 1984 it was discovered that synthetic THC inhibited adenylate cyclase (this enzyme occurs in plasma cell membranes) in nerve cells and these chemicals were involved in brain receptor operations. Research continued and in 1988 scientists found that cannabinoid receptors did indeed exist and that these receptors have a direct relationship to cannabinoids. In 1990 the receptors were located by using a "G-protein inhibitory second messenger" technique. A synthetic cannabinoid called CP55940 was found to bind to a receptor called CB1. Scientists hypothesized that the brain must produce its own types of "endogenous cannabinoids" and one was indeed discovered in 1992 and shortly after named "anandamine". Next scientists found cannabinoid receptors in the immune system. This means that cannabinoids are also immunomodulators. This receptor became known as CB2. Both CB1 and CB2 have developed in the human body as a process of our evolution in symbiosis with the cannabis plant. There is a still a lot of work to be done but these receptors suggest what old hippies have been telling the world for years: cannabis is natural and has many natural properties.

23 | FLOWERING CONCEPTS AND CALYX DEVELOPMENT

OVER THE YEARS MANY GROWERS AND BREEDERS have found that force flowering can be somewhat troublesome. The term *force flowering* is used to suggest that the cannabis plant will flower when the 12/12 photoperiod is introduced. This notion is erroneous for a number of reasons and we will endeavor to set the record straight here.

Many growers and breeders have approached me with questions about force flowering. The most common complaint is: "I have switched to 12/12 but have not seen any flowers after 4 weeks. What's wrong?"

Although this may be a problem with light leakage during the 12/12 photoperiod, in most cases it is not and has to do with the grower's inability to effectively understand cannabis flowering. *The Cannabis Grow Bible* goes into some depth to explain calyx development, but many growers are still using old flawed concepts when trying to get their plants to flower, so we will expand on this issue a bit here. In the early '80s and '90s a string of grow books and magazines told growers that by switching to the 12/12 photoperiod they would induce flowering. This is only partially correct. In order for a plant to respond to the 12/12 photoperiod, it must be sufficiently sexually mature.

A plant's sexual maturity occurs one to two weeks before initial calyx development appears at the nodes. This initial calyx development is not photoperiod initiated. It is initiated by plant maturity, which has a lot to do with the plant's hormones and age, and the growing environment.

As a grower you should wait for calyx development to show before initiating the

12/12 photoperiod and even then you can still continue the vegetative cycle for longer by keeping the 24/0 or 16/8 photoperiod, depending on which vegetative photoperiod you choose. Once calyx development has appeared under the vegetative photoperiod, you can trigger flowering by commencing 12/12. It really is that simple. Initial calyx development is by far the best way to gauge maturity and readiness to flower.

Force flowering is a concept derived from clone growers. Again, since clones carry the same age as the parent plant they where taken from, they are also more sexually mature than they look. After rooting, clones should be put into vegetative growth for a few weeks depending on how much vegetative growth you need. Whether the clone was taken from a flowering female or a female in vegetative growth determines how long it should take for the clone to flower. Usually clone growers refer to inducing flowering in clones as force flowering. This simply means stopping vegetative growth by triggering flowering with the 12/12 photoperiod. Clones that are taken very early on, before the parent plant's flowering, must undergo a few weeks of growth before they are sexually mature enough to flower themselves; however, when factoring rooting time and vegetative growth into the equation we soon find that clones are nearly always sexually mature by the time the clone grower wants to flower.

Another procedure of interest that has generated false notions about force flowering comes from images of flowering plants that appear only a few inches high. This has led many to believe that the plant is a seedling that has been flowered early using the 12/12 photoperiod, when in truth what we are seeing is just a clone taken from a flowering mother that has been rooted and rejuvenated for a few days before flowering was triggered again. The result is like a cola of bud on a short stick.

Another reason why force flowering is misunderstood is that growers sometimes switch to the 12/12 photoperiod a week before initial calyx development occurs. During this time the plant may naturally produce initial calyx development that is not related to the photoperiod change but plant maturity. However because the 12/12 photoperiod is present in the growing environment the plant will start flowering shortly after calyx development. Thus the grower has mistaken calyx development and flowering as a response to the photoperiod when in fact the calyx development was a natural development unrelated to the photoperiod change, though the flowering after calyx development was.

Force flowering does have some effects on certain strains during the vegetative period but good growers and breeders will generally not employ it because of adverse effects it has on gender development. It also can lead to sexual dysfunctions. Usually the early 12/12 photoperiod stresses the strain into a hormone-related activity that promotes flowering to occur. In most cases this leads to the early flowering of hermaphrodites and is very strain dependent. For this reason most growers simply wait until calyxes show before flowering their plants. To understand more about the photoperiod and flowering we should take a close look at phytochrome and photoperiodism.

PHYTOCHROME

Phytochrome is a family of proteins with a small covalently-bound pigment molecule. It is a blue-green compound that has two forms that are interconvertible by the absorption of light, and which regulates many aspects of development in cannabis according to the nature and timing of the light it absorbs. Light regulates plant growth and development and is important for photosynthesis. There are two light-sensitive mechanisms involved in this process.

Blue light response mechanisms are generally not flowering related. Blue light response mechanisms include phototropism, chlorophyll synthesis and stomatal opening. Red light response mechanisms, including flowering, leaf senescence and chloroplast development.

PHOTOPERIODISM IN CANNABIS

If the photoperiod is interrupted during the flowering period it can inhibit cannabis flowering. If the flowering photoperiod is commenced before sexual maturity then phytochrome may react in two ways. It may simply not do anything and we must wait until the plant is sexually mature before it has an effect, or it may force the plant into a crisis flowering situation which usually leads to early flowering and hermaphrodites.

The best approach to flowering is to always pay attention to calyx development. 100% of growers who wait for calyx development until they start flowering will see flowering within the first week of switching to 12/12. Growers who try to flower their plants before calyx development generally find the following problems:

- They wait weeks for flowering to occur.
- They find hermaphrodites.
- They have problems gauging the correct harvest time.

Some growers start counting the harvest time from the moment they switch to

12/12. If they switch to 12/12 before calyx development occurs, then chances are they will harvest early if they are going by the breeder's recommended flowering times. The best way to count the flowering time is after calyx development has occurred. Then when you switch to 12/12 you can start counting down to harvest time with a better likelihood of meeting the breeder's recommended flowering times. Still the best harvest indicators are the professional expert harvest indicators outlined in *The Cannabis Grow Bible.*

| RESOURCES

CANNABIS WEBSITES
http://www.hightimes.com -- High Times Magazine
http://www.marijuananews.com -- Marijuana News and Legal Information
http: //www.cannabistimes.com -- Cannabis Times Newspaper
http://www.cannabis.com -- General Cannabis Information Website
http://www.yahooka.com -- General Cannabis Information Website
http://www.cannabisculture.com -- Cannabis Culture Magazine
http://www.overgrow.com -- Cannabis Growing Website
http://www.cannabisworld.com -- Cannabis Growing Website
http://www.cannabishealth.com -- Cannabis Health Website
http://www.erowid.org -- Drug Information Website
http://www.lycaeum.org -- Drug Information Website
http ://www.icmag.com - Cannabis Growing Magazine
http://www.newlines.nl - Cannabis Cloning Organization
http://www.planetganja.com - Cannabis Cultivation Community

HASH AND PROCESSING
http://www.bubblebag.com
http://www.pollinator.nl
http://www.mixnball.com

HYDROPONICS AND LIGHTING
http://www.hydroponics101.com -- Hydroponics Shop Locator USA
http://www.hydroponic-shop.com -- Greenfields Hydroponics UK
http://www.greenthings.co.uk -- Green Things Hydroponics UK
http://www.allamericanhydro.com -- Online reseller Michigan USA

http://www.bchydroponics.com -- BC Canada
http://www.blunt.co.uk -- Esoteric Hydroponics, Surrey UK
http://www.hydrogrowth.co.uk -- Hydrogrowth Wigan UK
http://www.hydroponics.com -- Ontario Canada
http://www.hydromall.com -- Worldwide Store Search (Over 500 entries)

MEDICAL CANNABIS INFORMATION

Now that you are able to grow your own medicine why not join up with the International Association for Cannabis as Medicine (IACM). They can be contacted at the following address below.

Arnimstrasse 1A
50825 Cologne
Germany
Phone: +49-221-9543 9229
Fax: +49-221-1300591
E-mail: info@cannabis-med.org
Website: http://www.cannabis-med.org

The members of the board of directors is composed of eight medical doctors. Ask them to send you information on medical cannabis and they will invite you to become a member of the International Association for Cannabis as Medicine. This is an excellent resource for updates on medical cannabis information which includes a publication called the Journal of Cannabis Therapeutics.

SEEDBANKS

http://www.geocities.com/stonedas72/AussieSPC.html -- Australian Seeds
http://www.africanseeds.com -- African Seeds Canada and Europe (Breeders)
http://www.hempdepot.ca -- Hemp Depot Canada
http://www.hempqc.com -- Heaven's Stairway Canada
http://www.eurohemp.com -- Heaven's Stairway UK
http://www.hemcy.com -- Hemcy Seeds Holland
http://www.legendsseeds.com -- Legends Canada
http://www.emeryseeds.com -- Marc Emery Direct Marijuana Seeds Canada
http://www.peakseeds.com -- Peak Seeds Canada
http://www.seedsdirect.to -- Seeds Direct UK
http://www.worldwideseeds.com -- World Wide Seeds Switzerland
http://www.sensiseeds.com -- Sensi Seed Bank (Breeders)
http://www.cannabisworld.com/cgi000/auction.cgi -- Seed Auction Worldwide

http://www.greenhouse.org -- Green House Seeds Amsterdam (Breeders)
http://www.dutch-passion.nl -- Dutch Passion Seeds Amsterdam (Breeders)
http://www.seriousseeds.com -- Serious Seeds Amsterdam (Breeders)
http://www.flyingdutchmen.com -- The Flying Dutchmen Seeds (Breeders)
http://www.homegrownfantasy.com -- Homegrown Fantasy (Breeders)
http://www.kcbrains.com -- KC Brains Amsterdam (Breeders)

VAPORIZERS
http://www.xijix.com -- Digital Herbal Vaporizers
http://www.plasticsmithbc.com -- The BC Vaporizer
http://www.vaportechco.com -- Vapor Tech Vaporizer
http://www.vriptech.com -- Vriptech Vaporizer

CANNABISBOOK.COM
http://www.cannabisbook.com
Feel free to contact us...

The Grow Forums
The Greg Green cannabis grow forums can be found at
http://www.cannabisbook.com/forums

Register a username and feel free to chat with other growers and ask cultivation
questions. Also has an image gallery section.

Contacting Greg Green
Greg is unusual because he is a very busy stoner, but will try to respond to your
emails. If you have any cultivation questions or information that you would like
to share with Greg please contact him at greg@cannabisbook.com

Book Submissions
Submissions for the book should be made to book@cannabisbook.com
Please learn about our photography requirements at the web site below.
http://www.cannabisbook.com/photography.htm

We look forward to hearing from you!

++ GLOSSARY OF TERMS

A

ABAXIAL: Facing away from the axis of an organ or organism; "the abaxial surface of a leaf is the underside or side facing away from the stem".

ADAPTATION: An alteration or adjustment in structure or habits, often hereditary, by which a species or individual improves its condition in relationship to its environment.

ADVENTITIOUS ROOT: Roots growing in an unusual location e.g. from a stem. Of or belonging to a root structure that develops in an unusual place on the plant.

AERATION: To supply with air or expose to the circulation of air. To aerate the growing medium.

AEROPONICS: A technique for growing plants without soil or hydroponic media. The plants are held above a system that constantly mists the roots with nutrient-laden water. Also called aeroculture.

ALLELE: One member of a pair or series of genes that occupy a specific position on a specific chromosome.

ANEUPLOID: Having a chromosome number that is not a multiple of the haploid number for the species.

ANNUAL: Living or growing for only one year or season.

ANTHER: The pollen-bearing part of the stamen.

ANTHOCYANIN: Any of various water-soluble pigments that impart to flowers and other plant parts colors ranging from violet and blue to most shades of red.

APHID: Any of various small, soft-bodied insects of the family Aphididae that have mouthparts specially adapted for piercing and feed by sucking sap from plants. Also called plant louse.

APICAL DOMINANCE: Inhibition of the growth of lateral buds by the terminal bud of a plant shoot.

ASEXUAL REPRODUCTION: Relating to, produced by, or involving reproduction that occurs without the union of male and female gametes, as in cloning and tissue culture.

AUTOFLOWERING: A plant that flowers only according to plant maturity and is not flowering photoperiod responsive.

AUTOSOME: A chromosome that is not a sex chromosome.

AUXIN: Any of several plant hormones that regulate various functions, including cell elongation.

AXIAL: Located on, around, or in the direction of an axis.

B

BACKCROSS: To cross (a hybrid) with one of its parents or with an individual genetically identical to one of its parents.

BRACT: A leaflike or scalelike plant part, usually small, sometimes showy or brightly colored, and located just below a flower, a flower stalk, or an inflorescence.

C

CALYX: The sepals of a flower considered as a group.

CANNABINOID: Any of various organic substances, such as THC, found in cannabis.

CANNABIS INDICA: A cannabis of a variety noted by its short squat traits and shorter flowering period. It has a more physical, body stone, type of effect.

CANNABIS RUDERALIS: A cannabis of a variety noted for its autoflowering properties.

CANNABIS SATIVA: A cannabis of a variety noted by its long broad traits and longer flowering period. It has a more head high type of effect and is less physical.

CAPITATE STALKED TRICHOME: The most common type of trichome, typically mushroom shaped and somewhat long.

CARBON DIOXIDE: A colorless, odorless, incombustible gas, CO_2, formed during respiration, combustion, and organic decomposition and used in food refrigeration, carbonated beverages, inert atmospheres, fire extinguishers, and aerosols. Also called carbonic acid gas.

CAROTENOID: Any of a class of yellow to red pigments, including the carotenes and the xanthophylls.

CELL: The smallest structural unit of an organism that is capable of independent functioning, consisting of one or more nuclei, cytoplasm, and various organelles, all surrounded by a semipermeable cell membrane.

CHLOROPHYLL: the green photosynthetic coloring matter of plants found in chloroplasts and made up chiefly of a blue-black ester $C_{55}H_{72}MgN_4O_5$ and a dark green ester $C_{55}H_{70}MgN_4O_6$ called also respectively chlorophyll a, chlorophyll b.

CHLOROSIS: The yellowing or whitening of normally green plant tissue because of a decreased amount of chlorophyll, often as a result of disease or nutrient deficiency.

CHROMOSOME: A threadlike linear strand of DNA and associated proteins in the nucleus of eukaryotic cells that carries the genes and functions in the transmission of hereditary information.

CLONE: An asexually propagated living organism. A clone is different from a cutting because it has a root mass.

COLCHICINE: A poisonous, pale-yellow alkaloid, $C_{22}H_{25}NO_6$, obtained from the autumn crocus and used in plant breeding to induce chromosome doubling.

COTYLEDON: A leaf of the embryo of a seed plant, which upon germination either remains in the seed or emerges, enlarges, and becomes green. Also called seed leaf.

CROSS-POLLINATE: To pollinate (a flower) by means of cross-pollination.

CUBING: Selective, but random, mating of a female by using all of her off-spring's pollen in a backcrossing operation to produce a population of off-spring for further breeding selection.

CULTIVAR: A race or variety of a plant that has been created or selected intentionally and maintained through cultivation.

CURING: To prepare, preserve, or finish (a substance) by a chemical or physical process.

CUTTING: To remove a branch with leaves from the plant using a blade to be later transplanted and grown into a clone. Cuttings do not have roots. Cutting that have grown a new root mass are called clones.

CYTOKININ: Any of a class of plant hormones that promote cell division and growth and delay the senescence of leaves.

D

DIOECIOUS: Having the male and female reproductive organs borne on separate individuals of the same species. Characterized by species in which the male and female reproductive organs occur on different individuals; sexually distinct.

DIPLOID: Having a pair of each type of chromosome, so that the basic chromosome number is doubled: diploid somatic cells.

DOMINANT: Of, relating to, or being an allele that produces the same phenotypic effect whether inherited with a homozygous or heterozygous allele.

E

ELONGATE: To make or grow longer.

ENZYME: Any of numerous proteins or conjugated proteins produced by living organisms and functioning as biochemical catalysts.

EPISTASIS: An interaction between nonallelic genes, especially an interaction in which one gene suppresses the expression of another.

EVOLUTION: Change in the genetic composition of a population during successive generations, as a result of natural selection acting on the genetic variation among individuals, and resulting in the development of new species. The historical development of a related group of organisms; phylogeny.

F

FATHER: Any male donor in a breeding project or a specific male that contributes to the mother plant to produce a stable population of offspring.

FILIAL: Of or relating to a generation or the sequence of generations following the parental generation; Filial Generation 1 = F1, Filial Generation 2 = F2.

FITNESS: The extent to which an organism is adapted to or able to produce offspring in a particular environment.

FLOWERING: The final stage of plant growth where the plant develops its sexual organs for reproduction.

FUNGICIDE: A chemical substance that destroys or inhibits the growth of fungi.

FUNGUS: Any of numerous eukaryotic organisms of the kingdom Fungi, which lack chlorophyll and vascular tissue and range in form from a single cell to a body mass of branched filamentous hyphae that often produce specialized fruiting bodies. The kingdom includes the yeasts, molds, smuts, and mushrooms.

G

GAMETE: A reproductive cell having the haploid number of chromosomes, especially a mature sperm or egg capable of fusing with a gamete of the opposite sex to produce the fertilized egg.

GENE: A hereditary unit consisting of a sequence of DNA that occupies a specific location on a chromosome and determines a particular characteristic in an organism. Genes undergo mutation when their DNA sequence changes.

GENOTYPE: The genetic makeup, as distinguished from the physical appearance, of an organism or a group of organisms. The combination of alleles located on homologous chromosomes that determines a specific characteristic or trait.

GENUS: A taxonomic category ranking below a family and above a species and generally consisting of a group of species exhibiting similar characteristics. In taxonomic nomenclature the genus name is used, either alone or followed by a Latin adjective or epithet, to form the name of a species.

GIBBERELLIN: Any of several plant hormones, such as gibberellic acid, used to promote stem elongation.

H
HEMP: Cannabis. The tough, coarse fiber of the cannabis plant, used to make cordage. Any of various plants similar to cannabis, especially one yielding a similar fiber. The fiber of such a plant.

HERMAPHRODITE: An animal or plant exhibiting hermaphroditism.

HERMAPHRODITISM/HERMAPHRODISM: An anomalous condition in humans and animals in which both male and female reproductive organs and secondary sexual characteristics are present in the same individual.

HETEROSIS: A marked vigor or capacity for growth that is often shown by crossbred animals or plants called also hybrid vigor.

HETEROZYGOUS: Having different alleles at one or more corresponding chromosomal loci. Of or relating to a heterozygote.

HID: High Intensity Discharge (lighting)

HPS: High Pressure Sodium (HID bulb in red spectrum for flowering)

HOMOGENEOUS/HOMOZYGOUS: Having the same alleles at a particular gene locus on homologous chromosomes.

HORMONE: A synthetic compound, or naturally produced similar substances found in plants and that regulate their development.

HUMIDITY: The amount of water vapour in the environment.

HYBRID: The offspring of genetically dissimilar parents or stock, especially the offspring produced by breeding plants or animals of different varieties, species, or races.

HYBRID VIGOUR: See Heterosis

I

IBL: Abbreviation for In Bred Line and refers to a strain that is stable for the vast majority of its traits and will breed true in the offspring.

INBREEDING: To breed by the continued mating of closely related individuals, especially to preserve desirable traits in a stock. To breed or develop within; engender.

INCANDESCENT: A kind of bulb in which the light is produced by a thin filament of conducting material, usually carbon.

INSECTICIDE: A chemical substance used to kill insects.

INTERNODE: A section or part between two node regions. Also called the Internode distance.

L

LADYBETTLE/LADYBIRD/LADYBUG: Any of numerous small, rounded, usually brightly colored beetles of the family Coccinellidae, often reddish with black spots and feeding primarily on insect pests, such as scale insects and aphids.

LANDRACE: A population of plants, commonly found in the wild, with some manmade influences suggesting cultivation in its lineage, even though it may now grow wild.

LIFE-CYCLE: The stages of the plant's natural growth from start to finish.

LIGHT-MOVER: An electrical motor that allows movement of a HID light, typically in a circular motion. Also called a Light-Rail.

LINKAGE: An association between two or more genes such that the traits they control tend to be inherited together.

LOCI: The plural of Locus.

LOCUS: The position that a given gene occupies on a chromosome.

M
MANICURING: To clip undesirable parts of the plant for either drying or curing.

MATURITY: A plant reaches maturity when it is capable of displaying it sex.

MEIOSIS: The process of cell division in sexually reproducing organisms that reduces the number of chromosomes in reproductive cells from diploid to haploid, leading to the production of gametes in plants.

MERISTEM: The undifferentiated plant tissue from which new cells are formed, as that at the tip of a stem or root.

MH: Metal Halide (HID bulb in blue spectrum for vegetative growth)

MITOSIS: The process in cell division by which the nucleus divides, typically consisting of four stages, prophase, metaphase, anaphase, and telophase, and normally resulting in two new nuclei, each of which contains a complete copy of the parental chromosomes. Also called karyokinesis.

MONOECIOUS: Having unisexual reproductive organs or flowers, with the organs or flowers of both sexes borne on a single plant, as in corn and pines. Relating to or exhibiting hermaphroditism.

MOTHER: Any female donor in a breeding project or a specific female that produces a stable population of offspring with the right male.

MUTATION: A change of the DNA sequence within a gene or chromosome of an organism resulting in the creation of a new character or trait not found in the parental type. The process by which such a change occurs in a chromosome, either through an alteration in the nucleotide sequence of the DNA coding for a gene or through a change in the physical arrangement of a chromosome.

N

NECROSIS: Death of cells or tissues through injury or disease.

NODE: The point on a stem or a branch, where a leaf or branch is attached or has been attached. The region where a leaf is joined to a petiole or where the petiole is joined to a branch, or where a branch meets the stem.

NUTRIENT: A source of nourishment, especially nourishing substances. Minerals used for plant food.

O

OFFSPRING: See Progeny

ORGANELLE: A differentiated structure within a cell, such as a mitochondrion, vacuole, or chloroplast, that performs a specific function.

ORGANIC: Of, relating to, or derived from living organism.

OUTBREEDING: The interbreeding of individuals or strains that are relatively unrelated.

OVERDOMINANCE: The condition of a heterozygote having a phenotype that is more pronounced or better adapted than that of either homozygote.

OVULE: A minute structure in seed plants, containing the embryo sac and surrounded by the nucellus, that develops into a seed after fertilization.

OXYGEN: A nonmetallic element constituting 21 percent of the atmosphere by volume that occurs as a diatomic gas, O_2, and in many compounds such as water and iron ore. It combines with most elements, is essential for plant and animal respiration, and is required for nearly all combustion.

P

PERENNIAL: Living three or more years.

PETIOLE: The stalk by which a leaf is attached to a stem. Also called leafstalk.

PH: A measure of the acidity or alkalinity of a solution, numerically equal to 7 for neutral solutions, increasing with increasing alkalinity and decreasing with increasing acidity. The pH scale commonly in use ranges from 0 to 14.

PHENOTYPE: The observable physical or biochemical characteristics of an organism, as determined by both genetic makeup and environmental influences. The expression of a specific trait, such as stature or blood type, based on genetic and environmental influences. An individual or group of organisms exhibiting a particular phenotype.

PHOTOPERIOD: The duration of an organism's daily exposure to light, considered especially with regard to the effect of the exposure on growth and development.

PHOTOSYNTHESIS: The process in green plants and certain other organisms by which carbohydrates are synthesized from carbon dioxide and water using light as an energy source. Most forms of photosynthesis release oxygen as a byproduct.

PHOTOTROPISM: The tendency of growing plant organs to move or curve under the influence of light. In ordinary use the term is practically synonymous with heliotropism.

PHYLLOTAXY: The arrangement of leaves on a stem.

PHYTOCHROME: A cytoplasmic pigment of green plants that absorbs light and regulates dormancy, seed germination, and flowering.

PIGMENT: A substance used as coloring. A substance, such as chlorophyll that produces a characteristic color in plant tissue.

PISTIL: The female, ovule-bearing organ of a flower, including the stigma, style, and ovary.

PISTILLATE: Having one or more pistils. Having pistils but no stamens; pistillate flowers.

POLLEN: The fine powderlike material consisting of pollen grains that is produced by the anthers of seed plants.

POLLINATE: To transfer pollen from an anther to the stigma of (a flower).

POLYPLOID: Having one or more extra sets of chromosomes: a polyploid species; a polyploid cell.

PRE-FLOWERING: Calyx development before flowering. Also called Primordia.

PROGENY: Offspring or descendants considered as a group.

PRUNE: To cut off or remove dead or living parts to improve shape or growth.

PUNNETT SQUARE: In genetics, a type of grid used to show the gametes of each parent and their possible offspring; a type of grid that can indicate all the possible outcomes of a genetic cross.

PURE BREED: See IBL

R
RACE: See landrace.

RADICLE: The part of a plant embryo that develops into a root.

RANDOM MATING: Mating without selective pressures.

RECESSIVE: Tending to go backward or recede. Of, relating to, or designating an allele that does not produce a characteristic effect when present with a dominant allele. Of or relating to a trait that is expressed only when the determining allele is present in the homozygous condition.

REGENERATE: To flower the plant again after harvest. Also called rejuvenation, reflowering and revegetation.

S
SCROG: Stands for Screen Of Green, a SOG style grow with a mesh type canopy to train top cola growth.

SEEDLING: A young plant that is grown from a seed.

SEXING: Determining your plant's gender.

SEXUAL REPRODUCTION: Relating to, produced by, or involving reproduction that occurs with the union of male and female gametes, as in seed production.

SHOOT: A young branch or growth.

SINSEMILLA: Unpollinated female buds.

SOG: Stands for Sea Of Green, a group of clones flowered quickly together to produce an even canopy of bud.

SPIDER MITE: Any one of several species of parasitic mites of the genus Argas and allied genera. Any one of numerous small mites injurious to plants.

STAGNANT: A term used to describe growth stunting because of a problem.

STAMEN: The pollen-producing reproductive organ of a flower, usually consisting of a filament and an anther.

STAMINATE: Having stamens but lacking pistils.

STEM: The main ascending axis of a plant; a stalk or trunk.

STIPULE: One of the usually small, paired appendages at the base of a leafstalk

STOMA/STOMATA: One of the minute pores in the epidermis of a leaf or stem through which gases and water vapor pass. Also called stomate.

T
TAPROOT: The main root of a plant, usually stouter than the lateral roots and growing straight downward from the stem.

TERPENE/TERPINOIDS: Any of various unsaturated hydrocarbons, $C_{10}H_{16}$, found in plants and used in organic syntheses.

TETRAPLOID: Having four times the haploid number of chromosomes in the cell nucleus.

THC: A compound, $C_{21}H_{30}O_2$, obtained from cannabis or made synthetically, that is the primary intoxicant in marijuana and hashish.

TRANSLOCATION: A transfer of a chromosomal segment to a new position, especially on a nonhomologous chromosome. A chromosomal segment that is translocated.

TRANSPIRATION: The emission of water vapor from the leaves of plants.

TRICHOME: A mushroom shaped cannabinoid containing outgrowth on the pistil of a cannabis plant.

TRIPLOID: Having three times the haploid number of chromosomes in the cell nucleus.

TRUE-BREEDING: See IBL

W
WATT: An International System unit of power equal to one joule per second.

WHORLED PHYLLOTAXY: Having more than two branches form at the same axis area.

X
XYLEM: The supporting and water-conducting tissue of vascular plants, consisting primarily of tracheids and vessels; woody tissue.

Z
ZYGOTE: The cell resulting from the union of an ovum and a spermatozoon (including the organism that develops from that cell.

++ INDEX

Note: Page numbers in italics refer to photographs or illustrations. Numbers followed by "t" refer to charts or tables.

F

F1 generation, 35, 108, 113–115, 195
fan leaf mutations, 148
female plants
  and gender, 132–139
  hormones to promote, 70, 73, 87–88
  identification of, 51, 52–53, 53
  male selection for, 50–52
  maturity of, 182
  pollination of, 55–56
  reversal of sexual expression in,
    141–143, 142
  segregation from males, 53–54
  treatment to produce feminized seeds,
    133
feminized seeds, 132–139
  from sexually reversed females, 143
filial generations, 195
Fischer, M., 156
Fisher, Ronald Alymer, 150–152
flowering phase, 136
  and calyx development, 52–53
  force flowering, 207–210
flowering traits, 108, 186–193
  auto-flowering, 15, 107
  and calyx development, 207–210
  floral characteristics of cannabis,
    179–183
  maturity, 181–183, 183t
  stages of devlopment, 186–189
  test crosses for, 189
fluorescent lighting, 54, 93, 103
flushing, side effect of, 200
force flowering, 207–210
Formula 1, 72
fungi. See molds and fungi

G

gametes, 65, 76–77
gender
  dioecious strains, 43–44
  effects of environmental conditions on,
    132–139
  effects of force flowering on, 209
  identification by calyx development,
    52–53
  monoecious strains, 43–44
  reversal of sexual expression in females,
    141–143
  sex-inherited traits, 132–139

sex-linked traits, 140–143
and stress, 134–135
use of parent plants in multiple strains,
  47–52
gene frequency ratios, 24–25, 196
  determining, 25–26, 28–29
  manipulation of, 38–41
  Punnett square calculations, 33–34
gene migration (introgression), 37
genes, 20, 76–77
  types of, 196–198
genetically modified cannabis, 194–195
genetic drift, 37
genetic frequencies, 36–37
genetic notation, 24, 76
genetics, 20–44, 194–199
  alleles, 22
  biogenetics, 79
  breeding principles, 194–199
  cell structure and molecular genetics,
    65–69
  chromosomes, 22, 75–77
  dioecious strains, 43–44
  dominant genes, 20, 22
  dominant/recessive expression, 24, 29–34
  gene migration (introgression), 37
  genes, 20, 76–77, 196–198
  genetic drift, 37
  genetic notation, 24
  Hardy-Weinberg model of genetic equi-
    librium, 24–34, 37–38
  heterozygous traits, 22
  homozygous traits, 22
  inbreeding depression, 152–158
  lock down (of traits), 38–41
  locus/loci, 22
  monoecious strains, 43–44
  of propagation, 47–49
  Punnett square calculations, 31–34
  recessive genes, 20, 23
  and yields, 185
  . See also genotype; phenotype
genotype, 22
  and crop productivity, 195
  determining by test crosses, 29–33, 108
  environmental influences on, 180
  expression of, 65
  as factor in mutations, 83, 84
  and gender in phenotype, 132
  importance of in IBL breeding, 38–41

use in assessing breeding qualities, 50–52
offspring calculations
  hybrid generations, 34–36
  and Punnett squares, 31–32, 33–34
organelles, 67–69
outbreeding depression, 156
outdoor strains, 11, 129
  adaptability of, 165–166
overfeeding, 84
ovules, 65
Ozi Tonic, 70–71

P
parent plants
  assessing breeding qualities, 50–57
  compatibility in, 62–64
  and strain stability, 50
  use of in multiple strains, 47
peroxisomes, 67, 69
pest attacks, *176, 178*
  and crop productivity, 195
  defense against, 177–179
  and quarantine of foreign cuttings, 103–105
  resistance to, 72
  and stress, 84, 137
phenotype, 22
  changes in clones, 84–86
  environmental influences on, 109, 180
  expression of, 65
  and gender, 132
  and recessive traits, 29–33
  and sex-linked traits, 140–143
pH levels
  and stress, 84, 137
  for tissue culture, 93
phloem, 69, 70
photographs
  alteration of, 90–91
  photo rights, 131
photoperiods, 15, 107
  for flowering, 53, 209
  for force flowering, 207–210
  manipulation of, 44, 45, 53–54, 127, 137
  and photosynthesis, 202
  and seed production, 56
  for vegetative growth, 53, 138
photo rights, 131
photosynthesis, 67, 69–70
  chemistry of, 200–202

flow chart, 201t
process of, 201–202
phototropism, 70, 74
phytochrome, light response mechanisms, 209
plant selection, breeders on, 106–107
plant shape, 183–184
plant size, 184
plasma membrane, 67–68
plastids, 67, *191*
point mutations, 82
point of sale, 8
pollen and pollen production, 52–53, *54*, 65
  collection and storage of, 18–19, 54–55, 120
  control of outdoors, 54
  mutations in, 157
pollination, 52
  application of pollen, 55–56
  importance of record keeping during, 56
  and pollen production, 52–53
  self-pollination, 5, 43–44, 150
  timing of, 55, *57*
  wild pollination, *27*
polygamy in cannabis, 57–58
polyploid state (polyploidy), 77, 88–89, *89*, 141, 147, *147*
potency, 107–108, 127
  and calyx/leaf ratio, 172
  and mutations, 89–90
  and plant size, 91
  and polyploid state, 77
  psychoactive compounds, 203–205
  and THC content, 204
PowerBloom, 72–73
presentation strains, 101
pricing, 95–102
product testing, 123–124
propagation
  genetics of, 47–49
  types of, 1–5
protein kinesis, 68, 69
pruning, 137
psychoactive compounds, 203–205
Punnett squares
  genotype calculations, 31–32
  offspring calculations, 33–34
pure species type strains
  compatibility of, 62
  vs mostly-type strains, 13

++ INDEX 237

Skunk strains, *96, 97, 99,* 101, 145,
168–169
Willem's Wonder, 117
stress
and calyx development, 136–137
effect on gender, 134–135, 137
as factor in mutations, 83, 84, 127,
135–136
and hermaphrodite condition, 135–136
hormones to reduce, 72–73
nitrogen-deficiency-related, 72
photoperiod manipulation, 45, 127, 137
transplant shock, 71, 73
Superthrive, 73, 88
suppressor genes, 197
surface cleaning, 92–93
Sutton, Walter, 140

T
taproot, 161–162, *162*
temperature, 118, 138, 202
terpenoids, 190
test crosses, 29–33
in assessing breeding qualities, 50–52
record keeping of, 40
tetrahydrocannabivarin (THCV), 205
tetraploid chromosomes, 141
THC, 189, *191,* 204
synthetic, 206
thiamine, 73
tissue culture, 92–94
as factor in mutations, 86
mediums for, 93
top colas, 162, *167, 187*
and calyx/leaf ratio, 171–172
. *See also* buds; colas
topping, 137
toxicity of treated crops, 87, 88–89, 143
transfer techniques, as factor in mutations,
83, 86
transition, 82
translocations, 83
transplant shock, 71, 73, 137
as factor in mutations, 86
transversion, 82
trichomes
anatomy of, *191*
types of, 190–193
trilateral branching, 145, *146,* 147
triploid chromosomes, 141

tropism, types of, 73–74
true breeding traits, 5, 11, 38–41, 115
and adaptability, 165–166
and color, 174
and compatibility, 64
hybrid strains, 48–50
true strains, 18
turgor, 67
Tween 20, 92
twinning, 147

U
Urey, Harold C., 79

V
vacuoles and vacuole membrane, *66, 67, 191*
Vavilov, Nicolai, 16
vegetative characteristics, 159–164
breeding traits of, 164–185
vegetative stage, *53*
gender manipulation during, 136
and growth hormone application, 87–88
maturity, 181, 182
nutrient ratios, 138
ventilation, 119, *120,* 122
vesicles, *191*
viability
of pollen, 18–19
of seeds, 19, 59, 88
vigor, and adaptability, 184–185
vitamin B1 (thiamine), 73

W
Warmke, H.E., 77
warping, *146,* 147
watering, 84, 137, 138, 195
whorled phylotaxy, 145, *146,* 147
window lighting, 54, 93
Wood's Rooting Compound, 73

X
xylem, 69, 70

Y
yields
and calyx development, 172
effect of pruning on, 170
and growing environment, 185
and hormone use, 72–73, 87

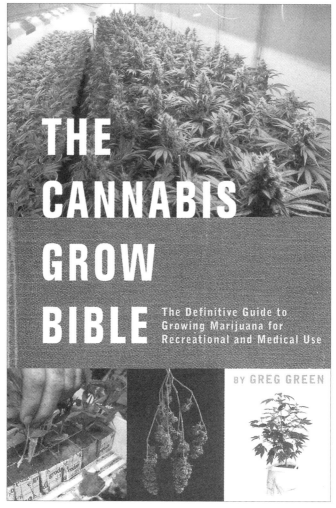

AVAILABLE AT YOUR LOCAL BOOKSTORE

CANNABIS CULTIVATION
MEL THOMAS
The easy-to-follow, step-by-step directions enable anyone to grow and harvest the highest quality marijuana using simple techniques and inexpensive, everyday gardening tools. An experienced grower, Mel Thomas pens a comprehensive manual that is both interesting and informative. Don't know the difference between soil and hydroponic gardens? Thomas will walk you through it. The book covers all of the important factors which can influence growth rate, yield and potency: lighting, planting mediums, pH, nutrients, water systems, air and temperature, and CO_2. *CANNABIS CULTIVATION* will help you turn almost any space into a high-yielding garden. $16.95

THE MARIJUANA CHEF COOKBOOK
BY S. T. ONER
THE MARIJUANA CHEF COOKBOOK gives a whole new meaning to cooking with herbs. With more than 40 first-rate recipes, this wonderful cookbook offers a multitude of ways to turn humble leaf into culinary treats that everyone can enjoy. In the mood for something sweet? Try Decadent Chocolate Bud Cake washed down with a delicious Mary Jane's Martini. A heady blend of theory and technique, *THE MARIJUANA CHEF COOKBOOK* is filled with delicious easy-to-follow recipes that will take you and your dinner guests on a natural high. $12.95

THE GRINGO TRAIL
MARK MANN
ASIA HAS THE HIPPIE TRAIL. SOUTH AMERICA HAS THE GRINGO TRAIL. Mark Mann and his girlfriend Melissa set of to explore the ancient monuments, mountains and rainforests of the southern continent. But for their friend, South America meant only one thing...drugs. Funny, shocking and revealing, *THE GRINGO TRAIL* is an *On the Road* for the Lonely Planet generation. A darkly comic road-trip and a journey of drama and discovery through South America's turbulent past and volatile present. $12.95

GREETINGS FROM CANNABIS COUNTRY
ANDRE GROSSMAN
GREETINGS FROM CANNABIS COUNTRY is a must have for enthusiasts! The book contains a collection of 30 beautifully detailed photo-postcards, taken by Andre Grossman at Trichome Technologies—the world's most sophisticated and largest marijuana growing operation. Fourteen of the potent strains of marijuana are displayed in both a colorful and playful way. The safest way to send pot through the mail! $11.95

ABC BOOK: A DRUG PRIMER
STEVEN CERIO
Steven Cerio's *ABC BOOK: A DRUG PRIMER* is a must-have for Ravers and Stoners alike. Come along for the ride from A-Z, and read the poems that accompany Steven's colorful psychedelic illustrations. Each letter represents a different type of drug, and its effects are stated in an accompanying poem. A lighthearted and amusing piece of work, this ABC book is pure fun! $12.95

ONLINE AT WWW.GREENCANDYPRESS.COM